The Right of Publicity

The Right of Publicity

Privacy Reimagined for a Public World

Jennifer E. Rothman

Harvard University Press

Cambridge, Massachusetts
London, England
2018

First printing

Library of Congress Cataloging-in-Publication Data

Names: Rothman, Jennifer E., 1969– author.
Title: The right of publicity : privacy reimagined for a public world /
Jennifer E. Rothman.
Description: Cambridge, Massachusetts : Harvard University Press, 2018. |
Includes bibliographical references and index.
Identifiers: LCCN 2017045240 | ISBN 9780674980983 (alk. paper)
Subjects: LCSH: Publicity (Law)—United States. | Privacy, Right of—United States. |
Personality (Law)—United States. | Intellectual property—United States.
Classification: LCC KF1262 .R68 2018 | DDC 342.7308/58—dc23
LC record available at https://lccn.loc.gov/2017045240

For Elijah and Hazel

Contents

The Right of Publicity

Introduction

IN AN AGE OF DRONES flying over our backyards recording images, people live streaming from smartphones what they are doing and where they are, online businesses collecting and selling our data, and widespread sharing of our photos, experiences, and thoughts online, there is little that remains unspoken, secret, or truly private. This has led some to conclude that privacy is dead. But privacy lives on—in part through the "right of publicity." The right of publicity is something we all have—it is the right to stop others from using our identities, particularly our names and likenesses, without permission. It is sometimes thought of as a property right in one's personality.

Most people outside of the entertainment business and the law are unfamiliar with the right, yet it is relevant to us all, and likely to be increasingly so in our Internet Age. To the extent people have heard of the right of publicity, it is likely in the context of celebrities, who often wield the right to prevent unwanted uses of their identities, or at least to reap the rewards of such uses. Basketball star Michael Jordan asserted his right of publicity and won more than $9 million against two supermarkets that used his name and jersey number along with their brand names to congratulate him in the pages of *Sports Illustrated* on his induction into the Basketball Hall of Fame. Tony and Grammy Award winner Bette Midler used the right to win a $400,000 verdict against a car company that used a song that she made famous in an advertisement, even though the company hired another singer to perform the song and licensed the music. Professional hockey player Tony Twist won a $15 million judgment on the basis of the right after the author of the comic book *Spawn* named a character

1

Tony Twistelli. Game show hostess Vanna White won a jury verdict of more than $400,000 by asserting her right of publicity against the electronics company Samsung when it used an image of a robot wearing a wig on the set of *Wheel of Fortune* in an advertisement, even though the robot looked nothing like White.

The right of publicity has given less well-known former National Collegiate Athletic Association (NCAA) basketball and football players the ability to stop future uses of their physical characteristics and playing statistics in video games, and to recover payments for past uses. It has given a circus performer (a human cannonball) the ability to recover damages when his act was shown on the nightly news. And the right of publicity has emboldened the troubled actor Lindsay Lohan to make repeated claims that her identity has been used without her permission, including a complaint that a starlet chased by paparazzi in the video game *Grand Theft Auto* V resembled her, and a complaint that a baby "milk-a-holic" named Lindsay in an E*Trade commercial was meant to be her. The right of publicity has even given a voice to the dead: from the Elvis estate suing a bar called the Velvet Elvis, to the Rosa Parks foundation suing to stop Target from selling plaques honoring the deceased civil rights hero, to dead pinup star Bettie Page's representatives objecting to uses of her name and likeness in stores and on websites that cater to fans of vintage clothing and the pinup aesthetic.

The right of publicity is not only for the famous. Nor need one be a performer or athlete to bring a right of publicity claim. Facebook users have relied on the right to sue the social media giant for using their names and likenesses in advertisements targeted to their online friends. Twitter users have asserted the right of publicity against that company for selling their names and photographs for use in a trading card game of "real-life people." Victims of sex traffickers have asserted right of publicity claims against online newspapers (like Backpage) and advertisers for using their images to offer their (nonconsensual) sex services. The right of publicity has also been asserted against mug-shot websites that "helpfully" offer to remove one's image for a fee.

There is no federal right of publicity, nor is such a right provided for in the United States Constitution, like the rights of liberty, freedom of speech, and freedom of religion. Instead, the right of publicity is a state law, and not a uniform one. Its contours differ from state to state. Nevertheless, it is described as a "right" because of a sentiment that we are each entitled to exercise some degree of control over how our identity is used by others, much as we have a right to speak (or not speak) or to marry (or not marry). But unlike these constitutionally protected rights, the right of publicity is created at the state level, either by judges creating common law rules in the context of deciding cases or by state legislatures passing right of publicity statutes. Because of the variability across states of what the right of publicity encompasses, defining the right of publicity is challenging. At its broadest, the right of publicity provides a basis to control the unwanted dissemination of one's name and likeness, and other indicia of identity for another's advantage.

Today, more than thirty states have such right of publicity laws, and the number will undoubtedly grow in the years to come. Some states limit their right of publicity to uses in advertising or in connection with products or services, or on merchandising, while other states allow claims arising out of virtually any use of a person's identity, including uses in news, movies, books, video games, and political campaigns. Some states allow only those who are residents (domiciled) in the state (or were at the time of death) to bring claims. Others allow anyone to sue. Some states limit claims to those with commercially valuable identities, while others do not. Some states require the use of a person's actual name, likeness, or voice, but others allow liability for any use that conjures up a person's identity. Some states limit right of publicity actions to the living, while others allow heirs to bring claims on the basis of uses of a deceased person's identity. The right of publicity, then, rather than a single, uniform right, is in reality many different laws. This variability itself makes these laws difficult to navigate and even to talk about in a coherent fashion.

Many states also (or instead) recognize a similar (sometimes identical) right to control uses of one's name, likeness, and often voice under those states' "right of privacy." Privacy is a term that has been used to mean many different things in the law. It sometimes is used to indicate the protection of secrets or spatial privacy (such as keeping snoops and the government out of your house). Sometimes privacy also refers to a broader notion of "decisional privacy" that has been used to justify a constitutionally protected right to use contraceptives or to have an abortion. This book does not seek to harmonize or disentangle the many strands of what is meant by privacy. Instead, the book addresses the first explicit right of privacy recognized in the United States, the one that emerged in the late 1800s in state tort laws.

At its origin, the right of privacy was primarily driven by the desire to protect individuals from having their names and likenesses used without permission. It was this concern that first motivated the adoption of the right of privacy in the United States, rather than concerns about intrusions into people's homes or the revelation of secrets. Privacy laws in the United States were first championed to stop unwanted "publicity." Yet, courts and commentators today frequently refer to the right of "publicity" as the "reverse side of the coin of privacy," as though they are opposites, and even deride early courts for confusing the two (allegedly) distinct claims. But the history of these two rights is far more intertwined than widely believed.

The frequently uttered and simplistic dichotomy—that privacy is about protecting the shrinking violets of the world, while the right of publicity is about protecting those who seek the limelight—was never true, and does a disservice to both those who wish to avoid publicity and those who seek it out. Actors do not want videos of them changing in a hotel room distributed online, their children followed, or their images slapped onto billboards or used in television commercials without their permission. This is not necessarily because they want to be paid for such uses, but because such uses are upsetting and disturbing, can destroy their reputations and ability to author their own identities, and turn them into puppets with others pulling the strings.

Nor do those of us who wish to live less public lives want to hide in our homes. We take walks, post family photographs to Facebook and Instagram, blog and tweet about our experiences, create YouTube channels showing how to prepare various recipes or master a video game, and leave traces behind when buying books on Amazon. These acts do not mean that private figures wish to cede the right to control how our names, likenesses, voices, and other information about ourselves are used by others. We all live our lives in public. But by doing so we should not become public property.

Privacy law at its origin was capacious enough to encompass our public lives and to evolve with a society that increasingly viewed the sharing of a photograph not as mortifying but as commonplace. But the law did not remain stagnant, and while privacy law and society developed, the common law (judge-made law) was moving in a different direction, largely based on myths about privacy law and misleading claims that privacy law did not adequately protect public figures who sought to commercialize their identities. It was this claim that purportedly led to the split of the right of publicity from the right of privacy—but, in truth, the primary difference

4

between the two rights was whether the right could be transferred and taken away from identity-holders and sold to corporations and others.

After the shift to the right of publicity took place, the myths about the differences between it and the right of privacy spread, and a cramped understanding of privacy law emerged—one focused on private figures, seclusion, secrecy, and injured feelings, rather than on the broader notions of autonomy and dignity that had reigned over the first sixty to seventy years of privacy law. Privacy, or the "right to be let alone," turned into something small and narrow. The true story of the evolution of the right of publicity has largely become lost in the mists of time. This book reveals the right of publicity's origins in and continued synergies with privacy law, and by doing so provides us with a way to avoid the dark side of today's right of publicity, without losing its ability to protect individuals. It also provides a path to reimagining what privacy means in our ever more public world.

The right of publicity can be a valuable mechanism for addressing a variety of twenty-first-century concerns about uses of people's images. But, despite the many benefits of having a right of publicity, its current incarnation comes with a host of dangers. The right of publicity limits what the public can say about public figures, even dead ones, and can bar the public from making sculptures, T-shirts, and posters honoring the recently deceased, such as Prince, Carrie Fisher, Robin Williams, and Muhammad Ali. It can block (and has blocked) the distribution and sale of busts of civil rights heroes, like Martin Luther King Jr. It has prevented video game makers from accurately depicting football players on historical team rosters, and television networks from using clips of their own broadcasts. The right has led to liability for comic book authors who name characters after their favorite hockey players, and a payout by the nightly news for showing a fifteen-second clip of a performer at a local fair. The right has blocked television and movie producers from making or licensing derivative works based on their copyrighted works, such as action figures, movie posters, and robots that remind people of fictional characters. The right can stop businesses from accurately reporting that celebrities are wearing their clothes or handbags or jewelry, or eating in their restaurants.

Perhaps worst of all, under many state laws, the right of publicity is treated as a fully transferable property right, meaning that your own name, likeness, and voice could be sold, given away, or taken by someone else— forever. Some models, actors, and recording artists have assigned their rights to managers and companies that can now use their names and

5

images without those individuals' additional permission, and even block them from appearing in public or making endorsements of their own choosing. The NCAA has claimed that student-athletes assigned (gave) their rights over their names and likenesses to the NCAA in perpetuity. Reality television producers have asked contestants to sign over their rights to their names and likenesses and life stories to the producers or production companies as a condition for participation in the shows. Both Facebook and Twitter have claimed to be able to use your name and picture to endorse and advertise products, and even on products, like trading cards. Social media sites' ever-changing terms of service (which you agree to simply by continuing to use their services) could do far more than this if the right of publicity is transferable—Facebook could become the owner of your own name and image in all contexts, not just on its website. Parents could transfer their children's rights to their names and likenesses, and nothing in the law provides for children to get those rights back, even when they turn eighteen. For those with more lucrative public personalities, if the rights are transferable, then creditors and ex-spouses could take ownership over (at least part of) their identities and, as a result, control and monetize them, without regard to whether the underlying person would approve of such uses.

The right of publicity can also force the commercialization of the dead against their own and their heirs' wishes. If the right of publicity is a transferable right, then it can (and will) be passed down to one's heirs after death. In fact, many of the most lucrative celebrities are now dead ones— such as Michael Jackson and Elvis Presley. Michael Jackson's heirs are currently fighting with the Internal Revenue Service (IRS) over the value of his postmortem right of publicity. The two are hundreds of millions of dollars apart in the valuation, with the estate claiming it is worth only a negligible amount, and the IRS claiming it is worth $400 million. The Jackson heirs are already actively commercializing the dead pop star—even approving his reanimation on the Vegas Strip and in award shows. But other heirs may wish to avoid such commercialization of their deceased loved ones. Unfortunately for them, if the right of publicity is a transferable property right (and estate taxes remain in force), then the IRS will value this property at its highest monetary worth—something that is determined by assuming that the property will be sold and fully commercialized. Such an approach will pressure heirs who do not have enough cash on hand to pay the tax bill to commercialize the deceased, even if that is not what they or the deceased person would want.

The right of publicity need not be such a negative force—suppressing speech, blocking otherwise lawful uses of songs and fictional characters, forcing commercialization of the dead, and stripping people of their own identities. The right of publicity has an important and powerful core insight that originated with the right of privacy—that we should have some control over how others use our names and likenesses. But the right has lost its way, becoming a misunderstood, misshapen, bloated monster that has turned against even its initial masters and proponents. The right of publicity got off track when it transformed from a personal right, rooted in the individual person (the "identity-holder"), into a powerful intellectual property right, external to the person, that can be sold to or taken by a non-identity-holding "publicity-holder."

These wrong turns by the right of publicity have been driven and continued by a host of mythologies that have sprung up surrounding both it and its predecessor, the right of privacy. This book challenges these common, though erroneous, stories about the two rights and by doing so provides a path to put the right of publicity back on course by reclaiming its origins in the right of privacy. In the process, the book provides an opportunity to reimagine both the right of publicity and the right of privacy for the Internet Age.

PART I

The Big Bang

1

The Original "Right of Publicity"

T HE RIGHT OF PUBLICITY is often thought to have been born in the
1950s in the United States. But in fact, its roots date much further
back—to the development of the right of privacy in the late 1800s, and even
earlier to a series of cases from England that preceded the right of privacy's adoption in this country. Many judges, lawyers, and scholars now think
of a right of privacy and a right of publicity as opposites, but at the origin
of the right to privacy, privacy was primarily about the right to control
"publicity"—when and how one's image and name could be used by others
in public. This was the animating impetus for the adoption of the right of
privacy in the United States.

The right of privacy was and remains the original right of publicity.
Many of the first cases to consider whether there was a right of privacy in
the United States were ones that involved situations that today would be
considered typical right of publicity cases, involving the nonconsensual
use of people's likenesses, often on products and in advertisements. Women
and men, both the famous and the anonymous, objected to the unwel-
come surprise of finding their photographs used in advertisements for
flour, life insurance, and medicinal preparations. Actors, dancers, and
singers objected to the taking of their photographs and the use of their images and names without permission, whether in promotions or newspaper
popularity contests. These were the cases that led to the creation of a right
of privacy, not ones about intrusion into secluded spaces or the publication of private facts. The right of privacy, once adopted, swept more broadly
than the misappropriation of identity cases, but it was with these cases,
starting in the late 1800s, that the right of publicity truly began.[1]

A Perfect Storm

Technological advancements and related cultural shifts in the mid to late 1800s led to calls for legal change, and in particular to the adoption of a right of "privacy" that included a right to control the use of one's image and name. The rise of portable, relatively easy-to-use "detective" cameras raised concerns over the unwanted taking and dissemination of photographs. Cheaper, more efficient printing techniques led to a burgeoning and increasingly competitive newspaper industry that sometimes resorted to salacious and prurient reporting to sell papers, the so-called era of yellow journalism. The development of the interstate railroad system and other aspects of the Industrial Revolution led to more attenuated markets in which consumers did not know sellers, and in which there were more fungible, mass-produced goods. These market changes required greater product differentiation for companies to succeed and encouraged the development of professionalized advertising, which increasingly used people's names and images to encourage sales.

By the late 1880s, it became possible for the average person to snap photographs of people on the street—often without the subject's knowledge. Prior to this time, photographic portraits were largely limited to those taken by professional photographers in their studios with willing sitters. Cameras had been large, unwieldy, and complex, and once film was exposed it needed to be quickly developed. New technology led to the production of easy-to-use and portable cameras, and an associated explosion in amateur photography. These amateur photographers were sometimes called "kodakers," a reference to the company that developed one of the most popular of the new consumer-friendly cameras. George Eastman put his Kodak camera on the market in 1888—it was touted as the "smallest, lightest, and simplest of all Detective Cameras." Advertisements at the time and in the decades that followed promoted these cameras' portability and ease of use, as well as the ability to take photographs of the unwilling without their knowledge.[2]

Photographers (both professionals and amateurs alike) followed the president, business leaders, and ordinary citizens as they navigated public spaces. The days of anonymity and "privacy" in public were over. Of course, being in public was never a private affair, but because it was rarely documented, people had previously perceived their public outings as private.[3]

Advertisement for Kodak Camera from 1889. Courtesy of The George Eastman Museum.

Courts, scholars, journalists, and ordinary citizens worried about the invasive nature of cameras and the nonconsensual taking of their photographs. People were embarrassed, shocked, and distressed when their images appeared in public without their permission. In 1902, the *New York Times* criticized the "outrages" of oppressive "kodakers" and noted that even well-known public figures who are "thick-skinned" and not at all "shrinking violet[s]" "revolt from the continuous ordeal of the camera." Judge John Clinton Gray, who sat on New York's highest court, its Court of Appeals, during this time, described the dissemination of a person's likeness without permission as an "act of invasion of the individual's privacy . . . possibly more formidable and more painful in its consequences than an actual bodily assault might be."[4]

The problems that photography raised were difficult to address under then-existing laws. Before the late 1800s, most portraits were taken in a professional photographer's studio with the consent of the sitter. If a photographer subsequently used a photograph without permission, claims were available under theories of breach of contract, breach of confidence, and copyright. But strangers on the street could not rely on such claims if

46

THE FOLMER & SCHWING MFG. CO.

The Deceptive Angle Graphic

Patent Applied For

This camera is in every sense of the word a detective camera, being thoroughly disguised to resemble a stereo camera and so arranged as to photograph subjects at right angles to its apparent line of vision.

It is of the twin lens type, fitted with regular lens and shutter for exposure and a matched lens through which the subject is seen in the same size as on the focusing screen.

This camera possesses unequalled advantages for detective camera work. It is carefully constructed of selected, kiln dried mahogany and covered with the best quality of black grained leather.

The side of the camera is fitted with a pair of dummy stereo lenses and imitation finder apparently in the direct line of vision when the operator is focusing.

The rack and pinion focusing device is concealed inside the camera with the exception of a small focusing lever operated by the thumb from the outside.

The point of the focusing lever acts as an index on a graduated focusing scale for off-hand, snapshot work when in use without focusing screens.

The front of the camera is hinged and may be opened to change or clean the lenses.

Two rectangular apertures are provided in the front through which the lenses work.

Advertisement for Folmer & Schwing Deceptive Angle Camera from 1904. Courtesy of The George Eastman Museum.

they later discovered that their picture had been taken and then used without permission.[5]

During the late 1800s, printing became cheaper and faster, leading to a proliferation of newspapers and magazines and the increased use of images in these publications. Photographs, as well as woodcuts and engravings of them, appeared in newspapers and magazines. The increased number of newspapers and magazines created greater competition—driving some papers to print more salacious articles to attract readers. This "yellow journalism" sometimes took the form of gossip about public figures, as well as about socialites who considered themselves private figures, and even about those who were not part of high society but had found themselves involved in a scandal, crime, or tragedy that journalists thought would sell papers. Gossip was of course nothing new, but the rise of mass media in the form of widely distributed newspapers and magazines meant that gossip moved from limited (often oral only) distribution to wide, printed dissemination. Today, such gossip is commonplace, but at the time the public, scholars, and even many journalists decried such "muckracking." Highbrow newspaper editors and reporters complained about the tactics of papers that operated in the gutter and that they deemed unseemly and abusive.[6]

The rise in the number of newspapers led to an increase in advertising space, as well as those advertisements becoming more valuable to potential advertisers given the increased circulation. The successes of the Industrial Revolution further encouraged a turn to professionalized advertising. Mass-produced goods, railroads, multistate corporations, and the resulting more attenuated markets created a need to differentiate products in the marketplace through advertising. During the late 1800s, advertising advanced from its primitive state of storefront signs, sandwich boards, and simple notices that factually described products and where to get them to more persuasion-based campaigns. As part of this shift, advertisers increasingly used images of both ordinary people and the well-known, as well as endorsements and testimonials (both legitimate and concocted). The rise of mass media also facilitated the creation of more valuable public personalities because of the ability to create a shared interest and recognition of particular celebrities across the country, and even across the globe.[7]

The focus on individualism and individual rights in the mid to late 1800s also amplified concerns about privacy. In 1888, Thomas M. Cooley published the second edition of his famous treatise on tort law—the subject of legal "wrongs which arise independent of contract" and criminal law, and for which private parties can sue to remedy their injuries. For the first time in his enumeration of personal rights, Cooley included a right of "personal immunity." He explained that "[t]he right to one's person may be said to be a right of complete immunity: to be let alone." He included nonphysical injuries, such as assault, in this category. (The harm of an assault in tort law is not a physical one; instead it is the apprehension of or perception of a likely and unwanted physical contact, without regard to whether such physical contact is ever made.) Although Cooley did not specifically consider the misappropriation of name or likeness, his expansive view of personal immunities led other scholars and courts to embrace his right "to be let alone" and to interpret it broadly as encompassing a right of privacy, including a right to control how or whether one's name or likeness could be used by others. Cooley's articulation of personal rights also marked a larger jurisprudential shift toward recognizing emotional as well as physical injuries. In the same edition of his treatise, Cooley advocated for the recognition of reputational injuries and for the protection of private letters to prevent injuries to feelings.[8]

Calls for Redress

These technological and cultural developments gave rise to new and amplified complaints about invasions of privacy. A surge of public and scholarly opinion advocated that something be done about uses of people's names and images without their permission in newspapers and magazines, and in advertising and on products. Previously, the use of famous individuals' images was tolerated, and even appreciated, by those depicted. Public figures rarely complained—at least publicly—about the use of their names and likenesses on merchandise. Merchandise that displayed images of famous people was deemed either part of the price of being a public figure (Benjamin Franklin's view in the 1700s) or part of a successful effort to generate interest in a particular performer to raise the person's profile and sell tickets—as was the case with merchandise displaying the name and likeness of famous Swedish singer Jenny Lind, who took the United States by storm in the 1850s with the aid of P. T. Barnum's shrewd promotion. The names and images of George Washington and other early American presidents were used on flour containers, mugs, and pitchers. In England,

Queen Victoria's image proliferated in advertising and merchandise beginning in the 1830s, and was thought of as "public property."[9]

In the mid to late 1800s the tide turned, and tolerance for such uses declined. The new photographic technology was thought more intrusive and invasive, both in the taking of the photographs and in the perceived intimacy and personal nature of the image. Conflicts began to arise over the use of photographs when a person had willingly sat for a portrait but did not intend for the photographer to make any use of the images without the person's permission. In 1894, a federal court in Massachusetts raised the question that was on many people's minds at the time: Does an "individual, in his lifetime, or his heirs at law after his death have the right to control the reproduction of his picture or photograph"?[10]

Numerous law review articles at the time considered the problem of who owned photographs—the sitter or the photographer—and often took the position that the sitter should own the images and be able to control any future prints made from the negatives. In 1869, the *American Law Register* published the article "The Legal Relations of Photographs," which commented on the new medium of photography. The article called for the recognition of a legal cause of action to prevent the selling of multiple copies of a person's photographic image without the person's permission. The article suggested that people have a "natural copyright" in their own "features" and that the appropriateness of providing liability when such "features" are used without permission was uncontroversial. In 1884, an article in the *Washington Law Reporter* advocated for a "portrait right" that would provide the right to control "publicity" about oneself and particularly to control the use of photographs of oneself.[11]

Advertisers and businesses used not only the images of public figures in their advertising and on products, but also those of private figures who were not accustomed to such public portraiture and did not think that they had donated their visages, names, or lives to the public. By the late 1880s, the use of faces (often without permission) had become commonplace in advertising, and opposition arose to the practice, particularly when women's images were used. In 1888, Congressman John Robert Thomas introduced a bill in Congress to "prohibit the use of likenesses, portraits, or representations of females for advertising purposes, without consent in writing." Such uses were considered "vulgar" and stirred up Thomas's and other congressmen's chivalrous interest in protecting their "wives, daughters, mothers, and sisters." The bill included protection for both the living and

17

the dead, and provided a criminal fine of "not less than five hundred dollars nor more than five thousand dollars" and possible prison time.[12]

The bill was motivated in large part by outrage over the nonconsensual use of the First Lady's likeness in advertisements. The drafters thought these uses of the much-celebrated young wife of President Grover Cleveland, Frances Folsom Cleveland, were to the "detriment of society, decency, and morality." Despite the widespread disapproval of the use of her and other women's portraits, the bill was never brought up for a vote and died in committee, perhaps due to a formal complaint lodged against it by a group of photographers.[13]

Despite the failure of this bill, women continued to lobby for statutory protections against unauthorized uses of their images. In 1899, an Illinois women's club was described as "waging a stern and relentless war" against uses of their likenesses without permission. The Fourteenth Congressional District Federation of Women's Clubs objected to the use of a woman's face as "an advertiser's fortune" and sought legislation prohibiting the use of the "face, form, or any portion of the figure of woman for advertising purposes, in either suggestive or an immodest or immoral manner."[14]

It was not just women and their protectors who objected to nonconsensual uses of names and likenesses. Men also objected to uses of their names, particularly when their names and likenesses were used in false testimonials or endorsements for suspect products like "quack" or "patent" medicines (direct-to-consumer products that made health claims of limited veracity that were popular in the mid to late 1800s). In 1891, a New York court heard Sir Morell Mackenzie's complaint that the Soden Mineral Springs Company used his name and (purported) signature to advertise its medicinal pastilles without his permission. The company claimed that the lozenges were beneficial for various maladies of the throat that Dr. Mackenzie was known to be an expert in treating. The court agreed with Dr. Mackenzie that the use of his name and signature violated his rights, noting that Dr. Mackenzie could "suffer damage to his professional standing and income as a physician, and an infringement of his right to the sole use of his own name."[15]

Even politicians objected to the use of their likenesses and introduced legislation to try to block such uses. In 1897, New York senator Timothy E. Ellsworth introduced a bill to "restrain the unauthorized printing, publishing or circulating of portraits or alleged portraits of individuals." Press coverage at the time dubbed the proposed legislation the "Anti-Cartoon" bill and indicated that his motivation was to limit the ability of newspapers to print political cartoons and photographs of politicians. The proposed law passed the state senate but died in the assembly.[16]

In 1899, California legislators were more successful. They passed a similar law, barring the circulation of people's likenesses without their permission—thereby enacting what is likely the first right of publicity statute in the United States. The law prohibited the publication "in any newspaper, handbill, poster, book or serial publication, or supplement thereto, the portrait of any living person a resident of California, other than that of a person holding a public office . . . without the written consent of such person." The statute was added to the penal code.

The California press also dubbed this law the "Anti-Cartoon Bill." Like the earlier bill floated in New York, this legislation was motivated by efforts to limit negative portraits of politicians in newspapers. The sponsors of the legislation had been stirred to action by political cartoons that portrayed them in an unflattering manner. The original bill allowed liability even for realistic portraits of public officials, but the state senate amended the bill to exclude state officeholders from the portraiture ban because of free speech concerns. Nevertheless, the law that passed still barred caricatures of public officials if the caricature "reflect[ed] upon the honor, integrity, manhood, virtue, reputation, or business or political motives of the person so caricatured, or which tend[ed] to expose the individual so caricatured to public hatred, ridicule, or contempt." There is no evidence that the law was ever enforced, and it was quietly repealed in 1915.[17]

Efforts to pass laws against the use of nonconsensual portraits and the increasing number of lawsuits arising out of false endorsements were part of a larger societal discussion about "privacy" and the ability to control when people's names, likenesses, and information about them could be publicized, particularly in the context of news reporting. In July 1890, *Scribner's Magazine* published an influential essay by Edwin Lawrence Godkin, a respected journalist and editor of the influential magazine *The Nation*. Godkin wrote passionately about the importance of privacy and in particular about being able to control "publicity" about oneself. Godkin complained that the newspapers were profiting from gossip and creating demand for low-quality journalism that incentivized intrusions into people's personal lives. Because of the rise of such widely published gossip, Godkin called for a right for people to control "how much or how little publicity should surround their daily lives."[18]

Like Godkin, lawyers Samuel Warren and Louis Brandeis (who later became a Supreme Court justice) advocated for a right of privacy to combat yellow journalism, as well as to address the nonconsensual taking and use of photographs. In their famous article, "The Right to Privacy," published in the *Harvard Law Review* in December of the same year as Godkin's essay, Warren and Brandeis focused on the "unauthorized circulation of portraits of private persons." They described the "simplest case" for a right to privacy as the "right of one who has remained a private individual[] to prevent his public portraiture." Warren and Brandeis called for the recognition at common law of Thomas Cooley's "right to be let alone." They described the "mental pain and distress" that follows in the wake of unwanted "publicity" as "far greater than could be inflicted by mere bodily injury."[19]

A Woman in Tights

One high-profile case involving a public figure influenced Warren and Brandeis and their call for a right to privacy. It also fomented broad and vocal public support for such a right. Several months before the publication of their article, the actress Marion Manola objected to the taking of her photograph during a theatrical performance. At the time, Manola had the leading role in a comic opera, *Castles in the Air*. The manager of the company had decided to photograph all of the troupe's members in costume for use in advertisements for the show. The manager's intent was to counter a dwindling audience, not to be intrusive. Manola refused to be photographed, noting that her costume involved wearing tights. Her objection was covered in newspapers across the country. In interviews Manola explained: "I am not prudish . . . I have no objection to wearing tights on the stage—that is a part of the business of my profession. But I object to being photographed in such a costume. My chief objection is that I have a young daughter, only 10 years old, and I don't want her to see pictures of her mother in shop windows in such costumes."

Taking advantage of the press coverage, the manager sent a photographer to take Manola's picture during a performance on June 14, 1890. While on stage performing, Manola realized that her photograph had been taken. The *New York Times* reported that she then "threw her mantle over her face and ran off the stage." Manola sought and obtained a preliminary injunction against the use of the photographs that had been taken against her will during the performance. The press coverage of the lawsuit generated helpful publicity that increased ticket sales for the show and built Manola's fame, leading at least some observers to wonder whether her objections had been part of a marketing scheme. The manager never published a photograph of Manola in tights, as his goal of increasing sales had been achieved without needing to do so.

Public sentiment at the time was squarely on Manola's side and supported her ability to control when and how she would be photographed and how such images would be used. The *Baltimore Sun* described Manola's claim as central to the "sacredness of the person" and the "rights of the individual [as] unquestionable in such a case."[20]

Flour of the Family

Like Manola's lawsuit, many of the other early cases to consider whether a right of privacy existed (or should exist) involved claims that a person's name or likeness was used without permission, often in the context of advertising or product packaging. The chief complaint was the giving of unwanted "publicity" to a person. Regardless of whether "privacy" was the appropriate term for such wrongs, courts referred to them as violations of a right "to" or "of" privacy in large part because of the use of that moniker in the influential article by Warren and Brandeis.

In 1893, a New York superior court followed Godkin and Warren and Brandeis's lead. The court held that a newspaper could not publish the name and picture of an actor, Rudolph Marks, in the context of a popularity contest between him and another actor. The court noted:

> No newspaper or institution, no matter how worthy, has the right to use the name or picture of any one for such a purpose without his consent. An individual is entitled to protection in person as well as property, and now the right to life has come to mean the privilege to enjoy life without the publicity or annoyance of a lottery contest waged without authority, on the result of which is made to depend, in public estimation at least, the worth of private character or value of ability.

The court thought that holding wholly uncontroversial, so much so that it stated that the "right of the plaintiff to relief seems too clear, both upon principle and authority, to require further discussion." Although the decision itself seems questionable today given current free speech law, the notion that one should be able to control how and when the press and advertisers use one's name and likeness was widely accepted by the late 1800s.[21]

The first high court of any state to consider whether a right of privacy existed was the New York Court of Appeals. In its 1895 decision in *Schuyler v. Curtis*, the court considered a privacy-based claim arising out of an objection to the intended use of the name and likeness of a famous, but deceased, society woman, Mary M. Hamilton Schuyler, in a statue at the Columbia Exposition of 1893, commonly known as the Chicago World's Fair. The statue was planned as a companion piece to a statue of Susan B. Anthony. Both statues were sponsored by a New York women's group to celebrate women who had made significant contributions to society either as a "philanthropist" or as a "reformer." Schuyler was the "philanthropist" and her surviving relatives objected to her appearing alongside the suffragette and "reformer" Anthony.

Although the court was (disappointingly) sympathetic to the offense that must have arisen from the association of Schuyler with a person supporting the right of women to vote, the court rejected her heirs' privacy-based claim. The court avoided the question of whether Schuyler would have been able to stop the use of her identity if she had been alive. Instead, the court concluded that if she had such a "right of privacy," it would be personal to her and would not survive her death. Judge John Clinton Gray dissented in *Schuyler* and contended that the right to privacy was as much a "form of property . . . as is the right of complete immunity of one's person." Because he thought a privacy right existed and that it was rooted in property, he concluded that the right survived Schuyler's death as other property rights did.[22]

Less than a decade later, the New York Court of Appeals squarely decided the question of whether a right of privacy existed for the living— this time in the context of the use of a person's likeness in advertising. In *Roberson v. Rochester Folding Box*, a flour company put Abigail Roberson's picture on approximately 25,000 lithographic advertisements with the words "Flour of the Family" above her image and the company's name— "Franklin Mills Flour"—below it.

Roberson's portrait had been taken with her consent at a photography studio, but she had not provided consent to Franklin Mills to use the photo-

THE FAMOUS PORTRAIT AS IT APPEARED ON A
LITHOGRAPHED HANGER.

Advertisement for Franklin Mills Flour with photograph of Abigail Roberson,
published in "The 'Right of Privacy,'" *Profitable Advertising* 12 (1902): 187.

graph, nor was she aware of the use until people that she knew told her about it. Roberson alleged that when she heard about it, "she was made sick, and suffered a severe nervous shock, and was confined to her bed, and compelled to employ a physician." She was "greatly humiliated by the scoffs and jeers of persons" who recognized her in the advertisements. The injury was to her "good name" and caused her emotional and physical suffering.[23]

The trial court framed the legal issue as one that many would recognize as a right of publicity claim—"whether the defendants have the right to print and circulate lithograph copies of plaintiff's likeness for the purpose of profit and gain to themselves without her consent." The court suggested that "it would certainly be a blot upon" the legal system if it could not provide Roberson with a remedy. The court noted that "[a]ny modest and refined young woman might naturally be extremely shocked and wounded in seeing a lithographic likeness of herself posted in public places as an advertisement of some enterprising business firm." The trial court concluded that "[e]very woman has a right to keep her face concealed from the observation of the public. Her face is her own private property" that "no man can take from her" without her permission. The court rooted her rights in a theory of property and ownership of her own likeness, as well as in Thomas Cooley's "right to be let alone."[24]

After being affirmed by the appellate division, the case went to the highest court in New York. On June 27, 1902, a closely divided Court of Appeals split four to three, reversed the lower appellate court, and held that there was no right of privacy in New York. The majority was not unsympathetic to Roberson's claim. Nonetheless, the judges thought that the vast array of line-drawing and free speech concerns that her claim raised indicated that the legislature was the appropriate place to fashion a remedy rather than the courts.[25]

The same Judge Gray who dissented in *Schuyler* dissented in *Roberson*, joined by two other judges. He thought Roberson should have a claim for the nonconsensual "display and use" of her "features [] for another's commercial purposes or gain." It is Gray's ardent dissent in *Roberson* that ultimately survived the test of time. His dissent was widely cited with approval and adopted outside of New York by other courts that confronted the question of whether a right of privacy existed.[26]

The reaction to the New York Court of Appeals' rejection of Roberson's claim was swift and critical. The *New York Times* published an editorial highlighting the "amazement among lawyers and jurists" and the public at the decision. The *Times* called for legislation to reverse the holding and to stop the "horrible" invasions of privacy of both public and private figures. The *American Law Review* similarly described the decision as one that "shocks and wounds the ordinary sense of justice."[27]

On the heels of this public uproar, legislation quickly followed. On April 6, 1903, less than a year after the *Roberson* decision, the governor of New York signed into law the Act to Prevent the Unauthorized Use of the Name or Picture of Any Person for the Purposes of Trade. The statute made it both a misdemeanor and a civil injury to use "for advertising purposes, or for purposes of trade, the name, portrait or picture of any living person" without written consent. Although often referred to as New York's right of privacy law, on its face the law describes a typical right of publicity law. As of 2017, more than one hundred years later, the statute remains the sole basis for privacy- *and* publicity-based claims in New York. Virginia soon followed New York's lead and adopted a similar "privacy" statute.[28]

A few years after *Roberson*, the Supreme Court of Georgia was faced with the same legal issue and unanimously held that a right of privacy existed in the state and that it protected against the display and use of a person's likeness for another's "commercial purposes or gain." In *Pavesich v. New England Life Insurance*, the court held that such a right existed at common law, and therefore no new law needed to be passed to protect such a right. The opinion quoted substantially from Judge Gray's dissent in *Roberson* and boldly criticized its New York counterpart, suggesting that the "day will come that the American bar will marvel that [the *Roberson* court's] view was ever entertained." The court even compared the decision in *Roberson* to Lord Hale's decision in the 1600s "impos[ing] the death penalty for witchcraft upon ignorant and harmless women."[29]

The dispute in *Pavesich* revolved around the nonconsensual use of a photograph of an artist, Paolo Pavesich, in an advertisement for life insurance.

Justice Andrew J. Cobb's opinion for the unanimous court rooted the "right of privacy" in the constitutional right to "liberty." He noted that the right includes the ability to determine the level of "publicity" one may "desire."

> One may desire to live a life of seclusion; another may desire to live a life of publicity; still another may wish to live a life of privacy as to certain matters, and of publicity as to others. . . . Each is entitled to a liberty of choice as to his manner of life, and neither an individual nor the public has a right to arbitrarily take away from him this liberty.[30]

DO IT NOW.
THE MAN WHO DID.

DO IT WHILE YOU CAN.
THE MAN WHO DIDN'T.

THESE TWO PICTURES TELL THEIR OWN STORY.

"In my healthy and productive period of life I bought insurance in the New England Mutual Life Insurance Co., of Boston, Mass., and today my family is protected and I am drawing an annual dividend on my paid-up policies."

"When I had health, vigor and strength I felt the time would never come when I would need insurance. But I see my mistake. If I could recall my life I would buy one of the New England Mutual's 18-Pay Annual Dividen-Policies."

THOMAS B. LUMPKIN, General Agent,
1008-1009-1010 EMPIRE BUILDING.

Paolo Pavesich appears in the photograph on the left. Advertisement for Thomas B. Lumpkin, insurance agent for New England Mutual Life Insurance, published in *Atlanta Constitution*, November 15, 1903, p. 9.

After the Georgia Supreme Court held in *Pavesich* that a right of privacy existed in the state, most state courts to consider whether a right of privacy existed adopted one, and allowed claims arising out of the misappropriation of a person's name or likeness. In 1909, the Kentucky Court of Appeals, that state's highest court at the time, agreed with *Pavesich* and allowed a former senator's claim against a company that falsely advertised his approval of Doan's Kidney Pills and used his name and likeness to sell them. In 1911, a Missouri appellate court adopted a right of privacy, declaring that the right provided a "property right of value" in the "exclusive right to [one's] picture." By 1929, Kansas, Kentucky, Georgia, Louisiana,

Missouri, and New Jersey had all adopted a common law right of privacy. And New York and Virginia had each adopted such a right by statute.[31]

In 1931, California followed suit, recognizing a right of privacy at common law. In *Melvin v. Reid*, a California appellate court held that such a right could be asserted against the producers of a fact-based film that revealed the plaintiff's prior life as a prostitute. From this point forward, California embraced a right of privacy under its common law. By 1941, William L. Prosser observed in his *Handbook of the Law of Torts* that the "majority of the courts which have considered the question have recognized the existence of a right of 'privacy.'" There were a few holdouts, and many states simply had not considered the question, but by this time the right was an uncontroversial, established part of American tort law.[32]

"The Right of Publicity . . . Is No New Idea"

From the beginning, courts and commentators referred to a right to control "publicity" about oneself as central to a right of privacy. Godkin and other commentators advocated for a right to control "publicity" about oneself. Warren and Brandeis called for a right to privacy to limit unauthorized "publicity." Courts regularly held that people, even public performers, had the right to live "free from unwarranted publicity." In 1902, the *New York Times* called for limits on the "purveyors of publicity," including restrictions on the publication of portraits even in newspapers and of public figures to protect "privacy" interests.[33]

At its origin, the two most prominent decisions on the right of privacy were the *Roberson* and *Pavesich* cases, both of which involved the use of the plaintiffs' likenesses in advertising. New York's statutory "right of privacy," which followed in the wake of *Roberson*, was (and, as of 2017, still is) the only right of publicity in the state, and functions as such. In *Pavesich* the Supreme Court of Georgia justified its holding that there was a right of privacy, largely on the basis that there had long been a "right of publicity."

> The right of one to exhibit himself to the public at all proper times, in all proper places, and in a proper manner is embraced within the right of personal liberty. The right to withdraw from the public gaze at such times as a person may see fit, when his presence in public is not demanded by any rule of law, is also embraced within the right of personal liberty.

Publicity in one instance, and privacy in the other are each guarantied. If personal liberty embraces the right of publicity, it no less embraces the correlative right of privacy, and this is no new idea in Georgia law.[34]

What the Georgia Supreme Court meant by a "right of publicity" was likely something different from our current understanding of what is meant by a "right of publicity." Perhaps it meant that one had a right to appear in public, at a time of one's choosing, as an aspect of liberty. But other courts and scholars at the time expressly referred to a right to stop or control "publicity" about oneself and viewed this as central to the rights encompassed in the right of privacy, particularly the right to prevent the use of one's name or likeness. Public figures at the time, from politicians to actors to singers, were already in the business of promoting and building publicity about themselves, and it was widely accepted by the late 1800s that they should be able to control how they appeared in public.[35]

These unwanted publicity cases lay at the heart of the right of privacy at the time of its adoption and spread in the United States. In 1911, an article in the *Columbia Law Review* described the right of "privacy" as synonymous with the "Right to Immunity from Wrongful Publicity," a right that the article urged should continue to be adopted across the country. In 1927, the Kentucky Court of Appeals described the right of privacy as "the right to be let alone, that is, the right of a person to be free from unwarranted *publicity*, or the right to live without unwarranted interference by the public about matters with which the public is not necessarily concerned." In 1929, George Ragland Jr., writing in the *Kentucky Law Journal*, described the "typical" right of privacy cases as the "picture-ad" cases. Leon Green writing in 1932 similarly noted that the most frequent privacy claims were about the "appropriation" of "personality," including the use of a person's name or likeness.[36]

In 1939, in the first *Restatement of Torts*, the American Law Institute included a privacy-based tort in the section "Miscellaneous Rules." The *Restatement* described the cause of action as when a "person unreasonably and seriously interferes with another's interest in not having his affairs known to others or his likeness exhibited to the public. . . ." William Prosser included the "right of privacy" in his influential 1941 treatise on tort law, and described it as including the right to control "*publicity* given to [a person's] name or likeness, . . . and the commercial appropriation of elements of his personality." He observed that "[t]he greater number of privacy cases . . . have involved the appropriation of some element of the plaintiff's personality for a commercial use. The typical case is that of the unauthorized use of his picture in the defendant's advertising."[37]

In 1955, a California appellate court described one of the "most flagrant and common means of invasion of privacy" as "[t]he exploitation of another's personality for commercial purposes." The court defined the right of privacy as the "right of a person to be free from unauthorized and unwarranted *publicity*." This right to control "publicity" about oneself was a concern that long predated the creation and adoption of what we now consider the independent right of publicity, and was always central to the right of privacy and to the adoption of that right.[38]

◇ ◇ ◇

Although the first state high court to consider whether a right of privacy existed rejected its existence, the decision was swiftly overturned by the legislature after a public outcry. Fifty years after Warren and Brandeis, Godkin, and others called for such a right of privacy, it was firmly established and often was synonymous with, or exemplified by, the right to the exclusive use of one's name and likeness. Concerns over the misappropriation of identity and unwanted publicity were not novel when the right of publicity purportedly emerged in the early 1950s. To the contrary, they were long-standing and in large part the inciting incident for the development of the right of privacy itself. Such cases were the prototypical privacy claim at the right of privacy's inception.

2

From the Ashes of Privacy

THE CREATION OF A RIGHT of publicity and its divergence from the right of privacy were not driven by essential differences. The right of privacy always included the right to stop others from using one's name and likeness publicly—in fact, this was central to its adoption. From the beginning, the right of privacy was understood as providing a right to stop "unwarranted publicity" about oneself. The central concept of privacy law—the "right to be let alone"—thus encompassed far more than just protection against the revelation of secrets or the intrusion into secluded spots. The right of publicity was therefore neither novel in name nor in substance at the time of the turn toward today's independent right of publicity. It is often claimed that the shift to the right of publicity was the result of public figures losing their rights of privacy by entering the public arena, whether voluntarily as politicians or performers, or involuntarily in the wake of publicized successes or tragedies. But this revisionist claim, like those regarding the right of publicity's novelty, is also mistaken.

When the right of privacy was adopted, it protected both private and public figures alike, including those with commercially valuable identities who actively sought out publicity and promoted themselves. Although some outlier cases rejected claims by public figures and paved the way for a shift to a right of publicity, courts and scholars have exaggerated the frequency, relevance, and import of these cases. Most of these cases either did not in fact make such holdings or were later abandoned in the relevant jurisdictions. Many of the successful early privacy cases involved lawsuits by public luminaries, ranging from the famous inventor Thomas Edison, to a former senator, J. P. Chinn, to a Harvard University president,

Dr. Charles W. Eliot, to a professional golfer, Jack Redmond, to a host of actors and entertainers, from Nancy Flake to Rudolph Marks to Gladys Loftus to Fred Astaire.[1]

One of the first lawsuits to raise the awareness and ire of the public over the misappropriation of a person's image is one already discussed in Chapter 1—that of Marion Manola, a successful actress who objected to the taking of her picture in tights while she was on stage performing in front of an audience. In their influential call for a "right to privacy," Samuel Warren and Louis Brandeis explicitly supported Manola's claim, and by implication those of other public figures who objected to unauthorized uses of their identities. In fact, such objections were central to their thinking, given their concerns over the wrongs committed against likely well-known members of Boston's high society, who were often targets of yellow journalists. Even though Warren and Brandeis at times suggested that the right to privacy was necessary to protect "private" individuals, they either had a broad view of what constituted private figures or thought that public figures should also be able to control public uses of their identities.[2]

The *New York Times*, in its 1902 editorial calling for the adoption of a "right of privacy," advocated for a broad right that would protect not just private figures like Abigail Roberson but also public ones, like the president of the United States and the prominent businessman J. P. Morgan. The October 1902 issue of *Current Literature* similarly advocated that everyone, even the president, should have a "right of privacy" and be able to prevent others from taking their picture in public.[3]

After the passage of New York's statutory right of privacy in 1903, courts applied the law to public figures, including well-known actors, athletes, musicians, and renowned heroes, and continue to do so today. Other state courts also allowed public figures to bring privacy claims. The Supreme Court of Georgia, in its 1905 decision in *Pavesich v. New England Life Insurance*, explained in some detail why it thought that even the president and other public office-holders retained rights of privacy:

> [I]t cannot be that the mere fact that a man aspires to public office or holds public office subjects him to the humiliation and mortification of having his picture displayed in places where he would never go to be gazed upon, at times when and under circumstances where if he were personally present the sensibilities of his nature would be severely shocked. If one's picture may be used by another for advertising purposes,

it may be reproduced and exhibited anywhere. If it may be used in a newspaper, it may be used on a poster or a placard. It may be posted upon the walls of private dwellings or upon the streets. It may ornament the bar of the saloon keeper or decorate the walls of a brothel.

Whatever one thinks of the Georgia court's limits on free speech, its views highlight that at the time that the right of privacy emerged it was broad enough to encompass public figures, including even politicians running for office. In the 1938 decision in *Flake v. Greensboro News*, the Supreme Court of North Carolina held that a right of privacy existed in that state and allowed an action for damages by a well-known singer when her picture was used in an advertisement without her permission.[4]

Although William Prosser suggested in his 1941 torts treatise that there should be greater latitude to use the identities of public figures, he did not think such individuals waived their right of privacy. In fact, he cited favorably to an early privacy case from 1893, *Marks v. Jaffa*, in which a public figure, a well-known actor, prevailed against a newspaper that used his name and picture without his permission in a popularity contest. In Samuel Spring's 1952 treatise, *Risks and Rights in Publishing, Television, Radio, Motion Pictures, Advertising and the Theater*, Spring highlighted this role of "privacy" law in protecting the rights of performers, actors, models, and professional athletes to control how their names, pictures, and character portraits were used in advertising, trade, and even in "entertainment." In 1957, the Supreme Court of Alabama agreed that "public character[s]" do not waive their rights of privacy and can sue for commercial uses of their identities.[5]

Show Me the Money

Some scholars and courts have erroneously claimed that even if public figures were able to bring claims for a violation of the right of privacy, they were limited to injunctive relief (stopping the offending use) or only to nominal damages if they did not suffer emotional distress. This would indeed be a significant limitation on the right of privacy, especially for public figures who actively commercialize and promote their identities, but it turns out not to be true. Courts routinely allowed public figures to recover economic damages, even when they did not suffer wounded feelings. Many of the public figures who brought privacy claims early on had economic interests at stake, in addition to dignitary ones. As Prosser observed in 1941, privacy-based misappropriation cases allowed recovery for injuries both to "personal feelings" and to "commercial value."[6]

Although ascertaining final recoveries in cases from the early days of privacy litigation is challenging as many records have been lost, there is ample evidence that many public figures received substantial recoveries under the right of privacy. In 1908, the actress Felicite Skiff Riddle recovered $3,000 in damages, equivalent to approximately $75,000 today, when the defendant used her photograph to advertise a book about "hair culture" without her permission. The well-known public hero Jack Binns was awarded $12,500 in 1911, approximately $300,000 today, when his name and identity were used without his permission in a fictionalized movie about his real-life use of telegraph technology to save thousands of lives at sea. The New York Court of Appeals upheld the award despite the fact that Binns was a public figure who had actively commercialized his identity by participating in a show at Coney Island that used his name to promote attendance. In 1936, the same court upheld a $5,000 award, $90,000 today, for a professional bullfighter when his performance was captured in a newsreel without his permission. At least half of that award derived from a violation of his right of privacy. Even when courts did not award damages, they often indicated that public figures could collect money damages for professional injuries under other circumstances, or in the same case after further discovery and litigation.[7]

Although early on many plaintiffs who were public figures exclusively claimed reputational, dignity-based, and emotional harms, not all did. Some public personalities freely admitted that they actively commercialized, promoted, and publicized their own images and names for their professional benefit, and did not suffer emotional distress from the uses about which they complained. They recovered even when the particular images that they complained of were ones that they had agreed to appear in, and even when they had agreed to the wide circulation of the photos for publicity purposes. These performers were upset not about the use of their name or image in general, but about uses that they did not control or give permission for, and for which they were not paid. In 1918, Gladys Loftus, a well-known Ziegfeld Follies performer, sought $50,000 in damages when her likeness was used in advertising for a motion picture in which she did not appear. Loftus did not claim to have suffered emotional distress, indignity, or humiliation as a result. She instead simply claimed a right to control the use of her image. In 1936, the well-known "trick shot" golfer, Jack Redmond, sought $25,000 in damages when Columbia Pictures licensed and reused newsreel footage of him doing trick shots. Redmond's main basis for seeking damages was not for emotional distress or reputational harm, but for the lack of "compensation" and lost business, as he claimed that the use of the footage jeopardized a movie deal he was negotiating. Notably, he had voluntarily appeared in the original newsreel footage and regularly appeared in such newsreels as he thought they were useful promotional tools.[8]

Public figures and other plaintiffs often pleaded reputational harms and emotional distress when bringing privacy claims because the new law's boundaries were not established and the right of privacy's existence in many states was unknown. Accordingly, plaintiffs wanted to preserve defamation claims that require a showing that the use damaged their reputation. It also was not yet clearly established what the cognizable injuries of privacy violations were, so lawyers tried to fit the claims into the rubric of the harms first raised by the plaintiffs in *Roberson* and *Pavesich*, both of whom had claimed to suffer emotional distress and reputational harms from the uses of their photographs in advertisements.

Many plaintiffs therefore hedged their bets and claimed that they suffered some humiliation or mental distress, even when it was clear that these were not their main complaints. And they likely underplayed their commercial harms because those claims would undercut defamation claims— plaintiffs' reputations could not be damaged by uses that were similar to how they were already using their own names and likenesses. In the early 1900s, Jack Binns—famed hero of the telegraph—complained about the use of his identity in a movie in part because his "name and reputation are of great pecuniary value to him in his said business" and the use in the movie "greatly damaged [Binns's] business and made less valuable to him his [] name and pictures." Binns conceded that he appreciated the press coverage he received for his heroic deeds and did not find it "distasteful." He even surprisingly testified that he had never even seen the movie that was at issue and that he claimed had humiliated him. Nevertheless, he also claimed reputational injuries and that he suffered emotional distress, and his testimony primarily focused on these aspects of his injuries.[9]

As photographs and their dissemination became more common, it also became less shocking and debilitating to see one's image in public. Rather than being mortified when their image was used, both public and private figures simply wanted to choose when and how their images appeared. This shift predated the turn toward an independent right of publicity and was already well on its way when the right of privacy emerged. Celebrity endorsements were on the rise by the late 1800s. One of the most prominent series of advertisements in the 1880s was for Pears Soap, an English brand known for its innovative marketing. The series used personal endorsements from celebrities of the day, from famous American preacher Henry Ward Beecher, to the international acting sensation Lillie Langtry, to the world-renowned opera star Adelina Patti. By the 1920s, this trend had expanded even further and the number of celebrities had grown to include film stars. As James Playsted Wood wrote in *The Story of Advertising*, by this time, "[o]pera stars, society women, prize fighters, baseball players, [and] explorers were all available at a price. They like the publicity and the fees." The right of privacy protected all of them.[10]

"Privacy Is the One Thing He Did Not Want, or Need"

Despite the reality that public figures could recover under the right of privacy, including monetary damages for professional injuries, many have erroneously claimed that public figures could not do so. These mistaken views primarily stem from overreliance on dicta—comments neither required for the decisions nor binding on future courts—from various cases. Many of these decisions also predated the adoption of a right of privacy in the relevant state, and therefore were not indicative of the scope of privacy law in other states or even those states once they ultimately adopted such a right. Often the statements suggesting that public figures lacked a right of privacy arose in cases that involved *private* figures. In most of these cases, the claims by the private figures were allowed, and the language about the privacy rights of public figures justified the court's cursory dismissal of a speech-related defense in the context of a private person. In these instances, then, the courts never directly considered the rights of *public* figures, nor whether they would have a claim under similar circumstances.[11]

There were a few cases involving public figures in which courts appeared to limit their privacy rights. But these apparent conclusions were also often in dicta or arose in a context in which the countervailing free speech interests predominated. In these instances, courts frequently collapsed the privacy question with the primary issue, which was whether the defendant's use was newsworthy, and therefore permissible regardless of the privacy interests of the plaintiff. Today, these inquiries are usually distinct, but early on in the development of privacy and free speech law these considerations were often not distinguished.

Overlooked in the simplistic and erroneous claims that public figures waived their privacy rights is the reality that private figures were also held to waive their privacy rights when they were at the center of a matter deemed newsworthy or of public interest. The crucial inquiry was not whether a person was a public or private figure—both could bring privacy claims—but whether the use was newsworthy. Newsworthiness defenses were more likely to be successful in the context of a plaintiff who was a public figure, but that did not mean that such a person lacked a right of privacy.[12]

A closer look at the most frequently cited cases demonstrates the flaws in the assertion that public figures could not bring privacy claims. The 1894 decision in *Corliss v. E. W. Walker Company* has often been cited to support the proposition that public figures lack privacy rights because such "public characters" become public property. In dicta, the court in *Corliss* suggested:

> A statesman, author, artist, or inventor, who asks for and desires public recognition, may be said to have surrendered this right [of privacy] to the public. . . . It would be extending this right of protection too far to say that the general public can be prohibited from knowing the personal appearance of great public characters. Such characters may be said, of their own volition, to have dedicated to the public the right of any fair portraiture of themselves.

It is misleading to rely on this dicta from *Corliss* for a broad proposition that public figures have no right of privacy. Put in its proper context, the case focuses on the nature of the use—a photograph of a deceased inventor in a biography about him—not the scope of his postmortem privacy rights. There was no question that the use was a justified one; it was considered both newsworthy and in the public interest. The decision also had little precedential value given that it was made at a time when Massachusetts law, under which it was decided, had not yet recognized a right of privacy. Thus, *Corliss* tells us nothing of how the state would treat such a claim if made after the state recognized a right of privacy, or if the use had been in an advertisement or on merchandise, instead of in a biography, or if Corliss had been alive. Thus, despite being cited for the contention that a public figure cedes his right of privacy, the case actually tells us little of what rights public figures had by the 1950s, when there was purportedly a need for a new right to protect them.[13]

Others cases frequently cited for the proposition that public figures cede their privacy rights similarly do not stand up to scrutiny. In the 1949 decision in *Cohen v. Marx*, a California appellate court rejected a professional boxer's claim that his right of privacy prevented a popular quiz show, *You Bet Your Life*, from broadcasting a former manager's critical comment about his talent. In so holding, the court suggested:

> [W]hen plaintiff sought publicity and the adulation of the public, he relinquished his right to privacy on matters pertaining to his professional activity, and he could not at his will and whim draw himself like a snail into his shell and hold others liable for commenting upon the acts which had taken place when he had voluntarily exposed himself to the public eye.

No doubt the image of the boxer "Canvasback Cohen" drawing up into his snail shell had literary appeal, but the court never suggested that Cohen lost his privacy rights. Instead, it simply concluded that as to this particular use it was waived, again collapsing the newsworthiness defense with its analysis of the scope of the right of privacy.[14]

Another oft-cited case for the waiver of privacy rights by public figures is the 1952 decision in *Gautier v. Pro-Football*. Like *Corliss* and *Cohen*, *Gautier* involved a newsworthy use. In *Gautier*, the New York Court of Appeals held that the plaintiff, Arsene Gautier, an animal trainer, could not bring a claim under the state's privacy law when his performance in the halftime show of a professional football game was televised on ABC without his permission. Gautier's contract to perform during the show specifically required additional permission (and no doubt payment) for broadcasting his performance. There was no question that Gautier had a breach of contract claim against the defendant, but the court rejected his privacy-based claim.

The court contrasted the situation in *Gautier* with that in *Binns v. Vitagraph Company of America*. In *Binns*, the plaintiff, Jack Binns, was singled out, and his identity commercialized as the central figure in a fictional-ized film about his heroism at sea. In contrast, Gautier agreed to perform in front of 35,000 spectators, the broadcast documented this perfor-mance, and therefore disseminated news and information about the event. Although commentators often cite to *Gautier* claiming that his pri-vacy claim was rejected because he was a public figure, that is not what the court held. Instead, Gautier's claim was rejected because the broadcast was considered news, as opposed to a use for trade or advertising purposes—as required by the New York privacy statute. Fictional uses, such as the movie from *Binns*, were deemed exploitative and for trade purposes, while non-fiction uses were not.[15]

One reason *Gautier* may be erroneously (and frequently) cited for a broader proposition about public figures ceding their privacy rights is Judge Charles Stewart Desmond's concurrence. Desmond went further than the majority and suggested that Gautier had no right to privacy because he sought out publicity. Desmond wrote that "privacy is the one thing [Gautier] did not want, or need, in his occupation." Desmond highlighted that Gautier's real complaint was not his "right to be let alone" but his right to be compensated for the broadcast. Four judges joined the majority opinion that the use fell outside the statute, and two judges dissented (con-cluding that Gautier did have a privacy claim), but no one, not a single other judge, joined Desmond's opinion. Thus, the conclusion that this case is so often cited for was supported by only *one* out of the seven judges on the court, and has never been the law of New York. Nevertheless, *Gautier* has been frequently cited primarily by legal scholars for the proposition that public figures lose their right of privacy. Most courts, however, and virtually all applying New York law (under which *Gautier* was decided) have, instead, accurately concluded that *Gautier* allowed public figures to retain broad privacy rights.[16]

Many early privacy cases emphasized that public figures retained the ability to object to the taking of their pictures without permission, the making of merchandise using their identities, and the wide exhibition of their images or names, particularly in advertising. The right of privacy of "prominent public men" gave them the right to prevent manufacturers from publishing their "pictures," even if they did not have the same lati-tude to stop newspapers from doing so.[17]

One of the very few examples in which a court actually did deny a public figure a privacy-based recovery in an exploitative (rather than a newsworthy) context was the 1938 Ohio trial court decision in *Martin v. F.I.Y. Theatre*. The plaintiff in *Martin* was a successful actress who objected to the defendant's posting of her picture outside a burlesque theater with which she had no connection. Martin alleged that the use of her image was defamatory and also violated her right of privacy. The trial court noted that Ohio had not yet recognized a right of privacy, and erroneously suggested that there was a trend toward rejecting such a right. For this mistaken proposition, the court cited *Roberson* (without noting that it had been overruled by statute more than thirty years earlier!) and a California appellate court decision that it erroneously read as rejecting a right of privacy, when that decision actually held there *was* a right of privacy in California.

Not letting sound legal research stand in its way, the trial court declined to find a right of privacy under Ohio law. But the court didn't stop there. It also suggested that even if such a right existed, it would not apply to public figures, who should be understood to have waived their privacy rights by entering the public eye:

> Persons who expose themselves to public view for hire cannot expect to have the same privacy as the meek, plodding stay-at-home citizen. . . . Actresses and actors seek publicity and often adopt various and sundry ways of securing such notoriety as will attract attention to them. They cannot expect to lead quiet, secluded lives. . . . The Court is of the opinion that any person following the theatrical business for a life's work has no such right or privacy as plaintiff attempts to assert in her complaint. . . . An actress of [her] accomplishments and reputation . . . is no longer a private individual, but has become a public character and cannot complain that any right of privacy is trespassed upon by the mere unauthorized publication of a photograph.

The court did not consider Martin's economic injuries, and discounted her "injured feelings" at being associated with a low-rent and salacious troupe. Nevertheless, although rarely noted by commentators, the court allowed her libel claim to proceed.[18]

The Supreme Court of Ohio ultimately rejected the conclusion in *Martin* that public figures could not bring privacy claims. In 1956, it held that a right of privacy did exist in the state, and in another case, one that went to the United States Supreme Court, the Ohio court accepted the possibility that a public performer could bring a misappropriation claim under Ohio's privacy law and recover economic damages for the violation. The overruled *Martin* likely would have fallen into obscurity if enterprising litigants and legal scholars had not inflated its importance (and substantive merits). Despite being a suspect decision riddled with errors, having little precedential value as a trial court, and ultimately being rejected by the state's highest court, the dicta from *Martin*—which suggested that a public performer did not have a right of privacy—was (and continues to be) cited as evidence that public figures lose their privacy rights and therefore need an independent right of publicity to protect their interests.[19]

"The Publicity He Got Was Only That Which He Had Been Constantly Seeking"

The most prominent case cited as holding that public figures waive their right of privacy in the context of a potentially exploitative use is *O'Brien v. Pabst Sales*, a Fifth Circuit Court of Appeals decision from 1941. Like so many of the other cases cited for the erroneous claim that public figures lost their privacy rights, *O'Brien* made no such holding and is cited for this proposition only because of a comment made in dicta, in a state, Texas, that had not yet adopted a right of privacy at the time of the decision.

O'Brien involved the use of a well-known college football player's name and likeness on a calendar put out by a beer manufacturer. The plaintiff, David O'Brien, had been a quarterback for Texas Christian University (TCU) and was recognized as the top collegiate football player of 1938. He won the Heisman Trophy that year and then played professional football with the Philadelphia Eagles for a couple of years before becoming an FBI agent.

The defendant, Pabst Blue Ribbon, a beer producer, put out an annual calendar that provided the intercollegiate football schedule for the upcoming season and displayed images of some of the top college athletes from the prior year. O'Brien objected to the 1939 calendar in which he was prominently featured. A large picture of him appeared above the schedule, beneath the company's name, and next to a picture of a beer can. This particularly irked O'Brien, who was opposed to the consumption of alcohol and refused to endorse such products. A second image of O'Brien appeared on the calendar with other players in a box that con-

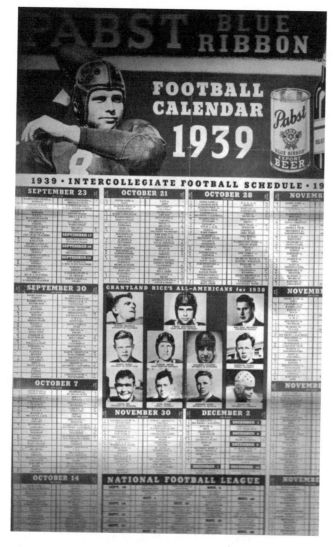

1939 Pabst Blue Ribbon football calendar from *O'Brien v. Pabst Sales*, 124 F.2d 167 (5th Cir. 1941), National Archives, Fort Worth, TX.

tained the names and photographs of Grantland Rice's All-Americans team for 1938.

Although the court ultimately agreed with Pabst that O'Brien did not have a claim, it never held that O'Brien waived his privacy rights because he was a well-known football player. Instead, the opinion noted that the specific photograph used by Pabst was one that O'Brien had consented to have taken, and to its use for publicizing himself and the team. As the court pointed out, Pabst's use of that photograph was specifically authorized by the TCU publicity department, which itself was authorized to do so by O'Brien. Thus, the primary basis for rejecting O'Brien's claim was that the "use of the photograph was by permission."[20]

This understanding of the case is further supported by the fact that the court was open to a variety of economic-damages claims by O'Brien despite his status as a public figure, or, perhaps, because of it. The court indicated that it might have recognized a claim of economic injury stemming from the use, including on the basis of an unjust enrichment claim, and an argument that O'Brien was owed the "reasonable value of his endorsement." But O'Brien and his lawyers had not made such an argument. O'Brien claimed that he suffered "humiliation, embarrassment, and damage to him in the actual sum of $25,000." He did not specify economic losses, though he did note that he routinely did endorsements, just not for alcohol. He primarily focused on the shame of appearing on a beer company's calendar given his well-known opposition to alcohol. This embarrassment only seemed likely to the court if people thought O'Brien agreed to be on the calendar, and therefore was perceived to be endorsing the beer. The court suggested it would have allowed such a false endorsement claim if there had been evidence of likely confusion as to sponsorship, but there was none. In the absence of such evidence O'Brien's claim of embarrassment was unconvincing.[21]

Judge Edwin R. Holmes's dissent in the case further supports this interpretation. Holmes disagreed with the majority, not about privacy law, which he thought was not the issue the majority decided, but instead about pleading requirements and evidentiary hurdles. Holmes thought O'Brien had presented sufficient proof to the jury that he should be compensated for the value of the use of his image, even if his complaint had not included a specific claim for professional damages or lost endorsement fees. Holmes pointed to trial testimony documenting that O'Brien had agreed to do various endorsements, and was compensated for doing so. Holmes thought denying O'Brien a claim in this case could interfere with his future endorsement deals. He noted that O'Brien had been paid $400 for similar uses and questioned whether further payments would be made given the majority's decision.[22]

Nevertheless, the case is regularly cited for the proposition that public figures cannot bring privacy claims because of the following dicta that suggested that O'Brien did not have a right of privacy claim: "[T]he publicity he got was only that which he had been constantly seeking and receiving." It is this one throwaway sentence that has gained the most attention in the case and that is so often cited without considering the rest of the case. This problematic dicta about O'Brien waiving his privacy right as a public figure likely emerged because Pabst's lawyer, in a legitimate moment of zealous, if overreaching, advocacy, incorrectly claimed that there was a "uniform[ity]" of opinion that public figures lose their right to privacy and become a "public possession." Pabst claimed that as a "football star [O'Brien's] likeness has become the possession of the public." As a result, O'Brien could not "choose what members of the public may reproduce it or the places where its reproduction may be hung."[23]

Holmes's dissent also may have supported this mistaken reading of the case because he distinguished a "right of privacy" from the "right to use one's name or picture for purposes of commercial advertisement." Holmes noted that because "commercial advertisers customarily pay for the right to use the name and likeness of a person who has become famous," there should be a cause of action when companies use the person's identity without permission. Holmes's distinction, however, was perplexing because such uses already were barred in jurisdictions that recognized a right of privacy. But Holmes's dissent, combined with the one line from the majority, skewed subsequent analyses of privacy-based misappropriation cases involving public figures.[24]

Texas ultimately rejected the alleged suggestion from *O'Brien* that public figures could not bring a right of privacy claim. In 1975, a Texas court of appeals held that a right of privacy existed in the state and explicitly extended the right to public figures, expressly including football players, and allowed for the recovery of economic damages. Nevertheless, *O'Brien*—and misguided reliance on dicta from that case—heavily influenced future courts and calls for adopting something new to address the needs of public figures, particularly those with potentially lucrative endorsement careers.[25]

○ ○ ○

By the 1950s, when the right of publicity emerged as something distinct from the right of privacy, some courts had indeed suggested that public figures had more limited privacy rights, but virtually none had actually held that they waived such rights. If anything, the weight of authority indicated that public figures retained a broad right of privacy and could enforce it, and even recover economic damages without regard to whether they suffered emotional distress or specific reputational harms. Nevertheless, the outlier decisions and dicta in several cases which suggested that public figures waived or had more limited privacy rights encouraged scholars and litigants to contend that something different was needed for public figures— even though privacy had long adequately protected their interests.

3

A Star Is Born?

B Y THE 1950S, the right of privacy was no longer controversial and was increasingly accepted across the country. This right included the ability to stop (or recover for) the unwanted use or misappropriation of a person's name or likeness, and was often described as a property right. It could be asserted by both public and private figures, and allowed recovery for economic and reputational harms, as well as for emotional distress. There was, therefore, no need for something new to address unauthorized and exploitative uses of public figures' names and likenesses. But the right of privacy did lack one thing—it was not a transferable right, meaning it could not be sold or given away to others, or inherited by heirs. This was not a problem for individuals who could adequately protect their interests, but it emerged as a concern for others, particularly businesses. Companies wanted the power to stop identity-holders from authorizing more than one use of their names and likenesses. This was the issue that arose in the 1953 decision in *Haelan Laboratories v. Topps Chewing Gum*, and that wound up unexpectedly changing the course of the right of privacy forever.

There is a widespread, almost universal belief held by virtually all courts and scholars that *Haelan* coined the term the "right of publicity" and that it created a "new" right—one that protected the economic interests of public figures who sought out publicity, and who were allegedly left out in the cold under privacy laws. Commentators even describe *Haelan* as protecting the rights of individuals to the economic value of their names and likenesses. But the decision did none of these things. The case was a battle between two gum manufacturers that were fighting over control of baseball players' names and pictures on trading cards. The baseball players themselves were never a part of the litigation and, if anything, were left worse off by the decision. This chapter tells the story of what really happened in *Haelan*.[1]

"Purely Personal and Not Assignable"

What is often thought of as the driving force behind the turn to the right of publicity was not in fact the impetus for its adoption. The problem was not that public figures lacked privacy rights, but instead that companies wanted stronger tools to prevent public personalities from giving permission to more than one company to use their names and likenesses. Particularly concerning to some companies were instances in which identity-holders (like actors and baseball players) did not want to sue third parties that used their names or likenesses (because they did not mind the publicity or did not want bad publicity from litigation), or more frequently could not sue (because they had consented to multiple and conflicting uses of their identities). These concerns had been raised in two cases before *Haelan*—one involving silent movie stars, and the other the famous Louisville Slugger baseball bats. It is with these two cases that the story of *Haelan* truly begins.

The first seeds of an independent right of publicity were actually sown in 1915, in a decision by a New York trial court in *Pakas Company v. Leslie*. *Pakas* involved the use of actresses' portraits in a collector series of posterettes, or poster stamps. The plaintiff, the Pakas Company, made five-year exclusive deals with a number of silent-movie actresses. The contracts provided no payments or other consideration to the actresses beyond the value of the free publicity in having the portraits circulate. The actresses allegedly did not know what the contracts said, did not read them, and had been told they were not exclusive. Pakas sued when Arthur Leslie and the other defendants in the case used some of the same actresses' pictures on portrait stamps. Pakas claimed that the contracts that the actresses signed gave it the right to assert the actresses' rights of privacy against the defendants, both to enjoin (stop) the uses and to collect damages.

It turned out that the actresses who signed the contracts with Pakas were employed at the time by the Vitagraph Company of America, one of the major motion-picture studios of the silent-film era—and coincidentally the defendant in Jack Binns's right of privacy lawsuit. The defendants in the case, including the named Arthur Leslie, had received permission from Vitagraph to use the actresses' names and images for publicity purposes, including on the *Famous Stars Series* stamps at issue in the litigation. Vitagraph held the copyright to most of the images used on the stamps and therefore could authorize the use of them. The actresses took Leslie and Vitagraph's side and asked the court not to issue an injunction against the uses by Leslie and the other defendants. The actresses emphasized that they did not authorize this or any lawsuit by Pakas asserting their rights. They had expressly approved of the defendants' uses of their names and images, and had no objections.[2]

The court did not question the conclusion that the actresses, despite being public figures, would have had a claim if any of the uses had been without their permission. Instead, the court addressed a different issue and held, as reported in the *New York Law Journal*, that privacy claims under New York law were "purely personal and not assignable" to Pakas. The court suggested that "[r]ights for outraged feelings are not more assignable than would be a claim arising from a libelous utterance." It is for this proposition that the case is usually cited. However, the *Journal*'s report appears to be of the court's order denying a preliminary injunction against the defendants rather than the final judgment in the case. Just over a month after the *Journal*'s report of the case, the trial court dismissed the complaint as to defendant Leslie's use of copyrighted photos owned and licensed by Vitagraph, but allowed a judgment against Leslie for the uses of other images of the actresses. Contrary to the conventional description of the case, the court actually allowed Pakas to enforce its contracts against Leslie via an injunction. Thus, even though the actresses' privacy claims under New York law were not assignable, Pakas could still enjoin uses over which it had superior rights. The only reason the company could not enjoin all of the uses was that Vitagraph held the copyright to many of the photographs and had lawfully licensed the photographs to Leslie. Leslie therefore had superior rights to Pakas as to those copyrighted images.[3]

Despite not knowing the actual outcome of the litigation, at least one law student at the time criticized the decision and claimed that companies needed a new tool in their kit to protect their interests in similar circumstances. At a time when law reviews were more widely read and student comments in them far more influential than they are today, a *Harvard Law Review* note on *Pakas* advocated for splitting the property-based claims of those who sought publicity from the privacy-based and reputational claims of private figures. The student's simplistic assessment—that the right of privacy was not a property right—was, and remains, historically inaccurate. From the start there was a property-based conception of the right of privacy. It was understood as a right of self-ownership. Many of the cases that supported the adoption of a right of privacy rested on property-based claims, such as analogies to common law copyright. Even before the adoption of a right of privacy, public figures who commercialized their identities were understood to have property rights over their names and likenesses. Once the right to privacy was broadly adopted, courts often described it as a "property" right, even when private figures were the plaintiffs. Nor was the student correct that public figures and corporations were left unprotected by either the decision in *Pakas* or New York's right of privacy law. Despite the failings of this student's assessment, future students, scholars, and courts cited to this note and repeated its misunderstanding of *Pakas* and of the right of privacy.[4]

As I will explore further in Chapter 6, mere status as property does not automatically translate to transferability—we limit transfers of property in a variety of instances. So even if the right of privacy (including the right to one's own name and likeness) is property, that does not necessarily mean it is transferable property. This is exactly what the Fifth Circuit Court of Appeals concluded in 1935, in the highest profile decision holding that privacy rights could not be transferred. The Fifth Circuit in *Hanna Manufacturing v. Hillerich & Bradsby* held that a company could not divest a person of his name even if that company had an exclusive right to its use. *Hanna Manufacturing* involved the use of baseball players' names on baseball bats. Hillerich & Bradsby made a number of deals with players giving it the exclusive authorization to use their names and often signatures on its famous Louisville Slugger "autograph bats." Hanna Manufacturing used some of the same players' names on its own bats and Hillerich & Bradsby objected. Hillerich & Bradsby's complaint alleged violations of trademark and unfair competition laws, as well as an interference with contract claim.

The trial court had held that the "baseball players, like any other individuals, have a property right in their names," that this right is "capable of assignment," and that these rights were transferred in some instances to the plaintiff, Hillerich & Bradsby. The court concluded that the uses by Hanna Manufacturing of these players' names on its bats violated this exclusive property right. The trial court's conclusion that the right could be assigned was not required, however, for the unfair competition claim on which the decision rested.[5]

The Fifth Circuit affirmed the trial court's conclusion that the use of the players' names constituted false representations and unfair competition, but limited the scope of the issued injunction so that the defendant could accurately indicate, including on the bat itself, that the bats were in the "style" of those used by particular players. The appellate court agreed that the players had "property" rights in their names, but concluded that this property was not "vendible in gross so as to pass from purchaser to purchaser unconnected with any trade or business." The court did not think that "fame" was "merchandise," nor that divesting players of their names would help the players nor "sportsmanship nor business." The court noted that to the extent there was confusion as to sponsorship or endorsement, which the district court held there might be, liability and an injunction were appropriate. The appellate court therefore allowed an injunction against Hanna despite the lack of assignability of the rights to players' names and likenesses to Hillerich & Bradsby.[6]

Perhaps attracted by the topic of baseball, many law students wrote comments about *Hanna Manufacturing*, and they were uniformly critical of the lack of assignability to corporations of the players' names. One student wrote in a 1936 issue of the *Harvard Law Review* that the holding in *Hanna Manufacturing* was "unfortunate" and advocated that companies, like Hillerich & Bradsby, should have a cause of action in such instances even if there is no likelihood of confusion. The comment discounted the sufficiency of unfair competition claims rooted in deception, and did not consider breach of contract claims or the torts of interference with contract or inducement of breach, even though those claims were well established at the time and could have protected Hillerich & Bradsby's Louisville Slugger bats if the players had given permission to both companies.

The student commentators also missed the free speech issue at the heart of the case—Hillerich & Bradsby could not and should not have been able to stop all uses of the players' names, because that would violate the public interest in receiving truthful information. This is exactly what the Fifth Circuit held. The public and the competing bat company, Hanna, had interests in accurately describing and receiving information about Hanna's bats, including that they were designed to match the bat preferences and styles of particular players. Even if the players' names and signatures had been assignable to the bat manufacturer, Hillerich & Bradsby, the company still would not have been able to stop such uses by Hanna.

The student comment in the *Harvard Law Review* also erroneously suggested that the holding in *Hanna Manufacturing* prevented players from controlling the "commercial use" of their names, when it did no such thing. *Hanna Manufacturing* did not address whether players could have sued directly, which they could have if the uses had been without permission. A Columbia Law School student similarly and erroneously claimed that *Hanna Manufacturing* indicated that a "public character" waived his right of privacy—even though the decision in *Hanna Manufacturing* made no such holding and in fact indicated the opposite.[7]

A more nuanced view came from a Yale Law School student who correctly observed that the individual players could have brought claims for privacy violations and that public figures waived rights only in the context of relevant news coverage. The note observed that the only issue was whether a licensee or assignee of those rights could sue a third party directly for using the players' names or likenesses. The student observed that it would be easier for a company like Hillerich & Bradsby if it could get an assignment of the players' rights to their names or likenesses. Of course, just because it is easier for the bat manufacturer does not make it the best rule, and the student-author did not elaborate any other reasons to allow such transfers. Despite their failings, these student notes influenced litigators and judges, including the judges in *Haelan*, who cited them as evidence that the weight of scholarly authority was against the decision in *Hanna Manufacturing* and in favor of a transferable right.[8]

Haelan Laboratories v. Topps Chewing Gum

Haelan is the case that has by far had the most influence on the development of the right of publicity, but it also is a case that has been profoundly misunderstood. Only by a careful review of the underlying facts, legal strategies, and theories advanced in the case can a full picture of what the case decided—and what it did not decide—become clear. *Haelan* involved a tangled web of contracts granting permission (usually exclusive for a limited period of time) to use various major league baseball players' names and images on trading cards included with gum or candy. Baseball cards originated as early as the 1880s and were the most popular of the many trading card series. By the late 1940s, the two major players in the field were the parties in *Haelan*—Bowman Gum (Haelan Laboratories' predecessor) and Topps Chewing Gum. During the years preceding the lawsuit, both companies raced to sign exclusive deals with ballplayers to use their names, likenesses, and biographies on their trading cards.[9]

Surprisingly, given its status in right of publicity folklore, neither the initial nor the amended complaints in *Haelan* included a privacy-based claim, a right of publicity claim, or anything similar to one. The litigation in *Haelan* initially focused on contracts from 1950 and 1951. Bowman filed suit in the United States District Court for the Eastern District of New York on June 22, 1951, to stop Topps from releasing its competing card series, or at least from including the cards of players who had also signed contracts with Bowman. The heart of the case was a claim for tortious interference with contract, a claim that first appeared in the amended complaint. The amended complaint set forth three causes of action: a trademark infringement claim for Topps's use of the word "baseball" on packages because one of Bowman's products was sold under the brand name "Baseball"; an unfair competition claim that Topps was trying to palm off its trading card candy as that of Bowman's by using confusingly similar trade dress—such as using a pink rectangular shape for its candy that resembled bubble gum; and a third and final claim that Topps had impaired Bowman's contract rights by knowingly inducing players to breach the exclusivity provisions of their agreements with Bowman.[10]

Although the first two claims occupied much of the litigation, they were rejected by the district court and Bowman did not appeal either of them. The trial court concluded that the use of "baseball" on the packaging was either generic or otherwise fair and descriptive of the contents of the product. The packages contained baseball picture cards, and there were no alternative ways to describe them, nor did the use of "baseball" by Topps indicate a trade name or source. The court held Topps's trade dress distinct and not infringing. The court also rejected the broader unfair competition claim because there was no evidence in the record of any likely confusion by consumers and the trade dress of both the packaging and the cards themselves was "outstandingly different."[11]

The third claim from the amended complaint was the one the case ultimately revolved around and was the subject of the appeal to the Second Circuit Court of Appeals. This claim—for interference with and impairment

Bowman 1951 package. Bowman Gum v. Topps Chewing Gum, No. 11852
(E.D.N.Y.), National Archives, New York, NY.

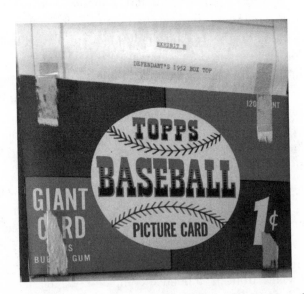

Topps 1952 package. Bowman Gum v. Topps Chewing Gum, No. 11852
(E.D.N.Y.), National Archives, New York, NY.

of Bowman's contracts—would have been a fairly straightforward one if Topps had directly contracted with the players knowing that the players had prior governing contracts with Bowman. Alas, things were complicated by the fact that Topps's licenses derived from ones obtained from the players by third parties. The claim was still possible, but more challenging; albeit not as challenging as it first appeared because one of the licensing agencies for Topps, Players Enterprises, was founded by the head of Topps and was held to be its agent. In addition, other courts had allowed claims for interference with contract against third parties even in the absence of evidence of inducement.[12]

A bigger challenge for the impairment of contract claim was that it was not clear that Topps or its licensing agents either induced breach or knowingly or wrongfully interfered with Bowman's contracts. The licensing agencies legitimately thought that many of the players were not under an exclusive contract with Bowman or anyone else. Many of the players themselves thought they were free to sign contracts because they thought that the Bowman contracts expired before the other licenses began or that the contracts simply did not conflict. There was evidence that the players (and Topps) were reasonable in so concluding. The initial Bowman contracts were for only a one-year period. But after players signed these contracts, Bowman added amendments extending the one-year term and expanding the contracts to cover confections (not only gum). Topps's initial uses were with candy, not chewing gum (albeit candy that looked like bubble gum), so Bowman wanted to expand the scope of its contracts to clarify that it had an exclusive right in the broader candy market. The validity of these Bowman amendments was one of many contract questions in the complex case.

If the Bowman contracts were invalid, no impairment or inducement claim could be based on them. Both Bowman and Topps suggested that the other company (or the involved licensing agencies) had taken advantage of the players and pulled a variety of sleazy tactics that called into question the validity of the contracts. The Bowman amendments were not always accompanied by additional consideration (such as payments), and at least some players claimed they were unaware of the alterations to the contracts. Some players never received the promised signing fees, subsequent payments, or royalties guaranteed under both parties' contracts. Players were often asked to sign the contracts while heading onto the field to play, sometimes after pressure from the team managers (who likely were paid for their encouragement), and appear to have been misled about the terms contained within the contracts. Most of the players signed the contracts without reading them, and without any legal representation. Topps's attorney snidely referred to the players as "child-like" and potentially illiterate: "I wouldn't go so far as to say they can't read; only that they don't." The validity of both sides' contracts also was relevant because Topps countersued Bowman claiming that Bowman had committed unfair competition and induced breaches of Topps's contracts. Topps pleaded this in the alternative, preferring to have the interference claims brought by the plaintiff thrown out, but to the extent that Bowman's claims could proceed, so could Topps's.[13]

Even though the baseball players' interests were never represented in the *Haelan* litigation, baseball players were called to testify about their understanding of the various contracts that they had signed. Wesley "Wes" Westrum provides a typical player's experience with the companies. Westrum was a well-regarded catcher for the New York Giants in the 1940s and 1950s. He signed a contract on September 7, 1950, with Bowman in exchange for $1 in cash and a men's Longines wristwatch, allegedly worth $140 at the time (approximately $1,400 today). Westrum also signed with Russell Publishing and Players Enterprises, which subsequently assigned those licenses to Topps. There were questions about whether Westrum ever received or was offered the promised payments under the Russell and Players contracts, and also whether he was misled into signing a second contract with Bowman that extended the duration of his commitment. The record suggests that he did not receive any additional payment for the expanded and extended contract with Bowman. Westrum claimed that he thought none of the contracts he signed conflicted with one another so he did not bother to tell any of the licensees about a potential conflict, or even to mention the existence of the other contracts.[14]

In part to avoid wading into the thousands of specific contracts at issue, and also because Bowman likely had more contracts with priority, Topps's attorney, George Middleton, started us down the path toward a right of publicity—even though that was far from his intention and worked against his client's interests. He told the judge that if his "view of the case is correct you won't even have to look at but few contracts." Middleton contended that Bowman's contracts were a "mere waiver of the ball players right of privacy, if any." Topps claimed that these waivers were unassignable, personal rights, and as such could not form the basis of an impair-

Front of 1951 Bowman Series Wes Westrum baseball card, in author's collection.

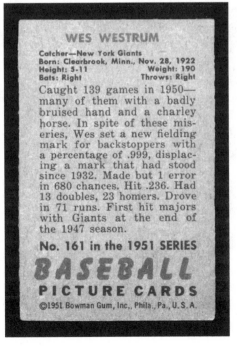

Back of 1951 Bowman Series Wes Westrum baseball card, in author's collection.

Front of 1951 Topps Series
Wes Westrum baseball
card, in author's collection.

Back of 1951 Topps Series
Wes Westrum baseball
card, in author's collection.

ment of contract claim because Bowman did not hold any property of value. Instead of having an ongoing contract with the players, Topps claimed, there was merely a release of liability or an agreement by the players not to sue Bowman for the use of their identities. According to Topps, Bowman therefore had nothing of value to assert against a third party. Notably, Topps's argument did not depend on whether Bowman held a property interest in the players' names or likenesses—instead it was an argument rooted in a narrow and creative reading of the interference with contract tort and a suggestion that one might not be able to obtain relief without an underlying property interest in the contract itself.[15]

The trial judge was initially skeptical of the relevance of privacy law. Judge Clarence G. Galston commented, "I do not see it in this case at all." Nor did he think such a holding was necessary for an injunction to issue. Galston viewed the contracts as similar to contracts for personal services, and therefore an injunction would be appropriate to enforce the exclusivity of the contracts. Even waivers of privacy rights, he contended, would be enforceable. A previous judge assigned to the case, Matthew T. Abruzzo, also had rejected a similar privacy-based argument by Topps, noting that whoever had priority rights via contract could enjoin the other company from using that player on its cards.[16]

Topps's attorney, Middleton, however, was a tenacious and persuasive attorney who was uncowed and refused to abandon his privacy-based argument. He insisted that the plaintiff would not have a case, at least not one against Topps, if the privacy rights of the players could not be assigned. The defendant's main merits brief focused on its claim that the right of privacy was not assignable and cited *Gautier v. Pro-Football, Pakas,* and *Hanna Manufacturing* to support its argument that privacy was personal and could not be transferred. The brief contrasted the right of privacy with patent law and claimed there was no general right to exclude others. Bowman was not the recipient of an exclusive license to a copyrighted or patented work or invention, and therefore could not enforce any rights against Topps.[17]

Topps argued against importing such an intellectual property (IP) model to control uses of one's name and likeness. It argued that using such an IP-like right would limit the players' freedom to contract and would be akin to slavery: "Baseball players are not plaintiff's bond slaves, though it seems to think so." Topps argued that the players were free to give permission to other companies (and receive compensation for) the use of their names and biographies. Topps noted that the players had not complained about its uses, which were consensual, and therefore Bowman should not be able to assert the players' rights against Topps. Bowman could sue the players directly for breach of contract, but could not block the players from authorizing other uses of their identities, or at least could not prevail against a party that had been given permission to use the players' names and likenesses. Topps pointed out that the "parties whose rights are the basis of the whole litigation—the ball players—are not present or represented" in the case.[18]

Perhaps as a result of better briefing and oral argument from the counsel for Topps, combined with a likely interest in avoiding sorting through the thousands of contracts, Judge Galston ultimately rethought his initial position. Galston concluded that Topps was correct that the contracts were mere waivers, and therefore they could not be enforced against Topps. Galston largely borrowed from Topps's brief for his analysis, citing the same cases (*Gautier, Pakas,* and *Hanna Manufacturing*) for support. The court held that Bowman could not sue third parties on the basis of its contracts absent a specific clause that transferred the players' rights—or at least the right to sue for a violation of the players' rights of privacy to Bowman or its licensing agency.[19]

If the case had stopped there, *Haelan* (or *Bowman* at the time) would now be a long-forgotten contract case. But Bowman appealed the case to the Second Circuit Court of Appeals. During the pendency of the appeal Bowman Gum was bought out by Haelan Laboratories, which became the named plaintiff. Because Haelan appealed the decision only on the impairment of contract claim, the appeal focused solely on the transferability and privacy issues. The Second Circuit's tunnel vision may have led it to see the case as being about the question of whether a broad transferable property right existed, but the plaintiff, Haelan, largely avoided making such a grand claim in its briefs submitted to the federal appellate court. Instead, Haelan contended that because the names and likenesses of the ballplayers were "commercially and pecuniarily valuable," the players' contracts had value and could be protected against interference by third parties regardless of transferability. Haelan's opening appellate brief correctly noted that the question at issue was not whether Sections 50 and 51 of the New York Civil Rights Law (the state's right of privacy) granted property rights, and transferable ones at that. Instead, the plaintiff contended that the right of privacy and the question of its assignability were beside the point. Privacy "has no bearing on the plaintiff's right which exists independent of the statute, *i.e.* for an injury to the plaintiff's not the players—property and/or valuable contract rights."[20]

As Haelan's attorney pointed out, if the contracts were valid and had priority, then Haelan was "entitled to equitable protection" even if property rights were not at issue. Its tortious interference with contract claim could succeed without regard to whether the rights of the players to their names and likenesses were transferable—"apart from statute, plaintiff is entitled to equitable protection against knowledgeable and intentional interference by defendant with economically valuable property and contract rights acquired by plaintiff." The exclusive grant of use—albeit for a limited time—was a sufficient basis to provide equitable relief. Haelan convincingly argued that "[t]here is no principle of law or other alchemy which changes that which business men consider valuable rights into nothing." Although Haelan did at times suggest that the rights to the players' names or likenesses were "vendible in gross" and had been assigned to it, this argument was a short afterthought in its briefs—and an understandable maneuver given the defendant's primary argument that the lack of transferability defeated Haelan's impairment of contract claim.[21]

The Second Circuit issued its opinion in *Haelan* on February 16, 1953. The majority opinion was a short one written by Judge Jerome Frank and joined by Judge Charles Edward Clark. Judge Frank's opinion noted that the facts (as to the conflicts of the contracts) had not been developed and therefore the panel for purposes of the appeal accepted Haelan's version of the facts. The court noted that if, as Haelan claimed, the "defendant, knowing of the contract, deliberately induced the ball-player to break that promise, [then] defendant behaved tortuously." The court directed the district court to decide the underlying facts that would determine the legitimacy of such a claim.[22]

But the opinion did not stop there. It also suggested that if Topps's view of the right of privacy was correct, then "in addition to and independent of that right of privacy[], a man has a right in the publicity value of his photograph." Frank dubbed this a "right of publicity." It is not clear that Frank or Clark thought they had created something new. But at times Frank's opinion did seem to take things a step further, suggesting that this "right to grant the exclusive privilege of publishing" a person's likeness may validly be granted "in gross" without any related transfer of an underlying business or ongoing connection to the individual player.[23]

The judges' files from the case suggest that they were worried that if Topps was correct that the contracts could not be enforced, the players might be left without protection against unwanted uses of their identities. Judge Clark in an internal memorandum to his fellow jurists noted that even if there was no breach of contract, "[s]urely a star should have the right to control the commercial use of his name, and a grant of its exclusive use to another must confer something in the nature of property rights on the latter." This was something that New York law already provided, but the federal judges seemed unfamiliar with the scope of the state's privacy statute.[24]

In the opinion, Judge Frank suggested that without the possibility of exclusive (and enforceable) assignment, an identity-holder could "yield no money" for the use of his identity. This conclusion was pure speculation for which the court had no evidence, and was patently wrong. Even absent assignability, the identity-holder could agree to endorse a product or give permission for the use of his image and be paid for doing so. By contract, he could also agree to make that endorsement or use exclusive, and be paid a premium for doing so. In fact, this had been working well for decades and athletes and actors had been receiving compensation for some time without any need of an additional right. The record was replete with evidence that baseball players had been engaged in such endorsements for many years. Frank and Clark also considered whether a fully transferable right existed (one that could be enforced against a third party like a patent or copyright could) because of the possibility that the inducement and impairment of contract claim would not apply if Topps lacked knowledge of the conflicting contracts.[25]

Judge Clark may have been particularly primed to advocate for something distinct from a right of privacy. In an internal memorandum to Judge Frank, Clark noted that he was persuaded by a book review by Herman Finkelstein, then the general counsel for the American Society of Composers, Authors and Publishers, that disagreed with the suggestion in Samuel Spring's book *Risks and Rights in Publishing, Television, Radio, Motion Pictures, Advertising, and the Theater* that public performers, such as professional models, would have claims under New York's privacy statute. Finkelstein thought, in contrast to Spring and the historical record, that privacy law did not address the commercial value of such individuals or others who "purposely pose in public for financial gain," but instead protected only those "who want to be let alone." Judge Clark, a former professor and dean of Yale Law School, likely routinely read the *Yale Law Journal*, but this book review particularly caught his eye because it coincidentally followed his own review of the book *Cases and Materials on Modern Procedure and Judicial Administration*, which appeared in the same issue. Clark conceded, in the memo, that he had never read Spring's book, but nevertheless concluded that Finkelstein's book review commentary and criticism of it was correct—even though Finkelstein misread New York case law, overlooking the historical record in which many public performers who had sought out publicity and financial success in the public eye had recovered under New York's privacy laws. Interestingly, Frank, who authored the majority opinion in *Haelan*, wrote back to Clark that he did not want to cite to Finkelstein's book review because he thought the review suggested disagreement with their "conclusion" about New York law.[26]

There was no question that the players would have had a claim against both companies under New York's privacy statute if the uses of their names and likenesses on the trading cards had been without permission. In fact, around the same time as the *Haelan* decision, a New York trial court held exactly that in *Jansen v. Hilo Packing Company*, a case involving baseball players who objected to the use of their pictures on popcorn containers and in packages of chewing gum. The court in that case noted that the players were public figures who were widely known. Nevertheless, it held that the players did not "waive[] the 'right to be let alone.'" The players could proceed with their lawsuit under Section 51 of New York's Civil Rights Law.[27]

Indeed, both Bowman and Topps understood that they needed to obtain releases from the players before using their identities on their trading cards, and both did exactly that. Neither company challenged the need to do so during the course of litigation. Haelan challenged the applicability of the New York Civil Rights Law only on appeal, and only after having lost in the district court on the grounds that such privacy claims were unassignable and therefore Haelan could not enforce its contracts against Topps. The suggestion by the Second Circuit—that absent a right of publicity the players would not have been able to prevent Topps's (or Haelan's) use of their names and likenesses if such uses had been without permission—was unquestionably wrong.

In so misreading state law, the federal appellate court in *Haelan* marked the beginning of federal courts taking the lead in improperly developing and expanding the right of publicity—a state law. Under the *Erie* doctrine, which emerged from the 1938 decision by the Supreme Court in *Erie Railroad v. Tompkins*, federal courts addressing state law issues must apply the relevant state's law rather than federal common law. While the Second Circuit in *Haelan* claimed to be predicting what New York courts would do, it guessed wrong. New York courts had always had a more capacious understanding of the state's privacy laws—one that encompassed public figures and protected baseball players in circumstances like *Haelan*. Unsurprisingly then, when the New York Court of Appeals, the highest court of New York, was presented years later with the question of whether an independent right of publicity existed in the state, it held that it did not. The state court thereby rejected the purported holding in *Haelan* that there was one, and concluded that the state's right of privacy statute was the only vehicle for preventing unauthorized uses of a person's name, likeness, or voice in the state.[28]

Judge Thomas Walter Swan, who was also on the panel, and another former dean of Yale Law School, wrote a concurrence in *Haelan*. He agreed that the case should be reversed and remanded, but thought the reversal should rest solely on an intentional inducement claim for encouraging players "to breach a contract which gave plaintiff the exclusive privilege of using [a ball-player's] picture." Swan therefore thought there was no need to engage with the right of privacy or create something new.[29]

"Our Old Friend"

Despite the common broad reading today of the majority opinion in *Haelan*—as creating a new legal right, a right of publicity—neither the parties to the litigation nor the district court on remand thought the opinion created a new, independent, quasi-intellectual property right under New York law. In its petition seeking the U.S. Supreme Court's review of the decision, Topps contended that "Judge Frank's newly created 'right of publicity' turns out to be our old friend, the right of privacy, in a different verbal dress." The petition observed that if, instead, this was in fact something different in kind, then such an "impersonal, assignable, bequeathable 'right of publicity' was never seen on sea or land before it sprang from the Jovian judicial brow," and violated the *Erie* doctrine that required federal courts to defer to state courts when it came to making and interpreting state law.[30]

Perhaps surprisingly from today's vantage point, Haelan's opposition to the petition for review agreed that the Second Circuit decision did *not* create a new right. Haelan said the decision simply enforced contracts and allowed interference with contract claims to proceed in the district court. Although Haelan noted that there was a property right in one's image and name separate from emotional distress claims, it emphasized that there was no transfer of such rights at issue in the case. The Supreme Court denied review, perhaps because of the centrality of state law to the decision.[31]

The best way of reading the Second Circuit decision is as an admonishment to the district court judge that he was going to have to actually sit down and read the thousands of relevant contracts, because if valid, the contracts that were signed first could be enforced against the competitor. On remand, Galston treated the case as an interference with contract case. (He still found a way to avoid reading all the contracts by assigning that task to a special master.) As the litigation dragged on, supplemental complaints were filed to add new, allegedly conflicting contracts to the ongoing dispute. Galston's temporary injunctions were routinely violated, and he expressed doubt and exasperation that the players or anyone else knew who had signed what or what had been agreed to in the now more than 1,700 contracts at issue in the litigation.[32]

On April 26, 1955, Haelan filed a separate complaint in New York state court that made essentially the same claims as Haelan had in its federal complaint—focusing on the impairment of contract claim. Notably absent from the state complaint was a right of publicity claim. The plaintiff's attorney either read the *Haelan* decision differently than we do today or was well aware that the New York courts would reject such an independent common law right. Shortly after the state filing, the litigation was terminated. In July 1955, Connelly Containers bought Haelan, and in 1956 Topps purchased Connelly, ending the years of ongoing litigation and the competition between Bowman, its successors, and Topps. Topps won in the marketplace, but American law was forever changed by Haelan's victory at the appellate court.[33]

☼ ☼ ☼

This thorough review of the case files in *Haelan* reveals that not only was the right of publicity not necessary for the decision, but it was not even central to the claims of the litigants. Ironically, to the extent that *Haelan* did create something new, New York state courts subsequently rejected its interpretation of New York law. New York does *not* recognize a common law right of publicity—as the Second Circuit in *Haelan* potentially suggested it would. Instead, New York limits the cause of action for appropriation of name and likeness to the state's statutory right of privacy. The only right of publicity in New York as of 2017 is its right of privacy. They are one and the same. To the extent that *Haelan* was understood—albeit likely incorrectly—to recognize an independent right of publicity under New York law, it has been expressly overruled.[34]

Nevertheless, from the time of *Haelan* forward, tort-based privacy claims were increasingly described as encompassing injuries to the feelings of private individuals suffering under the public's gaze, while the right of publicity was focused on the economic harms that befall public figures who seek out the public limelight and whose identities are commercialized. It would be claimed that *Haelan* created a new property right and extended protections to public figures, granting them the ability to recover economic as well as dignitary harms. But privacy laws did all this too. The mistaken revisionist reading of the right of privacy masked and obscured the one thing that really was potentially new about the *Haelan* court's right of publicity—its potential transferability. It was a savvy movie studio lawyer, an enterprising plaintiff's attorney, heirs of celebrities, and surprisingly influential student commentators (often with little knowledge of the history of privacy law) who, after the fact, took this ball from *Haelan* and ran with it.

PART II

The Inflationary Era

4

A Star Explodes

A CAREFUL READING of *Haelan Laboratories v. Topps Chewing Gum* indicates that it did not create anything new, but as more and more commentators claimed that the decision did, it was hard to put the genie back in the bottle. Although courts were initially reluctant to adopt an independent right of publicity, over the decades that followed *Haelan*, parties advocating for an expansive, transferable property-like right, distinct from a right of privacy, began to prevail in many states, particularly in federal courts applying their best guess about what state courts might decide about their own states' laws. The right of publicity then exploded across the country and expanded in scope far beyond what even its initial proponents had advocated.

It was ultimately not the decision in *Haelan* that launched the right of publicity. Instead, the right of publicity's successful journey into our jurisprudence was a product of slow creep in litigation briefs and court decisions after *Haelan*, combined with several pivotal events that led to the right's true launch. Two articles published on this "new" right of publicity were particularly influential in the right's development. The first was written by a lawyer at a Hollywood studio who saw the advantages for the movie industry of having a transferable right in actors' names and likenesses. The other article was written by a Chicago lawyer who represented the heirs of the mobster Al Capone, and the convicted murderer Nathan Leopold. He was looking for a legal hook to stop the distribution of movies and plays about these infamous historical figures.

These articles provided the platform in the 1970s for the right of publicity to finally catapult to stardom as a result of two major events. The first was a lawsuit brought by a circus performer who objected to the nightly news broadcasting his human cannonball act, and took his case all the way to the Supreme Court. The second was the death of Elvis Presley, "the King of Rock 'n' Roll," and the enterprising investors and heirs who sought to profit from him even when he was gone. It was these events, not *Haelan*, that made the right of publicity take flight, not in the 1950s, as is often claimed, but in the 1970s.

Privacy Fails to Meet the "Needs of Broadway and Hollywood"

Neither the litigants in *Haelan* nor the trial judge on remand thought the decision by the Second Circuit radically altered the law. The case "attracted singularly little notice in the press." One of the few exceptions was a short column on the decision by a well-regarded sports writer at the time, Red Smith, who suggested that *Haelan* created "a new and fascinating principle of law," and not necessarily a good one from his perspective as a journalist. One of the only other news reports of the case, published in *Sports Illustrated*, focused on the injunctions that issued in the case after it was remanded back to the trial court, rather than on any novel legal doctrine.[1]

In contrast to journalists who, other than Smith, largely ignored *Haelan*, law students looking for an interesting appellate case to write about—something often required of them—flocked to the appealing baseball-centered case. Like Smith, they interpreted the decision as creating something new and distinct from the right of privacy. The most influential and frequently cited of these comments on *Haelan* was published in the *Yale Law Journal* and referred to the right of publicity as a "doctrinal innovation." Many of the students erroneously suggested that *Haelan* was the first court to coin the term the "right of publicity," an error that persists today. The students also began the pervasive—but historically inaccurate—narrative about the "fundamental" differences between the right of publicity and the right of privacy, from the alleged lack of protection for public figures, to the perceived distinctiveness of economic versus dignitary claims. The uniformity of the students' views gave confidence to the courts, which then repeated the students' claims, as well as to the scholars that followed in their wake.[2]

On the heels of these student works came the first fully developed post-*Haelan* article on the right of publicity. In 1954, Melville Nimmer, an aspiring scholar, published "The Right of Publicity," which became the most influential article written on the topic. In the article, Nimmer advocated for the adoption of an independent and transferable right of publicity. At the time, Nimmer was an attorney at Paramount Pictures and was no doubt influenced by the interests and concerns of the movie studio.[3]

The early 1950s were a time of significant change in Hollywood. The studio system that had dominated the movie business had fallen apart. This system had been characterized by the studios cultivating and controlling actors using contracts that tied the actors to one specific studio. These long-term contracts regulated actors' public personas, careers, and even their personal lives. The system peaked in the 1930s but began to collapse by the mid-1940s. Actors started to challenge the employment contracts that studios had used to control them, claiming the long-term contracts were unconscionable and unduly restricted their freedom to take jobs and make decisions about their own lives. The studio contracts were finally defeated in court in 1944 as a result of a lawsuit brought by the great actress Olivia de Havilland. She successfully sued Warner Brothers to invalidate her contract with the studio after it had repeatedly extended the contract without her approval in violation of California's Labor Code, which limits personal services contracts to seven years. Film critic David Denby describes this court decision as a dramatic turning point. After it, "[s]ervitude [in Hollywood] was over," and the "modern era had begun."[4]

Given this sea change in Hollywood, the studios were looking for new ways to control their actors. It was therefore hardly a surprise that a studio lawyer, like Nimmer, would advocate for a transferable right of publicity. Such a right could take away the actors' ability to control uses of their own names and likenesses, and give legal control over their identities to the studios. Nimmer was upfront that this was his motivation. He contended that a right of publicity was needed because the "concept of privacy" did not "meet[] the needs of Broadway and Hollywood in 1954." The "entertainment and allied industries" needed to control their "employees' names and portraits," and he claimed they could not easily or fully do so under the current law. Nimmer expressed little concern over the actors or performers or whether their needs were adequately protected by then-existing laws—which they largely were. His focus was on how a right of publicity could assist employers like his. He even suggested that animal actors, like the collies that played Lassie, should have rights of publicity that the studios and producers should reap the rewards of owning.[5]

Nimmer's main objection to relying on privacy rights was that such rights are not assignable. He tellingly provided an example of privacy falling short in the context of an actress who allowed the use of her name and portrait by one bathing suit manufacturer, and then also gave permission to a competing company. Nimmer suggested that it would be better for the first company to "own" rights to her name and image, so it could bar her actions, rather than to rely on contract law to discourage her from double-booking.[6]

Like the student commentators before him, Nimmer undersold the usefulness of other legal actions the studios could take to enforce their rights, such as unfair competition laws, trademark infringement, false endorsement, breach of contract, and various interference with contract claims. Nimmer knew that some of these claims had already been successful, including in lawsuits filed by his own studio. Paramount had successfully stopped third parties from using actors' names and likenesses in unauthorized posters for Paramount movies without need of anything new. In the 1939 decision in *Paramount Pictures v. Leader Press*, a case Nimmer cited in his article, the Tenth Circuit Court of Appeals held that Paramount had a property right in its contracts with its actors, including to the actors' names and likenesses, that it could assert against third parties. Paramount successfully wielded such a right against a printer in the case, to prevent its printing of unsponsored movie advertisements. Thus, existing laws—absent a transferable right of publicity—were sufficient to protect Paramount's interests against third parties.[7]

A fully transferable right of publicity would undoubtedly be a more powerful tool, but it was not a necessary one. The main benefit of a distinct, transferable right is that it could be asserted more robustly by *publicity-holders* (such as movie studios or gum manufacturers) against the *identity-holders* themselves (such as actors or baseball players). The studios no doubt hoped to obtain, via the right of publicity, what they could no longer obtain via employment contracts after the de Haviland litigation—a broad right to control what their actors could and could not do, and how they were portrayed in public.

Also likely influencing Nimmer's thoughts on the subject was his interest in pursuing a job in academia. He no doubt wanted to write a groundbreaking article that would help him get a position as a law professor. Nothing could be more impressive than defining and developing a new legal right—something Warren and Brandeis had achieved in their famous article "The Right to Privacy." Nimmer described their article with glowing admiration as the "most famous and certainly the most influential law review article ever written." A modest comment on how the right of publicity was really nothing new, and was simply a component of the right of privacy, would not have had the same impact—nor would an enumeration of a panoply of existing actions that the movie studios could take to protect their interests in lieu of such a right. Despite the article's overstatement of both the novelty and the need for an independent and distinct right of publicity, courts frequently cited to it to support their adoption of such a right.[8]

"A Facet of the Right of Privacy"

Initially, courts were slow to embrace either a right of publicity or the expansive reading of *Haelan* provided by Nimmer and the student commentators. Nevertheless, litigants increasingly included causes of action for both a right of privacy and a right of publicity in their complaints. Given that at least some courts and prominent commentators had suggested that public figures might have only a right of publicity, lawyers were not sure which way the winds were blowing and appropriately wanted to cover their bases by pleading both claims. As more and more complaints and briefs included the right of publicity, courts were forced to confront the question of whether the right of publicity existed and, if it did, whether it was different from a right of privacy. This framing pushed courts further in the direction of distinguishing between claims brought by public figures and those brought by private figures, and toward treating the right of publicity as something different and independent from the right of privacy.[9]

Initially, most courts either rejected a right of publicity or understood it to be part and parcel of the right of privacy. Despite *Haelan* having been decided under New York law, most New York state courts rejected its holding and concluded that only the privacy statute governed unauthorized uses of a person's name or likeness in the state. All claims—whether by a public figure or private one, whether for economic injuries or emotional distress—had to be brought under the state's privacy statute. A few state courts in New York suggested that there might be a "right of publicity," but most of these suggested that it was simply a "facet of the right of privacy" that was of "particular significance to a public figure." New York state courts were not the only ones to reject the adoption of an independent right of publicity. In 1958, the first California court to consider adopting a right of publicity as a separate claim from a right of privacy also declined to do so. It should come as no surprise that the right of publicity claim was advanced in the case by Melville Nimmer, who was then in private practice representing the plaintiff in the case. To the extent that courts in other states adopted a right of publicity, they initially understood it as fitting squarely within the right of privacy, or a few courts placed it under state unfair competition laws.[10]

Over time, however, the tide began to turn, and the claim that the right of publicity was an independent cause of action picked up steam, particularly (and problematically) in federal courts, which should not have been in the vanguard of creating state laws. In 1969, the Eighth Circuit Court of Appeals in *Cepeda v. Swift & Company* cited to *Haelan*, suggesting that there was no "dispute that plaintiff [a famous baseball player] has a valuable property right in his name, photograph and image and that he may sell these property rights." In the oft-cited 1970s case *Uhlaender v. Henrickson*, a federal district court in Minnesota concluded that the right of privacy was about the right to be let alone (in the narrowest sense of seclusion), while the right of publicity focused solely on "pecuniary loss." *Uhlaender* involved a lawsuit brought by baseball players who objected to the use of their names and statistics in a board game. Although the court acknowledged that technically the right of publicity fit under the "privacy" umbrella, it emphasized that the right was different in kind from all other privacy torts.[11]

This having-it-both-ways approach—situating the right of publicity both within and outside of privacy—persisted for decades, and even remains in many jurisdictions today. The nominal rooting in privacy law of the "appropriation" tort (that courts and scholars noted was sometimes called the "right of publicity") was driven in large part by the great torts scholar William L. Prosser. In his influential 1960 article, "Privacy," Prosser looked at the seventy years of cases ostensibly decided under the right of privacy since Warren and Brandeis's influential article from 1890. He tried to make sense of what he contended was a series of seemingly unrelated decisions. Prosser was motivated in part by the statement by John Biggs Jr., the chief judge for the Third Circuit Court of Appeals, that privacy law was akin to a "haystack in a hurricane." To address this confusing area of the law, Prosser concluded that rather than being a single tort, the right of privacy was in reality four different torts: the tort of intrusion upon seclusion or solitude, the tort of public disclosure of embarrassing private facts, the tort of placing a person in a false light, and, finally, the tort of relevance here, the tort of "appropriation, for the defendant's advantage, of the plaintiff's name or likeness." Each of these torts "represents an interference with the right . . . 'to be let alone.' "[12]

Prosser cited to the *Haelan* decision and agreed that exclusive licenses should provide an enforceable property interest that can be asserted against third parties. But, in contrast to Nimmer, Prosser considered this "right of publicity" to be part of privacy law rather than independent of it. Nevertheless, Prosser agreed—without much development—that the interests served by this tort were more "proprietary" than "mental." Despite this conclusion, he did not suggest that such an interest was transferable or descendible to heirs after an identity-holder's death. Prosser also recognized that both dignitary and emotional injuries, and commercial and economic harms could result from the misappropriation of one's identity.[13]

Prosser's articulation of the privacy torts and particularly of the appropriation tort was widely accepted and unsurprisingly adopted by the American Law Institute in its influential *Restatement (Second) of Torts*—Prosser was the initial reporter for the *Restatement* and drafted the initial versions of the sections on privacy law. Many states today continue to follow Prosser's approach to evaluating misappropriation of name or likeness cases. Even some states that have a so-called right of publicity either continue to treat it as synonymous with a privacy claim for misappropriation of one's name or likeness or allow privacy-based appropriation claims without using the term "right of publicity."[14]

While Prosser's article generated harmony between privacy-based appropriation cases and the right of publicity, suggesting that they were one and the same, another article published the same year encouraged courts to separate the two claims. Harold R. Gordon, in his article "Right of Property in Name, Likeness, Personality and History," claimed that a private figure's interest in being "let alone" was distinct from a public figure's interest in the right to commercially exploit his identity. Gordon suggested that an independent action for commercial appropriation was needed.

Gordon practiced law in Chicago and became particularly interested in developing a claim that the famous (or infamous) could assert when their life stories were used without permission in motion pictures, books, plays, or television shows. In the late 1950s, Gordon took on as clients the descendants of famed gangster Al Capone, who objected to the use of Capone's name and likeness in a biographical movie and television series. Capone's sister, wife, and son ultimately sued over the television series *The Untouchables*, seeking $1 million in damages. Gordon contended that the companies had used Capone's name and likeness without the permission of his heirs for commercial profit both in violation of their property rights in Capone's name and likeness, and in violation of Capone's right of privacy under Illinois law. The district court, later affirmed by the Seventh Circuit Court of Appeals, rejected all of the Capone family's claims. The court concluded that the property-based claim was a privacy claim in disguise, and any privacy claim died with Capone.[15]

Around the same time, Gordon represented Nathan Leopold in his suit against the author, publishers, and producers of the novel, play, and movie *Compulsion*. *Compulsion* is based on the true story of Leopold's role in the murder and kidnapping of a fourteen-year-old boy—a crime that Leopold had pleaded guilty to having committed. A trial court had initially held that Leopold's right of privacy had been violated by the fictionalized account and related promotions, but that decision was vacated. The Illinois Supreme Court ultimately rejected Leopold's privacy claim, holding that the use of his name and life story was protected as newsworthy given that information about the crime was of public interest. Cases like these influenced Gordon's call for a "quasi-contractual right to recover for unjust enrichment against anyone who appropriated the name, likeness, life-story, and personality of another in a work of fiction that was distributed through the usual commercial channels." Gordon's co-counsel in the Leopold litigation noted that Gordon advocated for such a novel cause of action to avoid the short statute of limitations of libel and privacy laws—in which claims had to be brought within one year—and also to allow for the survival of claims after death.[16]

Although Gordon's primary goal was to establish a transferable property right to assist heirs in making claims against movie producers and playwrights, he also noted, like Nimmer, the benefit to corporations of such transferability. Gordon observed that the rights to a person's name, likeness, and personality could be transferred in gross to the "publishing and amusement industries." But more than anything, it was Gordon's suggestion that such a right could be protected and exploited after death that likely drove the right of publicity's expansion. Such survivability (after death) was essential to Gordon's lawsuit on behalf of the Capone heirs (and to his earlier representation of the widow of a deceased manager of Joe Louis, the well-known boxer).

Courts frequently cited Gordon's article, along with *Haelan*, to justify treating the right of privacy and the right of publicity differently, and also to justify distinguishing public and private figures' claims. Gordon described privacy as protecting against "injury to feelings," while the right of publicity (in his view) protected the "pecuniary value" of a person's identity. After Gordon's article it became increasingly common for courts to cast aspersions on their predecessors for having confused these two distinct claims. The connection between commercial and personal harms was severed.[17]

The "Me Decade"

From 1953 to 1970 few cases actually held that there was an independent right of publicity. The vast majority of cases during this era that involved the unauthorized uses of names and likenesses, including those by public figures and performers, continued to be considered under privacy laws. However, things changed dramatically in the 1970s. Part of the shift was the natural process of the law evolving over time as more litigants pleaded right of publicity claims and as there were more precedents to cite that indicated such an independent right existed. But two major events during the 1970s forever established the place of an independent right of publicity in our jurisprudence, and vastly expanded its scope and strength. In 1977, the first—and thus far only—right of publicity case reached the United States Supreme Court, *Zacchini v. Scripps-Howard Broadcasting*. That same year, the second major event took place—the death of Elvis Presley. After *Haelan* and the emergence of this potentially "new," transferable right of publicity, the estates of several celebrities saw opportunities for profit. The conclusion that there was a transferable right to one's name and likeness raised the possibility that it could be inherited like other property. The death of Elvis shifted the tide in these battles to establish a post-mortem right of publicity.

The Flying Zacchini and His Unexpected Flight
to the Supreme Court

The very same summer that Elvis died and courts went into overdrive trying to decide who was going to reap the windfall of the merchandising

75

that followed in his literal wake, the Supreme Court decided *Zacchini v. Scripps-Howard Broadcasting*. The Supreme Court's decision in *Zacchini* on June 28, 1977, cemented the right of publicity's place in our law and trumpeted it as a powerful right—one that could overpower even the First Amendment, even in the context of news reporting. Chapter 7 will address this case's far-reaching First Amendment implications, but here my focus is on its role in entrenching the right of publicity, and a conception of that right that is divergent from the right of privacy. Above all, *Zacchini* shifted the right of publicity to a strong property-based framework by analogizing it to IP entitlements like copyrights and patents. By doing so, the Supreme Court broke the right free of privacy law, broadened out the right, and legitimized it in jurisdictions that had not yet adopted it.

Today's strong IP-centered vision of the right of publicity largely stems from the unique facts of the *Zacchini* case. The case did not focus on the use of Zacchini's name or likeness, as in most right of publicity cases, but instead on the broadcast of his performance on the nightly news. The plaintiff, Hugo Zacchini, was a circus performer, known for his human cannonball act. Zacchini came from a long line of cannonballers. His father, also named Hugo, had developed the act while serving in the Italian army during World War I. The act consisted of being catapulted from a canon 200 feet into the air and landing in a net.[18]

On August 30, 1972, a news reporter for the Cleveland station WEWS, which was owned by Scripps-Howard Broadcasting, attended the Geauga County Fair in Burton, Ohio. As he was preparing to perform, Zacchini noticed the reporter and asked him not to film the performance. The reporter initially respected Zacchini's request, but when the reporter later told his producers about the amazing cannonball act, they instructed him to return to the fair to film it. The reporter did as he was told, and a fifteen-second clip of Zacchini's act aired on the local eleven o'clock news on September 1. The newscaster encouraged viewers to see the act for themselves, announcing while the clip was shown that "you really need to see it in person . . . to appreciate it."[19]

Almost a year later, on July 2, 1973, Zacchini filed a complaint in state court in Ohio. Ohio's pleading rules were minimal and the complaint extremely short. It mentioned neither the right of privacy nor the right of publicity. Instead, Zacchini complained that the "defendant showed and commercialized the film of his act without his consent and such conduct by the defendant was an unlawful appropriation of plaintiff's professional property." He sought a judgment for $25,000 but did not request an injunction against future broadcasts.[20]

The trial court rejected Zacchini's claim, but an Ohio court of appeals reversed. A majority of the appellate panel held that Zacchini had a property right in his performance, and that the defendant had unlawfully converted this property. In his concurring opinion, Judge John Manos agreed that the claim should proceed, but concluded that the appropriate claim was for the violation of Zacchini's right of publicity, rather than for conversion.[21]

The Supreme Court of Ohio reviewed the case. The court rejected the contention that this was a conversion case. The performance was not and could not be copyrighted, and therefore the court concluded it could not form the basis of a conversion action (nor obviously one for copyright infringement). Instead, the court adopted Prosser's tort of appropriation of one's name and likeness. The court noted that the appropriation tort was an aspect of the right of privacy under Ohio law, sometimes also called the "right of publicity." Under this theory, absent a competing privilege, Zacchini could stop the display of his name and likeness by WEWS. Zacchini had a "right to the publicity value of his performance, and the appropriation of that right over his objection without license or privilege is an invasion of his privacy."[22]

Despite holding that Zacchini had made—at least at the pleading stage—a case for the infringement of his right of privacy, the court concluded that the use was protected free speech. The news was privileged to show the performance because it was a "matter of legitimate public interest." A "TV station has a privilege to report in its newscasts on matters of legitimate public interest . . . unless the actual intent of the TV station was to appropriate the benefit of the publicity for some non-privileged private use, or unless the actual intent was to injure the individual."[23]

Zacchini filed a petition for review in the United States Supreme Court of the following question:

Where a performer has a protected "right of publicity"—the right of exclusive control over his professional affairs—and that right is held as a matter of state law to have been infringed by a television station's filming of his entire act over his specific objection and the broadcasting thereof on a nightly news show, is the television station's tortious conduct immunized as a matter of law by the First Amendment of the United States Constitution. . . .

The presented question provided an anomalous definition of the right of publicity—as being about control over "professional affairs," rather than the more common definition, involving the right to control the use of one's name and likeness.[24]

The Supreme Court granted review. In its decision, the Court agreed that the case was about the right of publicity—a right the Court defined (quoting the Ohio Supreme Court) as a person's right to control "commercial display and exploitation of his personality and the exercise of his talents." While the Ohio court considered the right of publicity to sit squarely within the rubric of the right of privacy, the U.S. Supreme Court described the right as a distinct species of IP that protected quite different interests than privacy law did. This view by the Supreme Court had no binding effect on how Ohio courts understood the right, but it had a dramatic effect nationwide by shoring up and reifying a distinction between the right of publicity and the right of privacy, and ultimately in narrowing our understanding of privacy. At the same time, the Supreme Court's decision vastly expanded what was meant by the right of publicity. This is true even though the Court's opinion nominally situated the right of publicity under the broader umbrella of privacy using Prosser's framework.[25]

Part of the emphasized distinction between privacy and publicity rights stemmed from the underlying First Amendment issue in the case. Zacchini's certiorari petition criticized the state court for relying on the Supreme Court's decision in *Time v. Hill* and falling into the "trap" of relying on the "label" privacy to decide the First Amendment defense. In *Hill*, the plaintiff objected to a *Life* magazine story that falsely described his family's experiences during a home invasion in the magazine's review of a play that was allegedly based on the real-life incident. The Supreme Court held in *Hill* that the First Amendment protected the publisher, *Time*, from a privacy-based claim brought under New York's Civil Rights Law § 51, unless *Time* (or its agents) knew that the story (or parts of it) was false or recklessly disregarded that likelihood. This "actual malice" standard was imported from the Court's decision in *New York Times v. Sullivan*, which established this standard in the context of defamation claims brought by public figures.

Zacchini's lawyer contended that the claim in *Hill* involved a different privacy tort—the false light tort—and therefore did not apply to the appropriation tort that was at stake in Zacchini's case. To support its argument that *Hill* didn't govern the case, Zacchini's opening brief contended that the right of publicity had "fundamental differences" with the right of privacy, the claim at issue in *Hill*. The brief contended that "for nearly twenty years the courts have been haunted by the 'myth' that the tort of appropriation (which encompasses the right of publicity) involves an actual right of privacy." The tort of appropriation, aka the right of publicity, "involves the commercial exploitation of a person before the public eye, whereas the traditional forms of invasion of privacy involve placing before the public either something theretofore secret or putting a 'false light' upon facts previously known." Putting aside the historical and analytical inaccuracies in that claim, the distinction had rhetorical appeal and was repeated by the majority of the Supreme Court and many courts and scholars thereafter.[26]

The Supreme Court, in a 5–4 decision, held that the First Amendment did *not* categorically protect news, and certainly did not protect the broadcast of an "entire act." The Court agreed that *Hill* had been a false light case, whereas the interests in *Zacchini* were different. The truth of the statements was irrelevant, and therefore so was the actual malice test. Here, the interests were primarily economic, and deserved more robust protection than those in *Hill*.[27]

Even though the Supreme Court focused on the distinction between the right of privacy and the right of publicity, such a distinction was a question of state law, and one that the Ohio Supreme Court had not considered, because it understood the right of publicity as part of that state's right of privacy. During the oral arguments before the U.S. Supreme Court, Justice Thurgood Marshall asked Zacchini's lawyer, John Lancione, to explain the "difference between the right of publicity and the right of privacy." Lancione answered that privacy was about "the right to have those matters kept away from the public which the public has no right to know about." Whereas, "the right of publicity is almost the opposite. An entertainer wants to be in front of the public, he wants to be publicized and advertised. . . ." The justices seemed persuaded by Lancione's position that publicity rights and privacy rights were radically different. One justice, likely Justice Potter Stewart, insisted that the right of publicity was a distinct property right and even admonished the attorney for Scripps-Howard during oral arguments to use the word "publicity," not "privacy," to describe the nature of Zacchini's legal claim.[28]

The Ohio Supreme Court had explicitly rooted Zacchini's claim in that state's right of privacy. But the U.S. Supreme Court was ultimately convinced by Zacchini's lawyer's argument, and unmoored the right of publicity from privacy. It defined the right of publicity as a strong, independent IP or quasi-IP right. In doing so, the Court set forth one of the first, and certainly the most influential, explanations of the reasons to protect the right of publicity. The Court concluded that the "State's interest in permitting a 'right of publicity' is in protecting the proprietary interest of the individual in his act." The Court noted that this was to produce an incentive effect—encouraging the production of "entertainment" in a way "analogous to the goals of patent and copyright law." The Court elaborated in the context of the case that the right of publicity "provides an economic incentive for [Zacchini] to make the investment required to produce a performance of interest to the public. This same consideration underlies the patent and copyright laws long enforced by this Court."[29]

The Court highlighted that this had "little to do with protecting feelings or reputation," in contrast to the claim in *Hill*. Instead, Zacchini's claim was about "reap[ing] the reward of his endeavors." Supporting this rationale, the Court noted that the broadcast of the entire act "pose[d] a substantial threat to the economic value of the performance." The Court suggested that if Zacchini could not stop such a broadcast, people might be less willing to pay to see it at the fair—the Court noted that the opposite could also be true (that the broadcast would encourage attendance), but thought this was a question of fact that should be decided at trial.[30]

The Court also provided an unjust enrichment explanation for the right of publicity. Quoting an influential essay by legal scholar Harry Kalven Jr., the Court concluded that if Zacchini was "ordinarily" paid for his performances, he should be compensated when his performance was used by another, even if the other was a news organization. "No social purpose is served by having the defendant get free some aspect of the plaintiff that would have market value, and for which he would normally pay." Kalven was actually critical of the privacy torts, and this oft-quoted language of his about the right of publicity was largely explaining Prosser's articulation of the tort of appropriation, rather than an effort by Kalven to develop a case for such a right.[31]

The Supreme Court remanded Zacchini's case, where it then settled on the second day of trial, without any determination of the facts. Both parties claimed victory. The television station claimed that the small settlement amount confirmed that it could continue to televise such events in the future, while Zacchini's lawyer claimed that the settlement established that the station had no right to do so. Regardless of what the parties thought, there can be no question that the Supreme Court's decision in

Zacchini forever altered the landscape of privacy and publicity laws. The decision changed our understanding of the right of publicity and forged it into a strong new independent IP right. In the process of doing so, it also changed and narrowed the right of privacy to focus primarily on seclusion, secrecy, and injuries to feelings and reputation.[32]

"I See Dead People"

Even before Zacchini's case started winding its way through the Ohio courts, another set of litigants was trying to erect a postmortem property right in the names and likenesses of famous dead people. The decision in *Haelan*, and the subsequent articles by Nimmer and Gordon, all suggested that an independent and transferable right existed in a person's name and likeness. If the right was in fact transferable, the right should transfer at death as other property does. So it was no surprise that dead celebrities started coming out of the woodwork. These IP zombies included Oliver Hardy and Stanley Laurel, Bela Lugosi, Rudolph Valentino, and Elvis Presley, and they wanted money and control—or at least their heirs did. Perhaps the most notable of these cases is the one brought on behalf of a different member of the walking dead: a vampire, or really by the heirs of the most famous actor who played one.

In the early 1960s, Bela George Lugosi, sometimes referred to as Bela Lugosi Jr., was an aspiring young attorney attending law school at the University of Southern California. He was also the son of a celebrity, Bela Lugosi, who was best known for his movie portrayals of Dracula. The actor died in 1956. A number of actors had played Dracula over the years, but Lugosi's version was by far the most famous. Lugosi Jr. graduated from law school in 1964 and no doubt realized that the novel area of the law called the right of publicity could be employed for his and his family's benefit. If someone was making money off his father's likeness, why shouldn't it be him?[33]

The litigation over who (if anyone) owned the dead Lugosi's name and likeness began while Lugosi Jr. was still in law school, perhaps having heard about the right of publicity in his torts class. In the complaint, Lugosi Jr. and his mother, Hope Linninger Lugosi, objected to Universal Pictures' licensing Lugosi's likeness for use on Dracula-related merchandise, such as shirts, cards, games, costumes, and masks. Lugosi's portrayal of Dracula had taken place decades earlier, but Universal launched a new merchandising effort in the 1960s to capitalize on the renewed interest in its classic horror characters. Dracula was only one of several promoted monsters at the time; others included Frankenstein, the Mummy, and the Wolf Man.[34]

The Lugosi family conceded that Universal could authorize Dracula merchandise, but said its Draculas could not look like Lugosi. The case is one of many that have raised the conflict between rights held by copyright holders—such as to market films using stills and to sell related merchandise—and the rights of publicity of those who appear in these copyrighted works, most often athletes and actors. This collision is something that will be discussed in more detail in Chapter 8. The key question of relevance here, however, is whether the deceased Lugosi or his heirs had any rights in Lugosi's name or likeness after his death. No one claimed that Lugosi's name (or likeness) rose to the level of a trademark—there was no business at the time operating under his name, nor was there a claim that the uses by Universal suggested false endorsement by the dead actor or his estate. The legal issue therefore boiled down to whether the right of publicity existed, and if it did, whether it survived his death.

Prior to *Lugosi v. Universal Pictures*, courts that had considered the question of descendibility of rights to one's name or likeness (that did not constitute trade names) had concluded that the rights terminated upon death. These holdings followed the conclusion that the rights at issue were personal, and therefore terminated when the person upon whom they were based died. In 1972, the California trial court that first considered Lugosi's case agreed that if Lugosi had only a right of privacy in his name and likeness, it would have died with him. But, the court did not stop its analysis there. It observed that if Lugosi had a property right in his name and likeness, it would indeed pass to his heirs. The court cited *Haelan* to support its conclusion that the right of publicity was such a "property right." Accordingly, Lugosi's right to control the use of his name and likeness descended to his heirs.[35]

Although the trial court's holding was ultimately reversed, the decision in favor of postmortem rights emboldened other courts to allow such claims, which then encouraged still more litigants to file such claims. Notably, in 1975, a federal district court in New York, in *Price v. Hal Roach Studios*, cited the trial court decision in *Lugosi* to support its holding under New York law that the famous comedians Stanley Laurel and Oliver Hardy had rights of publicity that survived their deaths. The case was decided under the federal court's interpretation of New York law and is no longer good law because the New York Court of Appeals has since expressly rejected the existence of a postmortem right in the state or any common law rights of privacy or publicity, limiting all claims to those under the state's privacy statutes.[36]

In 1977, a California appellate court reversed the trial court decision in *Lugosi*. The appellate court held that because Lugosi had not commercially exploited his name or likeness during his lifetime there was nothing that could pass to descendants. This exploitation requirement suggests that to succeed his name needed to qualify as a trademark (a source-identifier for products or services). The court concluded that the right at issue was still the right of privacy—which was not descendible. The appellate panel adopted Prosser's approach and understood the tort at issue to be the tort of appropriation of name or likeness. The court thought that this "so-called right of publicity" was in fact at the "heart of the law of privacy." The court noted that whether the right sounded in property was beside the point—the key was whether it could survive death, a question to which the court answered that it could not.[37]

The Supreme Court of California agreed with the appellate court's assessment in its 1979 decision in *Lugosi v. Universal Pictures*. Chief Justice Rose Bird wrote a lengthy dissent. She was heavily influenced by the United States Supreme Court's decision two years earlier in *Zacchini*. Much of her dissent focused on how the right of publicity was different from a right of privacy. Bird repeated the historically erroneous claims that privacy was solely about injuries to feelings, and publicity about injuries to one's pecuniary or commercial interests.[38]

Bird looked to the articulated justifications in *Zacchini* for the right of publicity and concluded that they indicated the appropriateness of extending such rights postmortem. The U.S. Supreme Court's analogy to IP laws was particularly persuasive to Bird. Given that patents and copyrights pass to heirs, Bird thought the right of publicity should also pass on after one's death. In contrast to patent and copyright laws, however, there were no governing statutes to describe the scope or duration of such postmortem publicity rights. Undeterred by this significant difference, Bird decided to arbitrarily borrow the copyright term, which at the time was fifty years after death (it is now seventy years), and concluded that that should be the term for California's common law right of publicity. Bird could have borrowed the much shorter term for patents, but did not, nor did she justify why she chose one over the other.[39]

Like Judge Gray, who won the war, if not the battle, in *Roberson*, Justice Bird's views did not carry the day, but they have carried the decades that followed as more and more states, including California, have adopted a postmortem right of publicity, and treat the right of publicity as something different in nature and independent of the right of privacy. As with the aftermath of *Roberson* in New York, the rejection of Lugosi's claim led the Screen Actors Guild and several of its members (prominent actors and their heirs) to champion the passage of California's postmortem statute, which was adopted in 1984 over the objections of the American Civil Liberties Union (ACLU), the Writers Guild of America, and a number of television and movie studios.[40]

While the *Lugosi* case was winding its way through the California courts, one of the most significant events in the right of publicity's history took place. On August 16, 1977, Elvis Presley, sometimes referred to as "the King of Rock 'n' Roll," died. Shortly after his death, lawsuits were filed across the country to stop the sale of unauthorized in-memoriam merchandise, such as T-shirts and posters. Hundreds of millions, maybe billions, of dollars were going to be made from such merchandise, and the question arose of who was going to make that money. Profits could be widely distributed across the public and different manufacturers and sellers, or aggregated in the hands of Presley's estate.[41]

Likely while Presley's body was still warm, the jockeying for rights to Elvis merchandising began. The Supreme Court's decision in *Zacchini* had been handed down only a few months before his death. The Court's strong endorsement of the right of publicity and its articulation of justifications behind the right added fuel to arguments that the right should survive death. Within two days of the star's death, Colonel Tom Parker negotiated an exclusive license with Factors Etc. (a commercial printing business) to use Presley's "likeness in connection with all souvenir merchandise." Parker, who was not a colonel of the military variety but used the honorific to indicate his Southern roots, owned 56 percent of Boxcar Enterprises, Presley's merchandising division (of which Presley had owned only 22 percent while he was alive). After Presley's death, his father, Vernon, the executor of his estate, agreed to the royalty agreement already in place with Boxcar (although Elvis's heirs would later fight Parker over the rights and royalties).[42]

The wave of litigation about who (if anyone) owned the rights to Presley's name and likeness after his death spanned decades and numerous states. The first courts to consider the question held that these rights survived death, at least under New York's common law right of publicity—a right which, as I have pointed out, was briefly recognized by federal courts after *Haelan* but ultimately was explicitly rejected by New York state courts. In 1977, a federal court in New York, relying on the later-discredited trial court decisions in *Price* and *Lugosi*, concluded that the in-memoriam money should go to Presley's heirs (and the entities that had licensing agreements with them), rather than to a disaggregated group of souvenir makers. The Second Circuit Court of Appeals affirmed this holding that the right of publicity survived death, relying heavily on *Zacchini*'s analogy to patent and copyright law. The court concluded that third parties should not reap a "windfall" from using Presley's name and likeness.[43]

Around the same time, a federal district court in Tennessee considered the identical issue—did Presley's rights survive his death? This time the challenged use was by a not-for-profit entity that sought to memorialize Presley in a bronze statue as a public monument in his hometown of Memphis, Tennessee. The court noted that no Tennessee court had ruled on the question. It then held that because Elvis had commercialized his identity during his lifetime he had a property interest in his name and likeness under Tennessee law that was descendible. A few years later, the Sixth Circuit Court of Appeals reversed, holding that there was *not* a postmortem right under Tennessee law. The appellate court questioned some of the justifications that had been suggested for extending a right of publicity after death. The panel did not think a descendible right would produce significant additional incentives to the deceased while alive. The court, like the Supreme Court of California, was concerned about line-drawing challenges better left to the state legislature, such as how long such a postmortem right should last and who should benefit from it. The court additionally expressed concerns about a postmortem right's restrictions on free speech and the robust engagement with deceased public figures.[44]

After the Sixth Circuit decision, the Second Circuit reconsidered its earlier decision extending postmortem rights to Presley. In 1981, it decided that the place of residency at the time of death determined whether postmortem rights existed. Because Elvis died domiciled in Tennessee his rights did not survive death, pursuant to the Sixth Circuit decision. Although the Second Circuit was not bound by the Sixth Circuit's interpretation of

Tennessee law, it deferred to the greater expertise of that circuit on that state's laws. In 1983, the case once again returned to the Second Circuit in light of conflicting Tennessee trial court decisions, one of which suggested that the right might be descendible under Tennessee law after all. The Second Circuit concluded that these trial court opinions were not determinative and did not require reconsideration of its holding. Like California, Tennessee then abrogated these decisions by passing legislation to provide the postmortem rights that the courts had denied to the Elvis estate. In 1984—the same year as California—Tennessee adopted a statutory right of publicity that included postmortem rights.[45]

○ ○ ○

The Second Circuit, in *Haelan*, suggested (even if unintentionally) the possibility of a transferable right, and the U.S. Supreme Court endorsed and expanded this right to encompass performance rights, and to stand up against First Amendment rights even in a news broadcast. By the end of the 1970s, the right of publicity was well established as an independent right—primarily framed as an exclusionary property right similar to long-standing IP rights, like patent and copyright laws. As this shift took place, a cramped understanding of privacy law—one focused more on private figures, seclusion, secrecy, and injured feelings—overtook the broader notions of autonomy and dignity that had reigned over the first seven to eight decades of privacy law. In contrast to the constitutional conception of privacy during the same era (which was expanding), privacy in the context of tort law turned into something for the shrinking violets of the world; the right to be let alone became something small, literal, and narrow, rather than the broader liberty-based right that first emerged at the turn of the nineteenth century. Meanwhile, the right of publicity only grew and grew.[46]

5

A Star Expands

ONCE THE SUPREME COURT in *Zacchini* officially placed the right of publicity in the pantheon of IP, it began to expand—and did so far beyond what its underlying justifications merited. Because IP is often thought to be in the public interest, courts and legislators often think that more of it is good, and the stronger the right, the better. Unsurprisingly, then, the right of publicity has proliferated across the United States and increasingly across the globe, and expanded in its breadth. Today, more than thirty states have right of publicity laws that are independent of a privacy-based appropriation tort, and that number is only likely to grow. At least twenty-five of those states recognize some form of a postmortem right of publicity. Most jurisdictions now protect against uses of a person's identity far beyond uses of name or likeness. Some states allow liability for simply evoking a person in the minds of viewers or listeners. The right of publicity has expanded in other ways too. As the right exploded across the country, states adopted very different versions of the right, particularly when adopting statutory rights. This variability among the laws leads to confusion, and ultimately to another form of rights expansion as potential users comply with the broadest and most speech-restrictive of these state laws.

Although it is frequently claimed that the scope of the right of publicity is narrowly limited to advertising and other commercial speech, the reality is that the right of publicity has long applied beyond uses in advertising and on products. The right has been successfully wielded against a variety of noncommercial speech, including uses in expressive works, from movies, to comic books, to video games, to busts of civil rights heroes, and even to uses in news reporting and political campaigns. So the right of publicity affects a much broader swath of speech than is often thought.[1]

The growth of the right of publicity has also been accompanied by efforts to justify such a broad, transferable right in a person's identity. But many of these justifications do not withstand scrutiny, and the most convincing justifications are the very same ones that support the right of privacy. This is no surprise given that, as this book has revealed, the original right of publicity was the right of privacy, and the differences between the two have long been exaggerated. Better understanding these justifications is crucial for getting the right of publicity back on track, and for navigating the right's increasing conflicts with other rights that are explored in the chapters that follow. Before considering these rationales in more depth, a brief detour into the expanded contours of the right is necessary. One needs to understand the right of publicity's current breadth and its extreme variability to fully engage with what does (or does not) justify the right.

Beyond Name and Likeness

Initially, the privacy-based tort of misappropriation was limited to actual uses of a person's name or likeness (often a photograph or representational drawing). Over time, however, misappropriation claims and right of publicity claims expanded to include other evocations of a person's identity, even if the person's image or name was never used. The least controversial expansion was to include protection from the appropriation of a person's voice. Using a person's voice is similar to using that person's image or name, but other expansions have gone far beyond actual uses of a person's name, likeness, or voice, and far beyond the initial parameters (and motivations) for protecting against unauthorized uses of a person's identity.[2]

Judges were originally skeptical of appropriation claims other than those arising out of the use of a person's name or likeness, and for good reason. In *RCA Manufacturing v. Whiteman*, a 1940 Second Circuit Court of Appeals case, Judge Robert Porter Patterson objected to a band leader's claim that he should be able to protect his personal style:

I think that these claims by the manufacturer of the phonograph record and by the orchestra leader are nothing but nonsense. The talk about a common law property of an orchestra leader in his manner or style of having a song played by an orchestra is particularly tiresome. It might as well be argued that no one but Al Smith has a right to wear a brown derby, on the ground that the wearing of a brown derby has become a property right belonging to him.[3]

Judge Patterson's hypothetical claim to a brown derby turned out to be prescient rather than far-fetched. Right of publicity and similar misappropriation claims have been allowed in a variety of contexts in which neither a person's image nor name nor voice is used. These cases run the gamut from liability for showing a red race car that some would recognize as being the car of a well-known race car driver, to using a phrase associated with a late-night talk show host ("Here's Johnny"), to showing a big band playing "Auld Lang Syne" on New Year's Eve that reminded viewers of a famous bandleader.[4]

Limiting the right of publicity primarily to uses of a person's likeness was sometimes read broadly, but it had boundaries. It encompassed the use of an actual image of the person, usually a photograph or film clip, as well as realistic re-creations, such as drawings or paintings. For liability to attach, the use had to actually look like and be identifiable as that particular person. But a broader concept arose over time, one often referred to as "persona." Liability for using someone's persona is much broader than liability for using a person's name or likeness because it encompasses any use—including the mere evocation—of that person's identity. So, for example, if a movie studio makes action figures of characters from a successful film, an actor can use a persona-based theory to claim a right of publicity violation even if the figure looks nothing like him. Once you have seen Robert Downey Jr. play Ironman, an Ironman action figure likely evokes Downey Jr.'s identity even if the figure is fully masked. When unmasked, a light-skinned, brown-haired, brown-eyed Tony Stark (Ironman's alter ego) doll will unquestionably evoke Downey Jr., even if the figure does not otherwise look like the actor.

This expansive approach is epitomized by the 1992 Ninth Circuit Court of Appeals decision in *White v. Samsung Electronics America*. *White* involved a lawsuit brought by Vanna White, the *Wheel of Fortune* game show hostess. White objected to a Samsung advertisement that she claimed used her identity. Samsung had developed a clever series of advertisements highlighting the longevity of its electronic products. The Ninth Circuit described the campaign as "hypothesizing outrageous future outcomes." The particular 1988 ad that White objected to suggested that Samsung's videocassette recorders (VCRs) would last so long that many decades in the future, 2012, a robot would be turning the letters on *Wheel of Fortune* instead of a human being. The advertisement depicted a robot in a wig turning letters on the *Wheel of Fortune* set. (Samsung got things really wrong—VCRs are obsolete, while Vanna White is still working the letter board.)[5]

Those who saw the advertisement were likely to infer that a robot had replaced White, but neither White's image nor her name was ever used. The robot and the real-life Vanna White look nothing like one another. It would therefore be readily apparent to all who saw the advertisement that the robot was distinctly *not* Vanna White. Although a showing of likely confusion is not required to make a right of publicity claim, members of the public would be unlikely to think that White had endorsed the Samsung ad (and if they were likely to be confused as to endorsement, other causes of action would have been available to her).

The Ninth Circuit agreed with the district court that White's claim under California's *statutory* right of publicity was barred because the statute limits claims to those in which a person's "name, voice, signature, photograph, or likeness" is used. The Ninth Circuit, however, disagreed with the district court's holding that the *common law* (judge-made) right of publicity also did not apply. California, like several other states, has both a common law and statutory right of publicity. The federal appellate court reversed the district court and held that California's common law right of publicity applies more broadly than the state's statute and covers any uses of a person's "identity." White was then allowed to proceed with her common law claim. On remand, a jury awarded White more than $400,000 for the violation of her right of publicity, the equivalent of approximately $675,000 in 2017 dollars.[6]

No doubt, anyone seeing the advertisement (who knew the show) would evoke White's identity. But allowing liability for the mere evocation of a person's identity rather than for the actual use of that person's name or likeness greatly expands the right of publicity's scope and radically limits free speech. Judge Alex Kozinski criticized this dramatic extension of right of publicity laws in his dissent from the Ninth Circuit's denial of a motion to rehear the case. He described the decision as "dangerous":

> The panel's opinion is a classic case of overprotection. Concerned about what it sees as a wrong done to Vanna White, the panel majority erects a property right of remarkable and dangerous breadth: Under the majori-

Longest-running game show.
2012 A.D.

The VCR you'll tape it on.
2012 A.D.
Samsung. The future of electronics.

Advertisement, Samsung,
Smithsonian Magazine,
November 1988, 235.

ty's opinion, it's now a tort for advertisers to *remind* the public of a celebrity. Not to use a celebrity's name, voice, signature or likeness; not to imply the celebrity endorses a product; but simply to evoke the celebrity's image in the public's mind. This Orwellian notion withdraws far more from the public domain than prudence and common sense allow. It conflicts with the Copyright Act and the Copyright Clause. It raises serious First Amendment problems. It's bad law, and it deserves a long, hard second look.

But the Ninth Circuit never gave it a second look and instead doubled down on the broad liability created by *White*.[7]

Image of Vanna White from *White v. Samsung Elecs. Am.*, 989 F.2d 1512, 1522 (9th Cir. 1993).

Enlarged image from Samsung advertisement from *White v. Samsung Elecs. Am.*, 989 F.2d 1512, 1523. (9th Cir. 1993).

As Kozinski had warned, the holding in *White* gave identity-holders (and publicity-holders) broad latitude to control ideas and references to themselves, and even to the characters they play. This is exactly what happened a few years later in *Wendt v. Host International*—Paramount Pictures licensed its characters, set pieces, décor, and trademarks from its hit television comedy series *Cheers* to Host International. *Cheers* was set in a Boston bar and remains one of the most successful television shows ever made. One of the themes of the show is that the bar is a place where "everybody knows your name"—a family of sorts away from home. Paramount and Host formed a partnership to provide this familiar and welcoming feeling to business travelers by re-creating part of the *Cheers* set in airport bars.

Two of the recurring characters in the series, Norm and Cliff, were considered part of the concept. The airport bars were to feature two animatronic robots representing those characters. Norm and Cliff usually sat together at the bar in the show and would provide built-in "friends" to guests at the airport bars. The Norm character was portrayed in the series as an overweight accountant who almost always wore a suit and tie, and Cliff was a mail carrier who usually wore his postal service uniform. For the entire run of the series, Norm was played by the actor George Wendt, and Cliff was played by John Ratzenberger. Wendt and Ratzenberger objected to the use of the robots in the bars because they claimed the robots evoked their identities without permission. In response, Host International, which had initially sought to license Wendt's and Ratzenberger's likenesses, renamed the robots Bob and Hank, and made them look more distinct from the actors. Host then installed these robots in several *Cheers* bars across the United States. Wendt and Ratzenberger sued, claiming that the robots wrongfully appropriated their likenesses in violation of California's statutory and common law rights of publicity.

The district court disagreed with the actors, concluding that the robots did not look like either Wendt or Ratzenberger. The Ninth Circuit Court of Appeals reversed, suggesting that whether the robots looked like the actors was a question of fact for a jury. But the appellate court went further and troublingly suggested that even if the robots did not look like the actors, there could be liability under California's common law right of publicity if the robots evoked the actors' "identity" more broadly, in a way similar to *White's* successful persona-based claim. No jury ever decided whether the robots looked like Wendt and Ratzenberger, or whether their personas were evoked, because after the Ninth Circuit decision the case settled for an undisclosed amount.[8]

Allowing liability in the absence of uses of the actual likenesses of the identity-holders—as happened in *White* and *Wendt*—greatly expands the scope of the right of publicity. One could avoid using the likenesses of Ratzenberger and Wendt—though the producers and copyright holders to the show should not always have to do so—but how can one use the characters Norm and Cliff without conjuring up the actors' images or identities in the minds of the public who are familiar with the show? Judge Kozinski again dissented from the expansive reading of right of publicity laws, bemoaning, "Robots again":

> According to the panel, Paramount and Host may not use Norm and Cliff in a way that reminds people of the actors who played them and whose identity is therefore fused in the public mind. This is a daunting burden. Can Warner Brothers exploit Rhett Butler without also reminding people of Clark Gable? Can Paramount cast Shelley Long in *The Brady Bunch Movie* without creating a triable issue of fact as to whether it is treading on Florence Henderson's right of publicity? How about Dracula and Bela Lugosi? Ripley and Sigourney Weaver? Kramer and Michael Richards? . . . When portraying a character who was portrayed by an actor, it is impossible to recreate the character without evoking the image of the actor in the minds of viewers.[9]

The expansion of the right of publicity to include voice combined with the expansion to cover persona has also led to liability on the basis that a vocal performance evokes an identity-holder even if only the style of a performer is used. It is one thing to hold someone liable for using a person's actual voice, but quite another to expand the right to allow liability for only conjuring up that person's identity. How could a person with a similar voice singing a song made famous by another performer not evoke the famous performer in the minds of listeners familiar with that rendition of the song? Should Beyoncé be required to get a waiver of Barbra Streisand's right of publicity before she performs or sells a version of "The Way We Were" (often referred to as "Memories"), a song made famous by Streisand, because people will think about Streisand while Beyoncé is singing?[10]

Voices can be distinctive, and it may be that we want to permit some actions arising out of sound-alike recordings when designed to trade off the

Photograph of Hank and Bob robots at Host International bar, Detroit Airport. Photograph by William Archie, published to accompany Cecilia Deck, "A Round for Robots," *Detroit Free Press*, February 12, 1991, p. 1E.

Screen shot of Cliff and Norm, "Norm and Cliff's Excellent Adventure," *Cheers* (1990).

value of the identity-holder's distinctive voice by confusing listeners into thinking it is the famous singer that is performing. But there must be latitude for performances of songs made famous by others, and for people to have similar sounding voices and styles. Current law does not clearly delineate distinctions among sound-alikes, uses of similar styles, or simply reminding listeners of particular recording artists, thereby greatly expanding the scope of the right of publicity in jurisdictions that do not explicitly limit the action to uses of name, likeness, or voice. In addition, as I will discuss in Chapter 8, copyright law expressly provides compulsory licenses for some sound-alike recordings of musical compositions, an allowance that could be set at naught if the right of publicity categorically barred such recordings.

The State(s) of Disarray

The expansion to cover persona is not the only expansion of the right that has taken place since the 1970s. While the right of privacy (and its appropriation tort from which the right of publicity emerged) is largely uniform across the more than forty states in which it has been explicitly recognized, right of publicity laws vary widely. In the right of publicity's continued march across the United States, individual states have adopted surprisingly different laws. Because of the widespread variations it is difficult to know exactly when a use will, or will not, violate a person's right of publicity. Even experts in the field have trouble keeping track of the many states' laws and legislative changes. In part to address this confusion, in late 2015 I launched a website, *Rothman's Roadmap to the Right of Publicity,* to provide a fifty-state database and analysis of the different state laws. But the chaos persists, as does uncertainty as to which state's law applies and what it entails. Such confusion broadens the scope of the right of publicity as a practical matter. Without clear answers to the most basic questions about when a use of another person's identity is unlawful or which law applies, the most expansive publicity laws often control creative decisions, and thereby limit speech.[11]

A small taste of some of the many variations across states is useful to understand how significant the discrepancies are. Some states limit actions to those in advertising, others to uses for trade purposes, while others allow claims arising out of any use for a defendant's advantage, whether for profit or not. Some states limit actions to uses of a person's name or likeness only;

others add to this uses of a person's voice. Some states allow broader liability when any "indicia of identity" is used, such as in Alabama, and other states protect against any broad evocation of a person's identity, such as California, at least as that state's common law has been interpreted by the federal appellate court, the Ninth Circuit Court of Appeals.[12]

Some states allow any identity-holder or publicity-holder to sue for right of publicity violations. Other states limit suits to those based on the identities of individuals with commercially valuable personalities, or even only to those who have exploited the commercial value of their identities. Even states that agree that a plaintiff (or underlying identity-holder) must have a commercially valuable identity to bring a claim do not agree on what it means to have such an identity. Some courts consider a person to have a commercially valuable identity solely by virtue of that person's identity being used in a commercial context. Pennsylvania, in contrast, requires identity-holders to have developed such a "commercial value" through the "investment of time, effort and money."[13]

The extent of the confusion over whether an identity-holder needs a valuable personality is highlighted in dueling lawsuits brought against Facebook by users when the company appropriated their names and images without permission to advertise products. Two federal courts concluded that the users needed to have commercially valuable identities to bring right of publicity claims, but disagreed on whether Facebook users had such identities. One district court concluded that there was no demonstrated independent commercial value to the plaintiffs' identities, and therefore no right of publicity claims could proceed. Another court in the very same district, applying the very same California law, disagreed, holding that the claims could proceed. That court concluded that Facebook's use itself demonstrated that the users' identities had commercial value, even though they did not have an independent commercial value. This intracircuit split in the Facebook cases about what is meant by a commercially valuable personality is particularly bizarre since California does not require that plaintiffs have a commercially valuable identity for either its statutory or common law right. In fact, the statutory right was specifically passed to protect those who lacked commercially valuable identities by providing statutory damages to discourage uses of their identities when economic recoveries were otherwise likely to be small.[14]

In the context of postmortem publicity rights there are similar variations among the states. Approximately twenty-five states provide postmortem rights, while the rest either have not considered the question or limit claims only to the living. Of the states that provide such rights, the boundaries vary widely. Some states require that the deceased be someone who had a commercially valuable personality while alive, or even that the person had commercially exploited her identity during life, but others do not. A few states limit postmortem rights to soldiers. Many states limit postmortem rights to those who died domiciled in the state, but others, such as Washington and Hawaii, allow anyone to sue if the use of the identity is made within the state. The duration of postmortem rights also varies widely depending on the jurisdiction, from lasting ten years after a person's death, to thirty, to forty, to fifty, to seventy, to one hundred years, to forever. Some states require registration of the names of the deceased for whom postmortem rights are sought; others have no such requirement.[15]

"Wanting, Needing, Waiting . . . for You to Justify My Love"

In the absence of an awareness of why we have such laws in the first place, it is no surprise that the boundaries of the laws vary widely, often without rhyme or reason. Developing a more convincing and coherent basis for the right could facilitate greater harmony in the laws across different states. To establish appropriate, limited boundaries for the right of publicity, we first must know why we need such a right, and what its objectives are.

Prior to the Supreme Court's decision in *Zacchini v. Scripps-Howard Broadcasting*, few courts and scholars spent much time providing justifications for having a right of publicity. Instead, scholars and courts focused on what was wrong or missing from the right of privacy, rather than why as an initial matter one should provide a right of publicity. It was primarily only after *Zacchini* that courts and scholars further developed theories to support the right's existence, at least those that differed from those supporting a right of privacy.

Scholars and courts have suggested a variety of justifications for right of publicity laws. These tend to fit into two broad categories. The first encompasses public-regarding justifications, such as the incentive rationale, consumer protection, and other efficiency-rooted welfare-maximizing claims. The second category consists of justifications that focus on the interests of identity-holders, ranging from protecting against economic harms to protecting against other injuries, such as emotional distress, as well as broader dignitary injuries stemming from the loss of control over one's own identity. This category also includes broad moral claims based on the alleged entitlement to the fruits of one's labor and the prevention of unjust enrichment of those who use a person's identity without permission for their own (usually financial) gain.

To evaluate the legitimacy of the justifications for right of publicity laws, one must take a broad view of the scope of the right, as a law that prohibits the unauthorized use of a person's identity. Such an approach is necessary because of the wide variations in state laws. The justifications (and their limitations) reveal much about what the right of publicity should look like, but we cannot presume at the outset whether the right should be treated as property, whether it should be transferable, whether it should apply to broad evocations of persona, whether it should apply only to individuals with commercially valuable identities, whether it should survive death, whether it should apply only to commercial speech, or whether only economic damages should be recoverable. To presume those features of the right of publicity at the outset is to put the proverbial cart before the horse. Only once explored can these justifications suggest answers to many of these questions.

The Incentive Rationale

The public-regarding goals of the right of publicity were front and center in the Supreme Court's first (and only) consideration of the right of publicity. In *Zacchini*, the Court fit the right of publicity into its understanding of IP laws. The Court explained that "the State's interest in permitting a 'right of publicity' is in protecting the proprietary interest of the individual in his act in part to encourage such entertainment." The Court claimed that the right of publicity "rests on more than a desire to compensate the performer for the time and effort invested in his act; the protection provides an economic incentive for him to make the investment required to produce a performance of interest to the public." The Court emphasized that this "same consideration underlies the patent and copyright laws long enforced by this Court." We protect copyrights to encourage authors to create works that ultimately "advance public welfare." The use of the copyright rubric was unsurprising given that *Zacchini* was really a quasi-copyright case in which a performer's "entire act" was allegedly used in a news broadcast. The Court's reliance on an incentive rationale, however, is far less convincing beyond the narrow set of circumstances in which an entire performance is appropriated.[16]

Nevertheless, many other courts and scholars picked up on the incentive rationale to justify the right of publicity. California Supreme Court Chief Justice Rose Bird, in her dissent from the decision in *Lugosi v. Universal Pictures*, relied in significant part on this rationale to justify both a right of publicity and its survival after an identity-holder's death.

> [P]roviding legal protection for the economic value in one's identity against unauthorized commercial exploitation creates a powerful incentive for expending time and resources to develop the skills or achievements prerequisite to public recognition. . . . While the immediate beneficiaries are those who establish professions or identities which are commercially valuable, the products of their enterprise are often beneficial to society generally. Their performances, inventions and endeavors enrich our society.[17]

The incentive rationale potentially justifies a broad right of publicity. If more protection produces more of an incentive to create, which increases social welfare, then as broad a right as possible is merited. The incentive rationale—if valid—could therefore justify protection for the mere evocation of a person's identity (such as a robot in a blond wig that makes people think of Vanna White) and postmortem rights. Under this logic, the contention is that giving White the right to either block or profit from any associations with her persona will incentivize her to develop her personality and pursue creative endeavors, thus benefiting society. Similarly, the claim is that by making it possible for heirs to inherit the value that a person builds in her identity, the person will have an incentive to develop her career and identity during her life.

This justification for publicity rights does not withstand scrutiny. The right of publicity likely has little additional incentive effect on already successful people, like White, who are adequately incentivized by their well-paid jobs to develop their careers and identities. There are ample incentives for such individuals apart from publicity rights. Actors with the most valuable names and likenesses can garner high salaries, win Academy Awards, achieve acclaim, and be rewarded by the simple pleasure of being able to act (and make a living out of it). Nor is the possibility that one's heirs might profit in the distant future likely to be much of an additional incentive to such an already successful individual. In contrast, those who most need an incentive to continue creative or noncreative pursuits are the least likely to receive any incentive from the right of publicity. No one pays large sums to use the names and likenesses of obscure musicians, actors, scientists, and journalists. So the very people that might need an incentive to continue will not receive one, and those who do not need any additional incentives will potentially reap even more rewards, furthering the vastly unequal distribution of wealth associated with commercializing one's persona.[18]

If the right of publicity incentivizes anything, it is not clear that it is incentivizing anything we might wish to encourage. Perhaps it produces more lucrative endorsement careers, though even this is questionable. Without a right of publicity the famous would still be able to demand endorsement fees, since many other laws bar false endorsements, and businesses will continue to want celebrities to wear their clothes in public or appear live in commercials. Perhaps it produces more people who are simply "famous for being famous," like the Kardashians or Paris Hilton, rather than those who make more meaningful contributions to society. It is unlikely that society substantially benefits from such an increase (if any) in endorsements, celebrity merchandise, or celebrity culture.[19]

This was one of Michael Madow's main concerns in his withering 1993 critique of the justifications that purportedly support a right of publicity. In his influential article "Private Ownership of Public Image: Popular Culture and Publicity Rights," he suggested that the right of publicity may be encouraging overinvestment in celebrity. Madow's conclusion is debatable, as there is little evidence that the right of publicity incentivizes much of anything, and the possibilities of becoming famous and earning massive salaries playing basketball or acting provide sufficient incentives without regard to the right of publicity. Nevertheless, he is absolutely correct that we cannot only consider whether the right of publicity produces any incentives, but must also consider exactly what it might be incentivizing.[20]

In addition, we need to consider what we lose out on by wielding this exclusionary property regime. If our primary objective and metric for evaluating the legitimacy of laws is to adopt those that maximize public welfare, then the downsides of the right of publicity must be figured into the calculation of its aggregate incentive (or disincentive) effect. We need to consider not only what performances and performers are encouraged by the right, but also what works are never made or are altered for the worse because of its existence. We lose out on commentary, expressive works, merchandise, and advertising about public personalities. Heirs of Martin Luther King Jr. can block sales of sculptures and merchandise that celebrate and spread King's vision of equality and justice. Athletes can discourage and stop their inclusion in comic books and video games. Vanna White can block Samsung's use of a robot to highlight the longevity of its electronics and to comment on the never-ending run of a popular television series. These social costs combined with the right of publicity's likely limited-to-nonexistent incentive effect make the incentive rationale a slender reed on which to base a broad and expansive right.

Consumer Protection

Another posited public-regarding justification, albeit a much less dominant one, is a consumer protection rationale. This justification claims that the right of publicity protects consumers from being deceived into thinking that a public personality has endorsed a specific product or service when that person's identity has been used without permission. Such confusion harms both the public that is deceived and the identity-holder, whose reputation is damaged as a result, causing both dignitary and economic harms.[21]

There are several problems, however, with relying on this rationale. Most importantly, the right of publicity does not require any showing of deception (other than in Utah), so the cause of action applies without regard to whether consumers are confused. The right of publicity even allows ample room to deceive consumers. Consumers can be duped by authorized uses of a person's identity. A celebrity actor, for example, could appear in an advertisement for an anti-aging skin cream that he does not use, and perhaps has never tried. Some consumers might then be deceived into thinking that he does use it and that the consumers' skin would look like the celebrity's if only they tried the same cream. Nor do we need the right of publicity to address this problem. There are already a variety of laws and regulations, including the federal Lanham Act, that provide protection against consumer confusion and prohibit such deceptive endorsements.

Economic Efficiency and Welfare Maximization

Because both the incentive-rationale and the consumer-protection justifications for a right of publicity are unconvincing, law-and-economics
scholars have tried to articulate alternative explanations for the right. These
scholars contend that the right of publicity maximizes the value of celebrity identities, and that this in turn benefits society. Their analyses focus
almost exclusively on celebrity-based claims. Although the right of publicity sweeps more broadly than this, I will take this framework as a given
for the purposes of considering as an initial matter whether these theories
work even on their own terms.

Mark Grady, who wrote one of the first economics-based analyses of
the right of publicity, contends that a "rent dissipation" theory explains the
right. He suggests that uses of a person's identity by third parties reduce
the "rent" that a publicity-holder can charge for uses of the identity. Although
the economic concept of rent dissipation focuses on a property owner not
reaping the full rent, because others are using some of the value of the
property without paying, Grady largely focuses on a slightly different
concern—that such uses would reduce the overall value of the underlying
identity. If someone can use a person's identity without permission, he
suggests there would be (over)use of the person's name or likeness that
would reduce the amount that person's name or likeness is worth, and
therefore the amount of "rent" that person could charge for an endorsement deal or appearance in an advertisement or on merchandise.[22]

William Landes and Richard Posner (who became a federal appellate
judge) justify the right of publicity using a similar theory of "congestion
externalities." They claim that in the absence of property protection a particular resource will be overused, thereby depleting its overall value. In the
context of the right of publicity, they claim that the "commercial value" of
a celebrity's name or likeness would be "prematurely exhaust[ed]" in the
absence of publicity rights. In the context of the living, the "overexposure"
from others using a celebrity's name or likeness "truncate[s] the period in
which his name or likeness retains commercial value." Similarly, after the
death of someone famous, free use by the public and merchandisers would
deplete the dead person's "commercial value."[23]

The law-and-economics account of the right of publicity largely depends
on a presumption that uses of a person's identity diminish rather than

increase its value. Such uses could have the opposite effect. Unauthorized uses of celebrity images on T-shirts and posters may generate more enthusiasm and value in that person. In the context of recording artists, the merchandise may increase sales for concert tickets, music, and even official merchandise. Landes and Posner concede that Shakespeare and Santa Claus are prominent examples of increased value with increased use, and in the absence of IP protections. Nevertheless, they claim that "total utility" could decline if anyone were free to use an actor's image. In such instances the value of "the image might become worthless" through confusion, tarnishment, or "sheer boredom on the part of the consuming public." Despite having some intuitive appeal, their tarnishment and confusion concerns ultimately are not convincing as a basis for right of publicity laws, at least not the ones we currently have. Neither showing is required to establish a violation of one's right of publicity (outside of Utah), and likelihood of confusion (and dilution) concerns are already addressed through separate federal and state laws. Trademark law may not protect all possible plaintiffs, particularly those who have not commercially exploited their identities, but Posner and Landes focus on examples of celebrities who would often be able to make such claims.[24]

These law-and-economics accounts also presume that a person (or her heirs) deserves the full value of her identity and that society is better off by maximizing that person's value, even postmortem. As I will discuss in more detail in the context of the labor-reward justification, the value of a person's identity is likely created by many contributors rather than solely by the underlying identity-holder. So one cannot simply presume as a starting point that a person deserves the entire value of her identity. Even from a purely efficiency-based rubric, it has not been established that maximizing the value of a person's identity and vesting it in a single person's (or company's) hands is better overall for society than letting the public freely use the person's identity. Society may be the poorer if public figures overcharge or refuse to allow certain uses of their identities, whether in movies, the news, or memorabilia. In addition, if the right is fully transferable, the identity-holder herself may be worse off under such a regime, as I will discuss further in Chapter 6. These economics-based models fail to adequately value control over one's own identity, as well as the interest in not commodifying one's own identity.

Landes and Posner contend that the right of publicity helps allocate resources efficiently—here a person's identity—thus maximizing the return on the "property." By propertizing (and allowing transfers of) a person's name, likeness, and other indicia of identity, they claim that the law ensures that the person or entity that most highly values the commodity will be the one who owns it. Without the protections the right of publicity affords, a person's identity could remain in the hands of an individual who may have limited interest in maximizing its value, or, in the absence of any publicity or privacy rights, be disseminated freely to the public. But, it is not clear how we could determine the optimal allocation of a right of publicity, or figure out who will most value a person's identity. It is possible that the best allocation of publicity rights is across many parties, but transaction costs and information costs may prevent such an allocation. This analysis also again fails to take into account the value in not commodifying a person's identity, or, at the very least, in not maximizing its commercial value.

As with many law-and-economics accounts, this justification for the right of publicity depends on fundamental and unanswered (perhaps unanswerable) questions, and presumes that everyone is a rational actor with perfect information, which of course they are not. Some of the insights of this approach support providing remedies for injuries to individuals, as I will discuss in more depth, but the analysis does not make the case for a robust right of publicity or provide specific guidance as to what constitutes a preferred allocation of publicity rights, or what the right's boundaries should be in the real world.[25]

Labor-Reward and Unjust Enrichment

The second broad category of justifications for right of publicity laws are those rooted in the underlying identity-holder, rather than those focused on maximizing overall social welfare. Of these more individual-focused justifications, the one highlighted by the Supreme Court in *Zacchini* is the prevention of unjust enrichment. This rationale focuses on a moral intuition that identity-holders (like IP creators) deserve to reap the financial rewards stemming from uses of their identities. This justification has two related aspects: rewarding laboring performers and preventing the "unjust" enrichment of those who reap the rewards of seeds sown by others. The Supreme Court claimed that the "rationale for (protecting the right of publicity) is the straightforward one of preventing unjust enrichment by the theft of good will. No social purpose is served by having the defendant get free some aspect of the plaintiff that would have market value and for which he would normally pay." The Court dismissed the relevance of "protecting feelings or reputation" and instead focused "on the right of the individual to reap the reward of his endeavors." Many scholars have agreed with this sentiment, deeming those who reap the rewards of using another's identity "poachers," "pirates," "free riders," and "scavengers."[26]

This unjust enrichment sentiment is undergirded by a contention that the identity-holder should be rewarded for her labor under a natural-rights theory, based in part on the philosophy of John Locke. The natural-rights justification for publicity rights contends that a person should be rewarded or compensated for uses of her identity because she has invested in cultivating the value of her personality. In the case of an actor, for example, one could contend that the commercial value associated with that actor's identity resulted from hard work on the part of that actor to develop her acting skills and her public image. She should accordingly reap the rewards of that labor.[27]

Many scholars and courts have posited this as one of the most robust of the justifications for a right of publicity. Although Melville Nimmer in his influential article on the right of publicity primarily focused on the interests of third parties and pointed out the limitations of privacy law, to the extent he made an affirmative case for the right of publicity based on the underlying identity-holder, he rooted it in the labor-reward model and the idea that "every person is entitled to the fruits of his labors." James Treece similarly contended that the celebrity's "work and sacrifice" should be rewarded with protection and the ability to control how one's name and picture are used. Justice Bird adopted this labor-reward rubric as well: "Often considerable money, time and energy are needed to develop one's prominence in a particular field. Years of labor may be required before one's skill, reputation, notoriety or virtues are sufficiently developed to permit an economic return through some medium of commercial promotion." Bird contended that if a person's identity has "potential economic value," that person should be the beneficiary of any value. She criticized the "windfall" to users who appropriate another's identity, "reaping one of the benefits of the celebrity's investment in himself." She viewed this windfall as illegitimate even after a celebrity's death.[28]

This labor-reward rubric, however, does not justify allowing a person to reap all the rewards of uses of her identity. Those with lucrative personalities are likely not the only ones who created the value in their identities. Actors, musicians, and athletes often have agents, managers, stylists, publicists, and others who create, shape, and distribute their public personas. Actors' public identities are also partially created by the roles they play, most often written by others, and shaped by costumers, makeup artists, directors, cinematographers, and editors. The media also shape these personalities and create "stars." The public itself imbues value and creates additional layers of meaning on top of the celebrities' identities. Vanna White has largely been the beneficiary of a successful show created and produced by others, and George Wendt and John Ratzenberger did not create Norm and Cliff, dress them, or write the words that they spoke. So the notion that the labor is all the identity-holder's is simply not true.

Celebrities also often free ride, pirate, borrow, or pay homage (depending on your perspective) to those who have gone before them. The pop music star Madonna based much of her public persona on those of other personalities who were stars before her, particularly Marilyn Monroe. Should she be paying fees to the Marilyn Monroe estate? Should Lady Gaga, who then relied in part on Madonna's persona to build her own, compensate both Madonna and Monroe's estate? Ultimately, even if we conclude that labor expended in service to the creation of public personalities is worth rewarding, it is likely impossible to fairly trace all who labored in their production and therefore should reap those rewards, or how to fairly distribute and disseminate such rewards.

In addition, what are we actually rewarding? There are many rewards for developing one's identity (such as fees, personal pride, and fame). Fame—the primary determinant of the monetary value of a person's identity—is often a product of luck and "serendipity" rather than actual labor. Madow tells the story, based on the historical research of Marshall Missner, of Albert Einstein's serendipitous path to becoming a celebrity. Missner notes that other physicists had theories at least as important and influential in science as Einstein's, such as Niels Bohr and Werner Karl Heisenberg, both of whom were working at the same time as Einstein, but only Einstein became a celebrity in the United States. Einstein's fame was driven in part by his own personality but also by other random events. One such event was the *New York Times* and *Washington Post* apparently (mis)reporting that when his ship arrived in the United States large crowds greeted him. It appears that the crowds were there to greet one of the leaders of the Zionist movement, Chaim Weizmann, rather than

Einstein. This is not to say that Einstein did not labor, but simply that a person's public and commercial value may not always be tied to that person's labors.[29]

Regardless, even though Einstein had a valuable identity while Bohr and Heisenberg had less valuable ones, this does not disprove the point that they should each be rewarded for their labor by reaping the benefits—if any—from uses of their identities. We all know that many talented, hardworking people never succeed or achieve fame, and some who seem to lack much talent (and may not work all that hard) sometimes rise to the top. But none of this ultimately challenges the intuition that one should reap rewards for one's labor, if rewards are to be had. At the same time, it does not establish that identity-holders or publicity-holders should reap the full value of their identities.

The labor-reward rubric provides virtually no support for postmortem rights. It is impossible to reward the dead. Nor do many of those who survive deserve the rewards that flow from owning and marketing a dead person's identity. Often they will have no more claim (sometimes even less claim) to the fruits of the deceased's personality than the public at large, a public that may have built the person's value in the first place. We imagine that heirs will be close, loved ones, a left-behind spouse or child, but this is often not true. In the aftermath of the death of the great performer and musician Prince, potential heirs came out of the woodwork claiming rights to his estate, from estranged siblings to people he had never met who claimed to be his children. There is no reason why such uninvolved individuals should reap a windfall from Prince's death, or why sharing DNA should be rewarded.[30]

Nor is there a labor-reward or unjust enrichment argument that explains why unrelated corporations or enterprising individuals should be able to scoop up the rights of aging celebrities who lack heirs. Bettie Page's right of publicity is now owned and managed by CMG Worldwide, one of the top management firms for dead celebrities. CMG has turned Page, a successful pinup model and actress, into an even more famous dead person who regularly appears as one of the ten most profitable deceased celebrities. CMG undoubtedly is laboring now to generate value, but it is unclear why CMG should reap the economic value of this iconic deceased celebrity, instead of the public that, at least in part, imbued her identity with some of its meaning and value. There is often discussion of a "windfall" to merchandisers that make posters or sell T-shirts after someone has died.

But in the absence of a postmortem right of publicity such benefits are disaggregated and no one gets exclusionary ownership rights in the deceased's identity. Whereas, by receiving Page's rights, CMG is the one to potentially receive a windfall. It may well be that close or chosen heirs deserve some limited and narrow postmortem control over uses of a deceased person's identity, but the best arguments for this are rooted in the dignitary interests and likely emotional distress of the survivors if others can exploit their loved ones after death.[31]

The unjust enrichment logic undoubtedly resonates intuitively for many jurists, scholars, and likely identity-holders, which is to say for everybody. And while a person is living, it makes some sense in conjunction with a dignitary and autonomy-based understanding of the right of publicity (and privacy)—which I will consider shortly—to start with a view that if someone is profiting from using your identity, it should usually be you. But when one digs a bit deeper into this justification, it starts to be less convincing and provides less guidance than it initially appears. To the extent that the unjust enrichment rationale holds up as a basis for an entitlement to (some) of the (monetary) rewards for uses of one's identity, it provides little to no guidance as to what the right of publicity's boundaries should be, or when uses are just or unjust.

Throughout the law we encourage competition and allow the use of other people's ideas and work, without permission or payment. IP laws often allow and encourage such "free riding." Public figures and celebrities are part of our culture and uses of their identities are often necessary and appropriate, rather than unjust. The crucial question, then, is not whether using others' identities is allowed, but when it should and should not be allowed. The unjust enrichment rubric does not provide enough information to tell us where to draw this line. In the context of trademark law, the primary dividing line is when consumers are likely to be deceived. The lack of any similar limit in right of publicity laws is problematic. All uses are deemed unjust under many state laws, at least as to showing as an initial matter that the right of publicity has been violated.[32]

In the context of *Zacchini*, we were far from the borderline of an appropriate use (at least according to the majority of the Supreme Court) because Zacchini's entire human cannonball act was broadcast; therefore, the value of his performance could have been destroyed in the absence of protection. *Zacchini* was an outlier, as the justices themselves noted at the time. The case never suggested that an identity-holder should reap all possible value from his identity, nor that he could block all uses of it. Ultimately, neither the labor-reward rubric nor the unjust enrichment rationale supports a robust right of publicity, a postmortem right, or the placement of all value in the hands of an identity-holder. Nor do they tell us when the right of publicity should yield to competing interests, or how to evaluate such conflicts—in other words, while justifying having a right of publicity generally, these rubrics fail to tell us exactly when a use of a person's identity should be allowed, and when it should not be.

Preventing Likely Injuries to Identity-Holders

One of the most convincing bases for having a right of publicity is rooted in the prevention and remedying of actual injuries to individual identity-holders. These concerns also justified the adoption of the right of privacy, and particularly its call to address the wrong of unauthorized uses of a person's name and likeness. Unauthorized uses of a person's identity can interfere with the ability to earn money from advertisers, and even with one's primary career if one's reputation and image are negatively affected, or if a use is substitutionary, as was potentially the case in *Zacchini*. Such uses can also cause emotional distress and reputational injuries. In contrast to the broad claims that a right of publicity produces a welfare-maximizing incentive effect or achieves allocative efficiency, it is easier to make the case that on an individual basis, a particular person has suffered economic (and other) injuries. If a particular use actually enhances the person's value, then this would eliminate the ability to recover for economic injuries in a specific case.

Often it is claimed that the right of publicity addresses economic injuries while the right of privacy addresses dignitary and emotional distress injuries. As I have revealed, such a division did not exist historically, is not enforced today, and makes little sense since injuries from the same harm of misappropriation can be economic, dignitary, and emotional. Many states today recognize this reality and allow the recovery of both economic and noneconomic damages (including emotional distress) under their right of publicity laws, even if the plaintiff is a celebrity. Just because a person seeks out publicity in some contexts does not mean that she is not harmed emotionally or in a dignitary sense by public uses of her identity without permission. Moreover, since many jurisdictions continue to root their "right of publicity" in the privacy-based appropriation tort, it makes no sense to force such a rigid, narrow-minded division between the rights, or between economic and noneconomic injuries.

Protecting Individual Liberty and Dignitary Interests

Even if a person does not suffer economic damages or mental distress, there are good reasons to provide control over how one's identity—particularly one's name, likeness, and voice—is used by others. In the absence of control over our own identities, we are all like puppets that can be used to speak others' words and messages. Our speech will be compelled, our liberty lost. Edward Bloustein's 1964 article, "Privacy as an Aspect of Human Dignity," powerfully argued:

> [U]sing a person's name or likeness for a commercial purpose without consent is a wrongful exercise of dominion over another even though there is no subjective sense of having been wronged, even, in fact, if the wrong was subjectively appreciated, and even though a commercial profit might accrue as a result. This is so because the wrong involved is the objective diminution of personal freedom rather than the infliction of personal suffering or the misappropriation of property.

To the extent that the right of publicity has deviated from this privacy-based foundation and insight, it has been made weaker, not stronger. As Alice Haemmerli has noted, the split from the right of privacy led to the right of publicity losing a "crucial part of its *raison d'être* as a right based on, and protective of, personal autonomy." Jonathan Kahn has called for "bringing dignity back" to the right of publicity. This was one of the core justifications that supported the adoption of the right of privacy in its original context of preventing nonconsensual uses of a person's name or likeness, and it remains one of the strongest justifications for the right of publicity.[33]

Valuing such dignitary concerns does not mean there should be absolute control over a person's identity, but instead that there should be a recognition that harm may flow from such uses. We then need to balance the harm to the individual against other competing interests, such as the countervailing free speech interest in commentary and information about

111

that person. No one should be able to fully control all constructions of her personality, but one should have some control over how others use one's name, image, and voice, particularly when injury is likely.

○ ○ ○

There are good reasons to have a right of publicity, but not for having the broad, expansive right we have in many states today. A serious interrogation of the purported justifications for the right of publicity suggests that the right makes the most sense when integrated with the right of privacy, rather than when aligned with its purported cousins, copyright and patent law. The most compelling justifications for a right of publicity are the same ones that justify the right of privacy—the promotion and protection of individual dignity, personhood, and liberty, and the recovery of (and prevention of) economic and emotional injuries to an individual. The unjust enrichment intuition supports having a right in the first place, as it does a right of privacy, but does not help determine what the right's boundaries should be, nor does it provide sufficient guidance for determining when it should be limited in the face of competing interests.

Concluding that the most convincing rationales for the right of publicity are those rooted in protecting individuals from harm and safeguarding their dignitary interests provides important guidance about the right of publicity's scope. Individuals (regardless of whether they have commercially valuable identities or are public figures) should have some control over uses of their identities. But the right should be narrower in many other ways, for example, limited to uses of a person's actual name, likeness, or voice, at least when there is no likelihood of confusion as to whether such a use took place, or as to the person's endorsement. A postmortem right may be appropriate, but only if it is more limited in scope, focused on protecting likely injuries to survivors, rather than granting a broad right and commercial windfall to distant relatives and corporations. This understanding of the right of publicity also calls into question the right's purported transferability, which works at cross-purposes with the interests of the very individuals who justify having such a right in the first place.

PART III

Dark Matter

6

The (In)alienable Right of Publicity

A S THE RIGHT OF PUBLICITY became uprooted from its privacy law origins, and instead was placed into the category of IP, it lost its way. The powerful IP rhetoric employed by courts, litigants, and scholars set the stage for the right to turn from a force protecting individual identity-holders to a potent, if as yet mostly untapped, force capable of destroying the very rights it is thought to protect. Today, the right is almost uniformly identified as a fully transferable property right, like copyrights and patents, or houses and cars—meaning that the right to use and stop others from using your name, likeness, and voice can be sold or taken away from you, potentially forever.[1]

The right of privacy was long thought of as a property right, but it was never thought of as a transferable one. Far from this being a liability, it was a blessing. The dangers that stem from a transferable right of publicity are the least appreciated and least criticized of the downsides of today's treatment of the right of publicity as a form of IP. Yet the possibility of a truly alienable right of publicity is a chilling one—such unfettered transferability would put control and ownership of a person's identity in the hands of third parties. Such a possibility directly contravenes the animating principles behind the emergence of the right of privacy, as well as the only convincing justifications for having a right of publicity.

Questioning the Unquestionable:
The "Rule of Free Assignability"

Courts, legislatures, and scholars routinely describe the right of publicity as a freely transferable or "alienable" property right. Complete (or full) alienability indicates that an entitlement is transferable in gross without any restrictions on its sale, donation, or ownership. The leading treatise author in the field of privacy and publicity rights, J. Thomas McCarthy, contends that the "rule of free assignability in gross of the right of publicity has never been seriously questioned." The Supreme Court of Georgia has claimed that "without assignability the right of publicity could hardly be called a 'right.'" The *Restatement (Third) of Unfair Competition* states matter-of-factly that "[t]he interest in the commercial value of a person's identity is in the nature of a property right and is freely assignable to others." And numerous state right of publicity laws expressly refer to the right as a "freely transferable" one.[2]

Despite such widespread claims, there is not even a common language to describe such a separation of rights from the underlying identity-holder, who is often referred to as the publicity-holder. I developed these distinct terms for my 2012 article, *The Inalienable Right of Publicity*, to facilitate a conversation about such transferability. If the right is truly separable and transferable, then the *identity-holder* (the person whose name or likeness is used) need not be the same as the *publicity-holder* (the person or entity that owns the rights to the name, likeness, or other indicia of that person's identity). If transferable, the publicity-holder, not the identity-holder, would be the one with the ability to legally enforce the right of publicity. So, for example, if the pop star Bruno Mars transferred his right of publicity to Atlantic Records, then Atlantic would be the publicity-holder and would have the exclusive rights to use his name and likeness, and to prevent others—even the identity-holder, Bruno Mars himself—from doing so.[3]

Achieving such transferability was indeed the primary motive for the shift away from the right of privacy and toward the right of publicity, but it has never served the interests of identity-holders upon whom the right is purportedly based. Scholars often point to *Haelan Laboratories v. Topps Chewing Gum* to demonstrate the need for a transferable right of publicity to "protect the ability of baseball players to profit from the use of their photographs." This common, though incorrect, description of *Haelan* obscures the reality that, as this book revealed in Chapter 3, the case was a dispute between two corporations that each claimed to have control over the baseball players' names and likenesses—the players and their interests were never part of the litigation. The players did not benefit from the holding and were not parties in the case. If anything, the holding in *Haelan* limited the players' ability to license uses of their names and likenesses, and reduced their likely payments for endorsements. The right of privacy already adequately protected the rights of the players to prevent unauthorized uses of their names and likenesses in the absence of transferability.[4]

Despite the dangers of such alienability, the Screen Actors Guild (now SAG-AFTRA) continues to advocate for the passage of expansive right of publicity laws that provide for such transferability. SAG-AFTRA so far has seemed unaware of the risks that these laws pose to the very people that it represents. If the right of publicity is truly transferable, then these laws, rather than furthering the interests of its constituents, allow for SAG-AFTRA's members to lose control over their own identities—potentially forever, even after they die. Aspiring musicians, actors, and models routinely sign predatory blanket, long-term (sometimes perpetual) assignments and licenses of their publicity rights as a condition of getting representation, a record deal, a role, or a photo shoot. Similarly, the NCAA has had student-athletes sign contracts as a condition of participation in college athletics that the NCAA claimed assigned to it the perpetual rights to those students' names and likenesses for use in any context. Social media sites already have claimed rights over photos and people's names and likenesses in their ever-changing and rarely read terms of service that their users all purportedly agree to in exchange for use of the sites. The profound and long-standing damage of assignments is perhaps most apparent when children are involved—parents can assign their children's publicity rights to third parties and neither the children (once grown) nor the parents can reclaim them.[5]

Many of the worst possibilities of having a transferable right have yet to come to pass because publicity-holders have rarely pressed the full extent of their rights against identity-holders—but the current law allows them to do so. As this book has already shown, the right of publicity is a story of expansion. No one would have thought at the outset that it would stretch to cover the evocation of people whose names and likenesses were never used, or to create a multibillion-dollar business in dead people, or to prevent statues of Martin Luther King Jr. from being made and sold without permission. But now it does. We ignore this danger at our peril. Many state laws expressly allow the total transfer of rights to a person's name, likeness, voice, and other indicia of identity to others, whether voluntarily or not, and usually without limitation. We should take them at their word.

Thus far, courts have shown some discomfort with enforcing the transferability of publicity rights against identity-holders, and at least one expressly rejected such a possibility. A California trial court refused to transfer O. J. Simpson's right of publicity to the Ron Goldman family, who had won a $33.5 million judgment against Simpson for killing their son. Although Simpson was acquitted of murder charges, he was found liable for the death of Goldman and Nicole Brown Simpson (O. J.'s ex-wife) under the lesser standard of proof in a civil wrongful death suit. Simpson vowed never to pay the judgment and moved out of California to Florida to shelter his primary residence from creditors. The court had no problem assigning the copyright to Simpson's book, *If I Did It*, to the Goldman estate—which the Goldmans then published with a preface that they wrote titled "He Did it." If the right of publicity were indeed fully transferable property, then it too should have been transferred. Instead, the judge held that a person's right of publicity could never be transferred to creditors. He likened such an alienation of Simpson's right of publicity to forcing him into "involuntary servitude."[6]

If publicity rights are fully alienable, more than simply the income that flows from the exercise of such rights would be transferred. Forcing the transfer of O. J. Simpson's right of publicity to the Goldmans, for example, would have meant several things. Although the Goldmans could not have forced Simpson to physically make appearances, they could have forced him to appear virtually in a variety of ways. The family would have been able to create and sell Simpson merchandise, such as T-shirts and mugs with Simpson's name and his photograph saying "I Did It." They also could have digitally created images (even animated ones) of him for use in both commercial and entertainment contexts. The Goldmans also would have had the ability to stop Simpson from exploiting his identity, including preventing him from making endorsements, participating in television shows, and even making some public appearances. If the Goldmans held his right of publicity, they could prevent others—including Simpson, the identity-holder—from using any indicia of his identity in public, certainly for any commercial purpose, but likely more broadly since many right of publicity laws apply beyond commercial speech, and even beyond for-profit uses.

Those who think Simpson did indeed murder his ex-wife and her friend might shed no tears if Simpson lost such control over his life and his identity, but a transferable right of publicity would allow any debtor to potentially lose control over her identity. Many individuals declare bankruptcy. Prominent celebrities such as Cyndi Lauper, Larry King, 50 Cent, Kim Basinger, and Marvin Gaye have each declared bankruptcy. If their rights of publicity had been transferred to creditors, they could have been subject to forced commercialization and exploitation of their identities, and potentially barred from making certain public appearances, including performing concerts, appearing on talk shows, and acting in movies without the publicity-holder's permission. The same would hold true for individuals who are not famous, and in the age of social media, each of our identities may be sufficiently valuable that creditors might wish to profit from taking ownership of our names and likenesses.[7]

Only a few state legislatures and courts so far have recognized the dangers of transferability. Nebraska expressly states that its right of publicity is not transferable, and Illinois does not allow the right to be forcibly transferred to creditors. But many states expressly permit the right to be transferred, and most of the laws passed in recent years, and those recently proposed, include transferability as a key feature. By doing so, these states have placed many of us at risk of losing control over our own identities.[8]

The potential transferability of the right of publicity arises in a variety of contexts from voluntary assignments, to involuntary transfers to creditors and ex-spouses, to transfers to heirs upon death. Allowing the transfer of a person's name and likeness and other indicia of identity significantly impairs the rights to liberty, freedom of speech, and freedom of association. Although identity-holders may garner short-term economic advantages from such transferability, the alienation of the right to one's own identity can cause long-term economic and dignitary harms that call into question the legitimacy of such alienability. Nor is it possible to truly separate the underlying identity-holder from her identity. This reality further supports an understanding of the right of publicity that, rather than being something different and independent from the right of privacy, is really part and parcel of it.

Voluntary Assignments

Even voluntary transfers of rights of publicity can destroy people's ability to control uses of their own name, likeness, and other indicia of identity, as well as limit their ability to take jobs and appear in public—potentially forever. Although identity-holders rarely sue assignees of their publicity rights, the few instances in which they have evocatively demonstrate the downside of permitting assignments of publicity rights. Aspiring actors, models, musicians, singers, and athletes are prime targets for agreeing to often nonnegotiable contracts that they sign to get representation from agents or managers, their first recording deal, a photo shoot, a paid role in a movie, a spot on a reality show, or even a chance to play competitive college sports. Musicians starting out in their careers have granted recording labels broad and sometimes perpetual rights to the use of their identities, including uses beyond the scope of particular recordings covered by their contracts. Some labels have obtained the ability to bar recording artists from approving any use of their identities in public, at least in the context of music, for the duration of their recording contracts. Such an occurrence led the famous composer and pop artist Prince to change his name to an unpronounceable symbol when Warner Brothers controlled the use of his name under a lengthy recording contract, and prevented him from making the music and public appearances that he wanted. Luckily for Prince the recording contract did have an end, and he was powerful enough to find a way around some of its most onerous provisions. When the contract terminated, Prince returned to his given name and celebrated his "emancipation."[9]

Reality television show contestants routinely sign away rights to their commercial personalities and their life stories. Shows that do not automatically assign contestants' publicity rights often contain a future assignment clause giving producers the option to force an exclusive assignment of a contestant's right of publicity at a later date. Some releases prevent former contestants from making future public appearances or publicizing themselves or their acts. These releases often expressly bar anyone from participating in the shows whose publicity rights are owned by or licensed to another party.

Models also often assign their publicity rights to others, and in the case of the adult entertainment industry, some companies routinely require their models to assign their rights of publicity in gross and in perpetuity. Some managers and agents also have their clients (most often actors) assign or exclusively license their publicity rights to them. As already noted, the NCAA has claimed ownership of its student-athletes' publicity rights. Social media sites now include in their terms of service the right to use their users' names, likenesses, and photos in advertisements, promotions, and otherwise without express permission. And without limits, users of social media sites, and those with successful YouTube channels, may find these companies increasingly trying to gain transfers of the rights to users' names, likenesses, and other indicia of their identities.[10]

Parents have assigned, often unwittingly, their children's rights of publicity with no opportunity for the children to recapture them. These are considered voluntary assignments, even though the children have no say in the agreements, because the parents have the legal authority to make them. In *Faloona ex rel. Fredrickson v. Hustler Magazine*, the Fifth Circuit Court of Appeals concluded that parents who had signed releases for the use of their children's images in photographs of their children in the nude could not reclaim those images or control unanticipated future uses of those photographs (including their use in hard-core pornographic forums). Nor could the children, who were the subjects of those photographs, do so, even upon reaching the age of majority. This is exactly what happened to the actor Brooke Shields. Her mother assigned her rights of publicity over nude photographs taken when the actor was a minor, and Shields was unable to reclaim any control or rights over the photographs as an adult.[11]

Courts often assume that parents will act in their children's best interests, but this is not always true. Some parents unfortunately exploit their children, particularly ones with economically valuable public personalities. The experience in the 1920s of child star Jackie Coogan led to the passage of a law in California that protects child actors from having their parents or guardians spend all their earnings before they reach the age of majority, as Coogan's parents did. But there is no similar law that protects children from having their rights of publicity transferred. Recently, a teenage performer, Olivia "Chachi" Gonzales, sued her mother, accusing her of assigning her rights of publicity and the trademark in her name and signature "Chachimomma pants" to a third party without Chachi's knowledge or permission. The case was withdrawn, hopefully due to a rapprochement between parent and child, but it raises the legitimate concern that parents will transfer their children's rights of publicity to third parties, potentially in perpetuity. Even well-intentioned parents may not fully understand the ramifications of what they are signing, and could unwittingly transfer their children's rights. If publicity rights truly can be assigned in gross, as claimed, rather than simply waived or assigned for the limited purpose of a single photograph, then parents can indeed assign future control over their children's public persona—not only for the children's entire lives (including their adult lives) but even after the children are dead.[12]

Although many of these voluntary assignments are limited in various ways, to particular time periods, or to the context of telecasts, or to a particular photograph, they are often broader—and can be perpetual and cover all uses of a person's identity in any context. And the more courts allow such contracts to be enforced, the broader they will get. Even though more powerful movie stars, athletes, and musicians may have the leverage to negotiate fair, or even favorable, contract terms related to the use of their identities, others will not be able to. Some assignments and licenses of publicity rights could be challenged on a variety of grounds other than alienability (for example, on contract or employment law grounds, such as being unconscionable or akin to disfavored noncompete clauses), but it is not appropriate in the first place to allow transfers of a person's right of publicity. In addition, contract law has done little thus far to limit or invalidate assignments or licenses of publicity rights.[13]

Involuntary Transfers

Even if such voluntary transfers were not problematic, the right of publicity is also subject to involuntary transfers to creditors and potentially in the dissolution of marital assets. If publicity rights are transferable property, then they should be "property of the estate" for bankruptcy purposes, could be subject to liens, and could be used as collateral and then lost if a debtor defaults on a loan, such as for a car or home. Other forms of IP routinely are included in debtors' estates and assigned to creditors, like banks, credit card companies, and the families of those wrongfully killed. Melissa Jacoby and Diane Zimmerman, therefore, have understandably concluded that the right of publicity is subject to capture by creditors.[14]

If the right of publicity is freely transferable property, then it may be subject to division in a divorce. Forced assignments of patents have been permitted in some divorces, as well as co-ownership of copyrighted works. Such assignments and co-ownership mean that the noninventor and nonauthor spouses may license or use the invention or work without the author's or inventor's permission. These noncreator spouses may even be able to grant exclusive licenses. If the same principles hold true in the context of the right of publicity, ex-spouses could become co-owners of their ex's names, likenesses, and voices.[15]

Postmortem Rights

Even though approximately half of the states provide postmortem rights of publicity, most do not treat them as naturally descendible property. Instead, they conclude that publicity rights can survive death only through specific, additional statutory provisions. These more limited and bounded postmortem rights are distinct from how traditional property is treated after death and challenge the (mis)perception that the right of publicity is a freely transferable property right. Regardless of this differential treatment, many states allow some form of publicity rights to transfer upon death. Such transfers are less problematic than ones of a living person's right of publicity because there are fewer concerns about a dead person losing control over her identity. But concerns remain. If the right of publicity is treated like other freely transferable property, including patents, trademarks, and copyrights, then it is subject to estate taxes. Such taxes may force the commercialization of a deceased person's identity.

Valuations of property are made on the basis of evaluating the property at its "highest and best use." The right of publicity would therefore be valued as a fully commercialized, transferable right, even if those who inherit do not want to market the deceased's identity. As Ray Madoff has noted, the "system . . . is incapable of recognizing the validity of the decision not to treat celebrity status as a commodity." The estate tax bill therefore could force heirs to commercialize the deceased person's identity to pay off this debt. Such involuntary commercialization would violate the most convincing justification for providing a postmortem right of publicity—that it allows the surviving relatives of the deceased to prevent exploitative uses that they would find "offensive" or degrading to the memory of their loved one.[16]

The question of whether the right of publicity can be classified as taxable property of the estate remains hotly contested, and no court to date has held that it is. The taxation issues related to the right of publicity go far beyond paying estate taxes, such as whether capital gains or ordinary income tax rates apply to income from assignments and licenses of individuals' names and likenesses. With regard to estate taxes, the IRS has now taken the position that the right of publicity is property of the estate and subject to taxation. The agency is currently engaged in active litigation with the estate of deceased pop star Michael Jackson about the valuation of his right of publicity, particularly the value of his name and likeness. The estate surprisingly has not yet challenged the inclusion of the right of publicity in its assets. The estate instead simply disagreed about its value, claiming unbelievably that it was worth only $2,000, while the IRS claims it was worth more than $400 million. Notably, both the estate in its filing and the IRS in litigation conflated the trademark-based value of Jackson's name and likeness, the value of the use of his name, image, and voice in copyrighted works (such as photographs, videos, films, and sound recordings), and his independent right of publicity, even though these three categories are distinct. Separating out these claims is no easy task, and raise valuation problems that weigh against the right of publicity being a transferable property right.[17]

In part to avoid the pitfall of his family being forced to commercialize his identity, the actor Robin Williams, who committed suicide in 2014, made a careful estate plan that barred any postmortem exploitation of his "right of publicity" for twenty-five years after his death. He vested ownership of the right, including "[a]ll ownership interest" in his "name, voice, signature, photograph, [and] likeness," in a nonprofit corporation expressly to avoid taxation. Otherwise, Williams's family could have been forced to pay off its debt to the IRS by selling mugs, T-shirts, bobble-head dolls, or posters with Williams on them even though such commercialization was something that would have been anathema to Williams and something that his wife and children also likely would have found distasteful, if not deeply upsetting.[18]

The Bankruptcy of the "Property Syllogism"

Despite this host of unsettling scenarios, the transferability of the right of publicity is rarely discussed, and to the extent it has been considered, the analysis most often has focused on determining whether publicity rights are property (and therefore assumed to be freely transferable), or whether they are really privacy-based, personal rights (and therefore not transferable). As David Westfall and David Landau have observed, this simplistic property-based analysis has eclipsed any other thinking about the scope of the right of publicity. They term this the "property syllogism," in which the classification "property" answers any presented question about publicity rights.[19]

Whether something is categorized as property does have some significance in certain contexts, such as determining whether something is taxable and how it will be taxed, and whether it is part of a debtor's estate or a divisible marital asset. Nevertheless, focusing on whether publicity rights are property sidesteps the fundamental question of whether—even if property—publicity rights *should* be transferable. As George Armstrong Jr. suggests, the "[c]haracterization of a value as property does not solve the question of content of this right." Limits can be, and have been, placed on the alienability of property in various contexts as a matter of public policy.[20]

Although most property is transferable, and this feature is an important stick in the bundle of sticks that constitute property, some property has restrictions placed on its transferability, and so should the right of publicity. Blood, babies, historic buildings, human organs, military service, voting rights, endangered species, and alcohol all have limits placed on their transferability. Some of these things cannot be sold, some cannot be transferred even for free, some have zoning restrictions that limit what can be done with them, and others can be transferred only to certain people, such as those who are at least twenty-one years of age. Several scholars have challenged the property status of certain items, such as voting rights or babies, but if they are characterized as property interests, they each have had bans or limits placed on their transferability.

Regardless of whether the right of publicity is categorized as property, its transferability can and should be limited. The alienability of property has been restricted when fundamental rights are at stake, the underlying property is one we wish not to commodify, or if transfers of the property are likely to be inefficient or even impossible. All of these bases to limit transfers of property apply to the right of publicity, and indicate that the right to control unauthorized uses of our own identities should not be transferable.

The Inseparable Right of Publicity

Most property is capable of separation from the underlying person who owns it. Even some of the most controversial questions surrounding the transfer (particularly sale) of property, such as babies and blood, have not raised the issue of separability because the "property" can easily be seen as separate (or separable) from the underlying person. Discussion of separability in such contexts, therefore, has focused not on the possibility of separation, but instead on limiting the separation of property from individuals when that property is intertwined with their personhood. Most prominently, Margaret Radin has suggested that when objects are intimately tied to our personality, inalienability rules should be used to make them inseparable from us.[21]

One's identity (even if limited to one's commercial, public persona) is not a separable "object" but instead an "attribute" of oneself. As such, one's identity—including its representation in one's name, likeness, voice, and other indicia—is not detachable from the underlying person. When property is physically or conceptually inseparable from the underlying person with whom it is connected, as is the case in the context of the right of publicity, then it is not capable of being transferred to others.[22]

Despite what seems an obvious conclusion, most courts and scholars today assume that publicity rights are separable from the underlying individual ipso facto because they are property rights. Richard Hoffman concludes that publicity rights are "inherently capable of being separated." Robert Post suggests, somewhat circularly, that "personality is commodified [when it] becomes 'something in the outside world, separate from oneself.'" McCarthy quotes this language from Post with approval and adds that the "property right in identity [] can be legally separated from the person in a way that privacy rights cannot." Neither courts nor these scholars, however, have convincingly explained how the separation of a person's identity from that person is possible.[23]

To the extent that courts and scholars have made any effort to explain how publicity rights could be separable from the underlying identity-holder, they have done so by contending that the right of publicity solely encompasses economic or "pecuniary" interests and that these interests can be divorced from the underlying identity-holder. Such a characterization of publicity rights is mistaken. The right of publicity encompasses rights far beyond the mere collection of income and entitlement to the economic value that flows from uses of a person's identity. The right of publicity provides control over the use of a person's identity and, therefore, ultimately over the person herself. It affords the ability to stop others from using her name, likeness, and other indicia of identity (in both commercial and noncommercial contexts) and, if transferable, allows a publicity-holder to stop an identity-holder from using her own identity in public. Publicity rights also encompass both dignitary and economic interests, and, as discussed, these dignitary and liberty-based justifications are central to the right's existence.[24]

In addition, the underlying cause of action for the infringement of the right of publicity is based solely on the identity-holder and can never be anything other than tied to that underlying person. Without reference to the underlying identity-holder, the right of publicity has no content and the cause of action cannot be satisfied. Because of this the identity-holder can affect the publicity-holder's interests and the publicity-holder can affect the identity-holder in a way not possible if separation took place. The economic nature—or lack thereof—of the right does not alter these facts.

The ability of an identity-holder to change the value of his publicity rights regardless of who "owns" them suggests that such rights cannot be unmoored from the underlying person. The identity-holder retains his identity and thereby some control over the value of the publicity rights even after assignment. Consider the debacle involving U.S. Olympic swimmer Ryan Lochte, who was a favorite of advertisers leading up to the 2016 Summer Olympics in Rio de Janeiro, Brazil. While in Rio, Lochte claimed that armed locals robbed him at a gas station. This turned out to be a very public lie to cover up for his drunken vandalization of the gas station. When the truth came out, many companies canceled his endorsement deals, including Speedo and Ralph Lauren. Suppose that in advance of the Olympics Lochte had assigned his right of publicity in perpetuity for $50 million to a company, Sports Titan. All of a sudden, through no fault of the publicity-holder, Sports Titan, Lochte's publicity rights lost much of their value.

Although Lochte appears not to have assigned his rights, this example demonstrates that identity-holders continue to wield control over their right of publicity's economic value even after a purported separation. The very attributes that constitute the right of publicity, the name and likeness (and other indicia of identity), cannot be fully divested and transferred from the underlying person—nor can even the economic value of those attributes (if it were possible to detach the two). The retention of related causes of action, such as false endorsement and false advertising claims, further demonstrates such inseparability, as these claims remain in the hands of identity-holders and can potentially be asserted against publicity-holders and their licensees.

At the same time, a publicity-holder can affect the identity-holder's public and private identity. The publicity-holder can not only harm the value of the underlying right of publicity—in which the identity-holder would have no economic stake (if the right had been transferred)—but also cause other economic harms (such as damage to the underlying career of the identity-holder), as well as dignitary and emotional harms. Publicity-holders can stop identity-holders from making public appearances and from approving public uses of their identities. Publicity-holders can produce merchandise, develop advertising campaigns, and create synthespians (animated digital actors) using the identity-holder's name, likeness, or voice. The publicity-holder also has the right to stop the public from using any indicia of the person's identity (barring the applicability of First Amendment and other defenses). These rights and powers far exceed the mere exercise of economic interests and affect the liberty of the identity-holder. Given the impossibility of disentangling the economic interests from the other interests at stake and the continued connection of the right to the identity-holder, the right of publicity is incapable of complete separation from the underlying identity-holder.

The Inalienable Right of Publicity

Even if one could somehow separate and disentangle a person's right of publicity from her, there are still good reasons not to do so. Placing the right of publicity in the hands of someone other than the identity-holder restricts the identity-holder's rights to liberty, freedom of speech, and freedom of association. Such rights are designated "inalienable rights" for a reason—these constitutionally protected rights cannot be given away or sold, even if a person wants to do so.

Scholars have developed a variety of justifications for prohibiting the alienation or transfer of fundamental rights. Guido Calabresi and Douglas Melamed suggest that fundamental rights are inalienable for paternalistic or self-paternalistic reasons. The state seeks to protect individuals from making bad decisions, or our past selves prevent our future selves from doing something dumb or shortsighted, like selling ourselves into slavery or abandoning our right to free speech. Also unwise is assigning the rights to your name, likeness, voice, and other aspects of your own identity to a third party forever.[25]

Margaret Radin justifies the inalienability of fundamental rights on the basis that such limits are "freedom-enhancing." From her perspective, we are free to do many things but not to give away or sell our freedom. This echoes John Stuart Mill's early articulation of the basis for preventing people from selling themselves into slavery. "It is not freedom, to be allowed to alienate [one's] freedom." Another posited justification for prohibiting the alienation of fundamental rights is the anticipated harm to third parties and to society from witnessing others lose their essential liberties. We all benefit from the universal protection of shared and fundamental freedoms, leading some to argue that we all are diminished by another person's loss of such freedoms.[26]

If fundamental rights are inalienable—which they should be—then, regardless of which foundation one chooses to justify that inalienability, there are reasons to significantly limit the transferability of the right of publicity. The right of publicity could itself be viewed as a fundamental right or, alternatively, as so rooted in the rights of liberty, freedom of speech, and freedom of association that any consideration of its alienability must be done in light of the long-standing inalienability of these fundamental rights. If the right is transferable, then publicity-holders could restrict a variety of fundamental rights held by identity-holders—such as controlling what an identity-holder can say or do, or compelling speech and associations by using the identity-holder's image, name, likeness, or voice.

The boundaries of what a publicity-holder could do, or block an identity-holder from doing, are unsettled, leaving a host of unanswered questions about what identity-holders who lack ownership of their publicity rights can (or cannot!) do. Would an identity-holder need to get permission from the publicity-holder before lending her name to a comic book? Could a bankrupt civil rights leader sell posters with his picture and an inspiring quote? Could a celebrity agree to an interview and fashion spread in a magazine without the publicity-holder's consent? Could an identity-holder sell or even give away her autograph? In each instance a publicity-holder could challenge and potentially bar such actions by identity-holders.

The ability to control how one's image is publicly presented plays a fundamental role in how our identity is created and develops. As Mark McKenna has observed, putting the control over one's identity in the hands of third parties permits others to author the "text of [that person's] identity." When publicity-holders control identity-holders' rights of publicity, they wield significant control over the construction of identity-holders' public personas. Such control implicates the right to liberty. It is therefore not surprising that courts and commentators have frequently compared nonconsensual uses of an individual's identity to involuntary servitude and even slavery. The Supreme Court of Georgia described losing control over how one's image and name are used as turning a person into someone who is "under the control of another . . . in reality a slave, without hope of freedom, held to service by a merciless master."[27]

Transferring a person's right of publicity to another can affect not only how identity-holders' names and images are used, but also their entire careers. If an actor cannot assign, license, or waive right of publicity claims for the limited purposes of a motion picture or television series because a third party owns her publicity rights, producers will not hire that actor. Studios might be willing to negotiate separately with the publicity-holder, but if the publicity-holder does not agree to the use or seeks a cost-prohibitive fee, the identity-holder will have no recourse. Studios may not want to get involved under such complex circumstances in which the publicity-holder and the identity-holder—the performer who will be in the limelight—may be at odds with one another.

The ability to control a person's right of publicity also interferes with an identity-holder's freedom of speech and of association. For example, the pop singer Ariana Grande is vegan. Suppose as part of an onerous agreement she signed with her first manager—who got her her first break and recording contract—she assigned him her right of publicity in perpetuity. (As far as I know this is not the case for Grande, but many artists from Prince to Ke$ha have found themselves trapped in recording contracts longer than they wish and that control their names, performances, and music.) Now suppose that Grande wishes to associate herself with a group that supports veganism, such as People for the Ethical Treatment of Animals (PETA). As part of her advocacy, she decides to encourage people to eat tofu by appearing in a billboard and television campaign cosponsored by PETA and Nasoya (a tofu maker). Her manager, the publicity-holder, could potentially block such an endorsement (even if uncompensated) because it is something that the publicity-holder would like to negotiate himself or prohibit for any number of reasons such as negotiating a lucrative deal for endorsing Oscar Mayer lunch meats instead (something Grande would find outrageous), or simply because associations with tofu are not in the publicity-holder's master plan for Grande's "brand."

Jacoby and Zimmerman, who have advocated for transferring rights of publicity to creditors, concede that such transfers may cause an identity-holder to "lose control over the use of her identity." They contend, however, that such limits on identity-holders' rights of association and free speech are both constitutional and normatively unproblematic, at least in the debtor–creditor context, because bankruptcy is voluntarily declared, and the limits on associational rights will not constrain "deep-seated belief systems, political affiliations, or concern with social causes." This conclusion fails to appreciate the depth of the injury to the identity-holder and the scope of what is transferred, as the Grande example demonstrates, while at the same time overselling the voluntariness of such transfers.[28]

The primary basis for making bankruptcy possible (or divorce for that matter) would be undermined by punitive penalties meted out on the basis of the "voluntariness" of filing such actions. We want people to be able to exit from bad relationships and from debt so burdensome that without the opportunity to make a (somewhat) fresh start, they would be trapped. Moreover, some bankruptcy declarations are expressly involuntary, and sometimes only one spouse wants a divorce. Even if bankruptcy and divorce were voluntary (or at least some instances of them), we do not permit even the voluntary alienation of fundamental rights. Creditors cannot force debtors to give up fundamental constitutional rights to satisfy their debts, nor should they or anyone else be able to force an identity-holder to cede control over her own identity.

Although no one has complete control over the creation of her identity, and public figures, in particular, relinquish some control over their persona to the public, there is a big difference between the general public shaping the construction of an identity that is largely controlled by the identity-holder, and a third-party publicity-holder controlling more directly the identity-holder's public image. The ability of an individual to participate in the conversation about her own identity should be protected. This remains true even when individuals have benefited from having third parties (often corporate entities) manufacture their images. Such third-party influence and shaping is not the same as involuntarily (or even voluntarily) and permanently handing over the reins of one's public persona to a third-party publicity-holder.

Justifying Transferability?

The right of publicity has been justified on the basis of the interests of identity-holders without regard to the economic (or other) interests of non-identity-holding publicity-holders. Transferring publicity rights from the underlying identity-holder defeats all of the justifications for having the right in the first place. Such alienation places control over a person's identity in the hands of a third party in direct contravention of the autonomy and dignity-based objectives of the right. Allowing a publicity-holder to control another person's identity also risks significant economic, reputational, and emotional harms to the underlying identity-holder, given the long-term effects on future income, career, and uses of that person's identity.

Nor is transferability needed to reward identity-holders. Identity-holders can receive endorsement fees and salaries regardless of whether publicity rights are assignable. Alienating publicity rights primarily rewards third parties rather than identity-holders. Although it is possible that identity-holders could get greater monetary payouts if publicity rights were assignable, they can be adequately compensated for their labor, including their labor in producing a celebrity persona, even if the rights have limited to no alienability. Short-term licensing can generate significant income. These licenses themselves must be significantly limited in scope and duration so as not to become default assignments, but there is a wide chasm between a transferable property right in which one's identity can be fully owned by others, and a license to use a person's name or photograph in a particular context (for example, selling perfume) for a limited period of time.

Transferability also does not protect against unjust enrichment. In fact, alienability may exacerbate unjust enrichment by granting windfalls to publicity-holders who buy up identity-holders' publicity rights before their value is ascertained or before a dramatic increase in the value of those rights. For example, if contestants are required to assign their rights of publicity to the producers of *American Idol* or *The Voice* when they are unknown, then those producers will reap the rewards if one of the contestants goes on to become a successful pop artist. Similarly, the NCAA allegedly purchased student-athletes' publicity rights at a bargain price—in exchange for either permission to play on a sports team or scholarship money—and then received a windfall in the sum of hundreds of millions of dollars from licensing these players' identities. Although the student-athletes won a partial victory in a lawsuit challenging the NCAA's agreement with them (primarily on antitrust grounds), the example highlights the likelihood that if free transferability is allowed, the least powerful will transfer their rights of publicity, and others will reap the rewards.[29]

To the extent that the incentive rationale holds any water in the context of the right of publicity—which, as discussed in Chapter 5, it likely does not—transferability is not necessary to incentivize the identity-holder's work or development of her personality. Even absent a transferable right, a person can still be compensated for waiving or licensing the use of her name or likeness. Additionally, if the right of publicity is alienated, an identity-holder may have a disincentive to continue to develop her personality and career since someone other than herself will reap (many of) the rewards. To the extent that the protection of consumers is a valid justification for the right of publicity, which it is not, alienability defeats its purpose by separating out the person whose endorsement is indicated (the identity-holder) from the person who has the authority to endorse (the publicity-holder). The value of the endorsement is dependent on its voluntariness and accuracy as a reflection of the identity-holder's preferences, not those of the publicity-holder.

It is possible, maybe even likely, that alienability benefits publicity-holders, who will have an enhanced incentive to develop the value of the publicity rights or who will be rewarded for their labor, but publicity rights have never been justified on the basis of these third-party interests. Additionally, if we were to reconceptualize publicity rights as promoting publicity-holders' interests, it would require deep engagement with the countervailing interests of identity-holders as well as those of the public who might have stronger use interests as compared with third-party publicity-holders. Ultimately, none of the convincing justifications for having a right of publicity—those rooted in the underlying individual—support its transfer to a non-identity-holding publicity-holder. When alienability works at such cross-purposes with the underlying entitlement, transferability must be limited or completely barred.[30]

The Inefficiency of Alienability

Although we usually favor the free transferability of property, when transferability is likely to be inefficient (for example, when there are negative externalities that the market cannot adequately address), or when there are significant challenges to valuing the relevant property, then even the strongest proponents of free, unregulated markets conclude that transferability should often be limited. Both of these features—inefficiency and valuation problems—are present in the context of publicity rights. Allowing the transfer of publicity rights produces a number of negative consequences that are not easily addressed by the market. Alienating publicity rights burdens liberty, free speech, and the rights of free association. These nonmonetary burdens are hard to quantify in economic terms and therefore hard for the market to address, but cannot be ignored when considering the value (and costs) of transferability.[31]

Setting aside such nonmonetary costs, the simple act of separating the right of publicity from identity-holders could lead to a number of other inefficiencies. If identity-holders are not the holders of their own publicity rights, then they may have less of an incentive to maintain or enhance the value of their identity. Identity-holders, as discussed, could even (intentionally or not) destroy (or reduce) the value of their publicity rights, and publicity-holders would have little power to stop them. Although golfer Tiger Woods bounced back from several scandals involving his "sex addiction," "failed marriage," and high-profile car crash (not to mention his continuing poor play on the greens), these scandals caused many companies that used his image to remove him from their advertisements. At the peak of his endorsements, estimates put Woods's annual total endorsement income in the range of $40 million to $60 million dollars. In the aftermath of the scandals, several economists estimated that billions of dollars in the value of his commercial identity were lost almost overnight. If someone other than Woods owned his publicity rights, Woods would not bear the full cost of his actions and would not necessarily have an incentive to maximize the value of his identity.[32]

Even if identity-holders have sufficient incentives to cultivate their personalities without owning their right of publicity, coordination problems may arise. A publicity-holder and an identity-holder might have different ideas about how to enhance the value of the person's identity. Such a lack of coordination could lead to mixed, and perhaps contradictory, public messages that are likely to lower the value of the relevant right of publicity. Such problems are exacerbated by the number of analogous causes of action that remain fully vested in the hands of identity-holders. The Lanham Act (as well as similar state law claims) still permits false endorsement and sponsorship claims by identity-holders as well as oppositions to the registration of trademarks on the basis that a mark falsely suggests a connection to the identity-holder, even if the right of publicity has been transferred. The identity-holder also retains the ability to sue for defamation, false light, and privacy torts. Moreover, some states permit identity-holders to sue for right of publicity violations even if they have "assigned" their rights to others. The continued ability of identity-holders to bring such identity-based claims increases the likelihood of conflicts with publicity-holders' management strategies and, as discussed, also challenges the possibility of separation.[33]

Undoubtedly, in some circumstances the assignment of publicity rights could facilitate the coordination and maximization of the value of publicity rights through a combination of cooperation and ongoing contractual control over an identity-holder. An identity-holder may not have the time, interest, or ability to adequately police and enforce her right of publicity, and some third parties may be better situated (and motivated) to publicize and manage a performer's identity than the identity-holder herself. But such cooperative management and policing by a third party does not require the transfer of the right.

The alienation of publicity rights could also lead to consumer confusion over endorsements and affiliation as well as over an identity-holder's actual allegiances and actions. A publicity-holder could endorse a product using an identity-holder's identity even though the particular identity-holder might not in fact use that product. Although publicity-holders would have to be careful in such situations not to cross the line into false advertising territory, even if they stayed within the legal bounds, there would be a social cost to such "endorsements" that do not accurately reflect the identity-holder's preferences—the exact information that consumers want and expect that they are receiving.

Publicity rights also pose a host of valuation problems that weigh against allowing alienability. To appropriately value publicity rights, one must assess not only how much a person could collect for commercial endorsements and other commercial (and noncommercial) uses of her identity, but also how much, if at all, a person would be willing to sacrifice control over her identity. Some individuals do not want to sell their publicity rights at any price. Others would sell for higher or lower prices based on their personal preferences for retaining control over their identities and their willingness to commercialize their identities. Additionally, the uncertain scope of the right of publicity across different states exacerbates valuation problems for both inter vivos and postmortem publicity rights. The right of publicity is not limited to commercial uses in all jurisdictions, and even when it is, what is considered commercial varies from advertising for products, such as flour or tortilla chips, to uses in comic books, television news, movies, and related merchandise. Common defenses to publicity rights, such as the First Amendment, newsworthiness, and copyright pre-emption (which I will discuss in Chapters 7 and 8), are also unpredictable. Valuing publicity rights, then, is more akin to a prediction of the likely success of a legal dispute than a valuation of a parcel of property.

Postmortem rights are particularly difficult to value. This is true in part because it is difficult to predict whether death will raise or lower the value of a deceased celebrity's image. James Dean, Marilyn Monroe, and Elvis Presley became more valuable after their respective deaths, but most en-tertainers have a significant drop-off in publicity value once they die and can no longer generate and maintain goodwill. As mentioned, the Michael Jackson estate and the IRS disagree by almost $400 million over the value of the deceased star's name and likeness. The estate claims that child mo-lestation charges virtually destroyed any postmortem value. The IRS's val-uation may be closer to the mark as the Jackson estate signed hundreds of millions of dollars worth of endorsement deals after Jackson's death, and Jackson has regularly topped Forbes's annual list of dead celebrities who make the most money after death, but the determination is murky at best.

It is therefore no surprise that the few times that courts have been called to do so, they have struggled to quantify the value of the right of publicity. In the context of valuing marital property, even when courts have decided that celebrity goodwill or publicity rights are marital property that could be divided upon dissolution, none has ultimately awarded ex-spouses any part of the property. In each instance, the courts were unable to value the publicity rights with sufficient certainty to make an award.[34]

An Existential Crisis?

Alienating the right of publicity—if even possible—burdens fundamental rights, works at cross-purposes with the right of publicity's purported objectives, sometimes forcibly commodifies a person, and is inefficient. Although we have not seen some of the most chilling consequences of transferability, all of the scenarios described in this chapter are plausible if the right of publicity is indeed transferable. Publicity-holders may cur-rently be hesitant to push the most extreme readings of their rights for fear of losing some of their power if a court decides against them and rejects the right's transferability. Conflicts with identity-holders can also make for bad publicity, as major performers can use the media to their benefit. When transfers involve less public and less commercially valuable individuals, the issues may simply not be worth the cost of litigation. These conflicts, however, will increasingly occur, and as once-private individuals have more value among their social media networks, publicity-holders may be more inclined to push their ownership rights against identity-holders. It will take only one case decided in favor of a publicity-holder and against an identity-holder in such a scenario to embolden others to seek and enforce transfers of individuals' publicity rights. As we saw with the *Lugosi* litigation and the development and proliferation of postmortem rights, it took just one victory in a trial court to set off a sea change.

Legislatures must step in and revise their right of publicity statutes to limit transferability, and new laws should make explicit that the rights are personal to the identity-holder, or to certain living heirs, in the context of a postmortem right. In the absence of such changes, courts themselves must step in to block such transfers as violations of the identity-holder's rights to liberty, freedom of speech, and freedom of association. In states where a common law right of publicity is recognized, or a statute is not explicit about transferability, courts should conclude that it is not a transferable right. In fact, a few courts have suggested both these things, even in California, the epicenter of right-of-publicity ownership and litigation.[35]

Limiting or precluding the transferability of the right of publicity, however, leads to an existential crisis for the right. Given that transferability is the primary and defining feature of the right, and is at the root of its split from the right of privacy, one can question whether, absent such alienability, it makes sense to have a separate right at all. It is unlikely at this point that the right of publicity will be extinguished, but changing our concept of the right so that it is understood as inalienable can fix many of the right's excesses. Absent transferability the right is less IP-like, and instead rooted once again in the individual. This understanding of the right of publicity as a narrower right provides guidance for resolving its growing conflicts with free speech and with copyright laws.

7

The Black Hole of the First Amendment

TRANSFERABILITY MAY BE one of the most concerning of the right of publicity's dangers, but its interference with free speech has been front and center in recent years. The right of publicity has been wielded to shut down, penalize, and discourage references to, commentary about, and depictions of real people in comic books, news, works of art, movies, dolls, video games, plays, T-shirts, songs, posters, and political campaigns. Publicity rights restrict uses of a person's name, likeness, and other indicia of identity, thereby limiting what others can say. The more broadly the right of publicity applies—for example, to news and expressive works, to dead people, and to mere evocations rather than actual uses of a person's identity—the more concerning such limits on speech are. From the beginning, the right of publicity and the First Amendment (which protects our constitutional right to free speech) have clashed. But such conflicts have worsened as the right of publicity's breadth has widened and as it has risen in status to an IP right. In trying to determine when speech is unconstitutionally limited by state right of publicity laws, courts have sown confusion and uncertainty, leaving the public and content creators with little guidance. This lack of clarity about how to mediate such conflicts has further chilled speech.

Many scholars and litigants have identified the current mess and some have tried to navigate ways out of it, but thus far no magic pill has been found to determine when the First Amendment bars right of publicity claims. This book about the larger story of the right of publicity's emergence, missteps, and opportunities cannot tackle this challenging issue in all its complexity, but there are some lessons that stem from better understanding the true origins and motivations behind the right of publicity. Determining when the First Amendment's protection of free speech should yield to the enforcement of state right of publicity laws requires a deep understanding and interrogation of the rationales behind the right of publicity. Unfortunately, most courts have rotely repeated the least convincing justifications for the right of publicity, those rooted in the IP paradigm—the incentive-rationale and labor-reward rubrics—and have unacceptably limited free speech as a result.[1]

Recalibrating the right of publicity and realigning it with its privacy-based origins can help refocus our First Amendment inquiries in a way that is more speech protective while still providing adequate safeguards for individuals whose identities are used without permission. Courts must revisit why states have adopted a right of publicity, and engage in more searching analyses of the legitimacy of these justifications. Only when the underlying identity-holders (and sometimes their heirs) are likely to be injured is it appropriate to limit the freedom of speech. Even under such circumstances, First Amendment defenses should often prevail depending on why and how the person's identity is used. This chapter considers how we got sucked into the current black hole of an underprotective and uncertain First Amendment defense to right of publicity claims, and suggests some possible routes of escape. This chapter begins with the human cannonball, and then takes us on a journey through hit hip-hop songs, fantasy sports leagues, popular video games, best-selling comic books, celebrity portraits, and Academy Award–winning films that have been impacted by this ongoing struggle between the right of publicity and the freedom of speech.

The Supreme Court's Cannonball

Because it is the only right of publicity case to be decided by the Supreme Court, *Zacchini v. Scripps-Howard Broadcasting* has had an outsized impact. Recall that in this decision from 1977, the Supreme Court rejected a First Amendment defense to a right of publicity claim when a television news broadcast aired Hugo Zacchini's fifteen-second human cannonball act. Prior to this decision, few judges (or litigants) thought that the right of publicity applied in the context of news reporting, and to the extent they did, they would have thought that the First Amendment or state-based "newsworthiness" defenses applied, which is exactly what the Supreme Court of Ohio had thought when it rejected Zacchini's claims. The United States Supreme Court's decision in *Zacchini* upended this view while providing little guidance for resolving future conflicts with the First Amendment. *Zacchini* also limited the success of First Amendment defenses to right of publicity claims by placing the right of publicity into the category of IP. Although you have a right to speak, the Supreme Court has held that you do not have the right to speak someone else's words or use someone else's private (intellectual) property to make your speech.[2]

The U.S. Supreme Court nearly did not hear *Zacchini*—which would have left in place the Ohio Supreme Court's rejection of Zacchini's claim, and a more speech-protective environment today. As was their usual protocol, the U.S. Supreme Court's law clerks wrote memoranda evaluating the case and advising whether they thought the Court should grant review. The clerks uniformly recommended against granting the petition for certiorari, noting that the record (the fact findings) in the case was not developed, nor was the law in the area, and also that the unique set of facts (a fifteen-second human cannonball act) was not likely to reoccur. Nevertheless, the clerks also commented that the case would be "a lot of fun," "fun-to-work-on," and "interesting," conclusions that Justice Lewis F. Powell Jr. may have found persuasive as he appears to have underlined and agreed with these comments in his copies of the clerks' memos. At the conference meeting to vote on whether to grant review, he ultimately was persuaded to vote to hear the case, noting, "I think this will be [an] interesting case." Although five justices voted to deny review of the Ohio decision, four votes to grant was enough. Justice Powell likely regretted casting the deciding vote to grant review, as he ultimately dissented in the five-to-four decision.[3]

The U.S. Supreme Court held that Ohio's newsworthiness defense was really a First Amendment inquiry. This meant that the defense relied on the U.S. Constitution, a document about which the U.S. Supreme Court had the ultimate say, rather than on a question of state law about which the Ohio Supreme Court would have had the final word. Having so concluded, the U.S. Supreme Court held that the First Amendment did not protect the station's use of Zacchini's "entire act." After rejecting the First Amendment and newsworthiness defenses, the Court remanded the case for fact-finding about whether Zacchini's entire act was in fact used, and whether that use reduced or instead improved his professional prospects.

Once back in state court, the case settled on the second day of trial for more than $10,000 with both parties claiming victory.[4]

The Supreme Court dismissed future line-drawing problems, observing that the case before it presented "what may be the strongest case for a 'right of publicity'—involving, not the appropriation of an entertainer's reputation to enhance the attractiveness of a commercial product, but the appropriation of the very activity by which the entertainer acquired his reputation in the first place." The complaint in *Zacchini* was not that the news used Zacchini's identity but that it used his *performance*. Tellingly, one of the justices suggested during oral arguments that the issue was "reproducing" rather than "reporting" on Zacchini's act. The justices in the majority worried that rejecting Zacchini's claim, even in the context of a news broadcast, would mean that the news and others could broadcast an entire play, boxing match, song, or symphony without permission, claiming that the use was news reporting. Justice Harry Blackmun was particularly concerned about this issue. He had seen a symphony at the Kennedy Center for the Performing Arts only two nights before the oral argument in the case and this musical experience was on his mind as he considered Zacchini's complaint. Blackmun included the program from the Minnesota Orchestra's performance of a Mahler symphony in his case file and referred to it during the oral arguments. He noted that the playbill explicitly prohibited the "taking of photographs and the use of recording equipment" in the auditorium. Blackmun was concerned that allowing the news to use Zacchini's fifteen-second cannonball act might lead to television stations being able to broadcast entire symphonies without permission under the guise of reporting the news.[5]

Unfortunately, instead of addressing this concern—about absolute immunity for the news, particularly the possibility that such broadcasts could reproduce entire (much longer) performances—the defense primarily focused in its briefs and oral argument on objecting to the review of what it deemed a state law issue. Scripps-Howard's attorney, Ezra K. Bryan, began his oral arguments with the unwise statement: "I still am perplexed . . . as to how we got here. When I first heard that certiorari had been granted in this case, I was at least seriously puzzled and, as a matter of fact, had the apocryphal thought that perhaps we had slipped back of the looking glass with Lewis Carroll with Alice."[6]

The limits of Bryan's advocacy were compounded by the case flying under the radar of others likely to be affected by the decision. No amicus briefs were filed at the petition stage or on the merits, a fact lamented by the justices' law clerks. Shortly before the oral arguments in the case, the National Association of Broadcasters filed a motion for leave to submit its amicus brief along with a copy of the brief. The Court denied the motion. Although the brief appears in the Court's records, there is no indication that any of the law clerks or justices read the brief. Without useful advice from content creators, broadcasters, and others with insight into privacy and publicity laws, and these laws' impact on free speech, the Court was left at sea with regard to future line drawing. The Court also lacked guidance on the state interests furthered by Ohio's right of publicity, which was actually part of that state's privacy law, rather than independent of it as the Court at times seemed to claim in its decision.[7]

In his dissent, Justice Powell (joined by Justices William Brennan and Thurgood Marshall) noted that the majority's "entire act" standard provided little guidance outside of Zacchini's case, and even within the case, what constituted the entire act was itself disputed. Powell thought the majority's rejection of the First Amendment defense would greatly chill news gatherers and other media, which would self-censor to avoid uncertain liability. This was the exact concern expressed in the only submitted (though unfiled) amicus brief. The National Association of Broadcasters warned that a decision rejecting a First Amendment defense in the case could impair press coverage of events such as Martin Luther King Jr.'s "I Have a Dream" speech—a speech that was widely broadcast and transcripts of which were published in newspapers around the country at the time King gave it. When the brief was written, this was a persuasive argument; it would have been shocking to think of limits on disseminating King's influential, masterful speech. But today, alas, in the aftermath of *Zacchini*, expansive right of publicity laws, and robust copyright laws, the Martin Luther King Jr. estate has successfully insisted on being paid for reprinting or broadcasting his speech, and regularly threatens to sue those who do not remove videos or transcripts of the speech from YouTube and other websites. Even the federal government (through a foundation) acceded in 2007 to the estate's demand to pay nearly $800,000 to license King's name, likeness, and words for use on a memorial sculpture of the great civil rights leader placed on the National Mall in Washington, D.C.[8]

Although the Supreme Court did not reach a final conclusion about whether there should be liability against the news station in *Zacchini*, the Court's rejection of the First Amendment defense and remand of the case left much confusion in its wake, and a much less robust free-speech defense to future right of publicity claims. Content creators and the public have been the losers ever since. *Zacchini* conveyed at least two powerful messages to lower courts with regard to First Amendment review in right of publicity cases, both of which limit free speech: First, that the right of publicity could apply to fully protected noncommercial speech without running afoul of the First Amendment, even in the highly protected context of news. This conclusion greatly undercut First Amendment defenses not just for uses in news but also for uses in expressive works more generally, like movies, books, and video games. Second, that the right of publicity should be treated like other IP laws, a signal that First Amendment defenses would be less likely to succeed against the claims brought by the (intellectual) property owners—in this context, the publicity-holders.

The IP Exception

The First Amendment prohibits restrictions on the "freedom of speech." Its language is absolute: "Congress shall make no law . . . abridging the freedom of speech." This admonishment blocks the enforcement of laws that limit speech. Despite the sweeping language of the constitutional provision, the First Amendment has rarely been treated as an absolute. There are categorical exceptions from its protection for certain types of speech that have been deemed less valuable or even without value. Examples of such speech include obscenity, fighting words, true threats, incitement, child pornography, and false or misleading commercial speech (primarily advertising about products or services). State and federal laws can ban these types of speech. But even speech that falls within the scope and protection of the First Amendment is not free from regulation. And some speech receives less First Amendment protection than other speech. For example, the First Amendment protects truthful commercial speech but has allowed greater regulation of such speech than of political speech.[9]

Although the Supreme Court has never explicitly said so, it has repeatedly indicated that First Amendment defenses have less traction against IP claims. IP laws are *content-based* speech restrictions, meaning that courts must look at what is said to determine whether the laws are violated. For example, to determine whether someone copied parts of your book in her book, courts need to look at the content of both works. In the context of trademark law, if Starbucks claims that someone is using its trademarked name as part of its coffee shop's name, courts need to evaluate the allegedly infringing name, Charbucks, to determine whether Starbucks's mark has been infringed. A *content-neutral* speech restriction, in contrast, focuses on the how, when, or where of speech, rather than on its content. So a law restricting the use of loudspeakers on motor vehicles because of the noise pollution they cause is content-neutral because it applies without regard to whether the sounds are speeches made by politicians or preachers, or music performed by a hip-hop group.

The difference between content-based and content-neutral laws matters because content-based speech restrictions are usually subject to the highest level of review, sometimes called "strict scrutiny," whereas content-neutral restrictions are subject to a less stringent review, under an intermediate scrutiny standard. The Supreme Court has explained that "[c]ontent-based laws—those that target speech based on its communicative content—are presumptively unconstitutional and may be justified only if the government proves that they are narrowly tailored to serve compelling state interests." When such a strict-scrutiny standard applies it is often the kiss of death for the challenged law. It is sometimes contended that such scrutiny is "strict in theory, but fatal in fact." So a lot rides on whether strict scrutiny applies, even if it is not in practice always fatal to the challenged law.[10]

Despite the usual heightened scrutiny of content-based laws, IP laws are not subjected to this level of scrutiny. One reason is that courts have adopted the view that people cannot usually use someone else's property to make their speeches. Uses of others' IP are also often devalued because they are mistakenly thought not to contribute anything new to the marketplace of ideas, and also not to be "self-expression in any meaningful sense," because the speaker "pirates the expression of another."[11]

In copyright cases, the Supreme Court has suggested that only rarely should a First Amendment defense be considered. This is partially true because the Court has concluded that copyright's built-in free-speech protections—which leave ideas and facts in the public domain and provide a fair use defense—adequately protect speech. The Court has also indicated that it tolerates greater speech restrictions in the copyright context because copyright is an "engine of free expression" given its purported incentive effect—in which copyright is understood to encourage the creation of new works (or speech) for the public good. The claim is that we tolerate copyright's limits on speech to promote the production of more speech overall. Whatever one thinks of that questionable logic, it has little traction in the context of the right of publicity, which cannot claim to be incentivizing (much, if any) speech, and lacks copyright's built-in speech-related safeguards. Yet, because of the Supreme Court's placement of the right of publicity into the IP box, courts have often imported this preference for copyright holders into right of publicity cases as a basis to prefer publicity-holders over the defendant speakers.[12]

Outside of copyright cases, First Amendment defenses to other IP claims, such as to trademark claims, also are evaluated without using the strict-scrutiny analysis that usually applies to such content-based speech restrictions. Instead, courts have developed a set of unique tests to evaluate First Amendment defenses in trademark cases that balance (in a variety of ways) the speech value of the use with the likely harm to trademark holders and the public if such uses are permitted. The Supreme Court has even held that in some instances trademark holders can prevent uses of their owned "words," in the absence of a showing of any likely confusion as to origin or sponsorship, because defendants cannot "harvest" for their own use the "legitimate property" of others.[13]

By creating and endorsing a vision of the right of publicity as an IP right in *Zacchini*, the Supreme Court undercut the role of the First Amendment as a strong defense in right of publicity cases. Like other IP laws, the right of publicity, despite being a content-based speech restriction, is rarely subject to strict scrutiny, and publicity-holders are often favored over speakers.

Zacchini's "Hurt Locker"

In their struggle to apply *Zacchini* to very different facts, courts have created a series of different and conflicting balancing tests to determine when the First Amendment protects a particular use of a person's identity from a right of publicity claim. The uncertainty of what a speaker can do has itself chilled speech because content creators do not want to risk litigation or liability. They therefore will often self-censor and adhere to the most speech-limiting interpretations of the law.

At least five balancing approaches have been applied to evaluate First Amendment defenses in right of publicity cases. The first is an *ad hoc balancing* approach that weighs the nature of the use against the likely injury to the publicity-holder. The Eighth Circuit took this approach in *C.B.C. Distribution & Marketing v. Major League Baseball Advanced Media,* holding that online fantasy baseball games could use players' names and statistics because the information was in the public domain, and the uses did not materially undermine baseball players' incentives to engage in "productive activities."[14]

The second approach is a *transformative-work* test. This test extracts a single consideration from copyright's fair use doctrine and asks "whether the work in question adds significant creative elements so as to be transformed into something more than a mere celebrity likeness or imitation." This approach was first adopted by the California Supreme Court in *Comedy III Productions v. Gary Saderup, Inc.,* in which the court held that a realistic portrait of the famous comedy troupe the Three Stooges infringed the comedians' right of publicity. The court rejected the First Amendment defense because the lithograph was imitative and realistic, and did not add significant additional material or commentary that would turn the work into something transformative.[15]

The third approach courts have taken is the *transformative-use* test. This is a narrower version of the transformative-work test that focuses on whether the person's identity itself is transformed rather than whether the overall work is transformative. This approach requires defendants to "distort[]" or "transmogrif[y]" the person's identity "for purposes of lampoon, parody, or caricature," or that the use be "more of a 'fanciful, creative character,' than an 'imitative character.'" The Third and Ninth Circuit Courts of Appeals have adopted this approach. Both of these federal appellate courts used the test to reject First Amendment defenses to the alleged use by Electronic Arts (EA) of athletes' likenesses in sports-themed video games that included rosters of actual teams from the past. The courts did not consider the substantial amount of additional material that EA contributed to these interactive sports games, but instead concluded that because the athletes were realistically depicted the uses were not transformative. In contrast, under the broader transformative-work test such additional materials would likely have been allowed by the First Amendment because of their transformative quality in the context of the larger work.[16]

A fourth approach to evaluating First Amendment defenses to right of publicity claims is the more speech-protective *relatedness* test. This approach allows uses of a person's identity in expressive works unless the underlying work is "'wholly unrelated' to the individual" or is a "disguised advertisement for the sale of goods or services or a collateral commercial product." Some courts have expanded this analysis to allow liability if the use is "solely to attract attention to a work." The Second, Fifth, and Sixth Circuit Courts of Appeals, as well as Kentucky and New York courts, have adopted some version of this relatedness approach, whether as an independent First Amendment test or as a narrowing of the scope of the right of publicity claim itself. The relatedness test is sometimes also called the *Rogers* test because it is (inaccurately) thought to originate with the Second Circuit's decision in *Rogers v. Grimaldi*. *Rogers* involved a lawsuit brought by Ginger Rogers arising out of a Federico Fellini movie called *Ginger and Fred*. The fictional movie tells the story of two Italian entertainers who imitate the famous American dancing and acting duo Ginger Rogers and Fred Astaire. The court allowed the use of Rogers's name in the movie title despite her objections because the use was relevant to the theme and content of the movie, and was not a disguised advertisement for some other product.[17]

The final (significant and independent) First Amendment approach is the *predominant-purpose* test. The determinative inquiry for this test is whether the use "predominantly exploits the commercial value" of a person's identity, or instead uses that person's identity with the "predominant purpose" of making "an expressive comment" about the "celebrity." Only Missouri has thus far adopted this approach. The Supreme Court of Missouri adopted the test in *Doe v. TCI Cablevision*, in which Tony Twist, a professional hockey player, sued over the use of a variation of his name, "Tony Twistelli," as a character in the successful comic book series *Spawn*. The court rejected the author's First Amendment defense, because it concluded that the use of Twist's name was "predominantly a ploy to sell comic books and related products rather than artistic or literary expression." The court thought that the use of hockey players' names in the comic book series was directed at ginning up sales of the comics to hockey fans, and therefore did not deserve the First Amendment's protection.[18]

This panoply of tests used to determine whether the First Amendment allows and protects uses of a person's identity has led to bizarre and conflicting outcomes in cases with similar facts. The Eighth Circuit (applying its general balancing test) held that the First Amendment allows uses of athletes' names and playing statistics in for-profit online fantasy sports leagues, while the Third and Ninth Circuits (applying the transformative-use test) barred similar uses of players' statistics and characteristics in sports-themed video games. The Missouri Supreme Court rejected a First

Amendment defense to the use of Twist's name in a comic book because it was deemed to be *predominantly* directed at generating sales, while the California Supreme Court held similar uses of professional rock musicians' names and likenesses in a comic book permissible because the uses *transformed* their identities. Realistic portraits of comedians have been barred by California's transformative-work test, while realistic portraits of golfers have been allowed when the Sixth Circuit applied the very same test.[19]

These contradictory results are no surprise given that all of the tests suffer from ambiguities and uncertainties that make results difficult to predict. What is "wholly unrelated"? What is "transformative"? What is "predominantly" commercial rather than expressive? Depending on which test is applied and how, the success of a First Amendment defense could be different even with identical facts. Consider in more detail the facts of *Comedy III*, the case in which the California Supreme Court first adopted the transformative-work test. The defendant was the eponymous company of Gary Saderup, an artist who primarily paints celebrity portraits. The litigation concerned Saderup's portrait of the Three Stooges, each of whom was deceased by the time of the case. Saderup sold both prints and T-shirts with their likenesses on them. The court rejected Saderup's First Amendment defense, concluding that the uses were not transformative but instead merely imitative realistic depictions of the comedians that did not add "significant expression."[20]

In the case, the court distinguished Saderup's lithograph from Andy Warhol's portraits of Marilyn Monroe and other celebrities, concluding that Warhol's works provide "subtle social criticism," while Saderup's work is merely imitative. Does this analysis indicate that if Saderup had painted the Three Stooges in color or added makeup or something surreal to the portrait that he would have had a First Amendment defense? Or perhaps Saderup's original work would have been allowed if an art critic had praised his skill and his overlay of seriousness and sadness on the comics' faces to comment on the facade of comedy. Or maybe Saderup's use would have been acceptable if he had simply been Warhol—a famous, sought-after, successful and celebrated artist. Or perhaps the use would have been permissible if Saderup had added some other comedians to the picture, like Charlie Chaplin and Lucille Ball. Such additions to a portrait of the golfer Tiger Woods by the artist Rick Rush were deemed transformative by the Sixth Circuit, and the use of Woods's

Gary Saderup, *The Three Stooges*, from *Comedy III Prods. v. Gary Saderup, Inc.*, 25 Cal. 4th 387, 411 (2001).

name and likeness were therefore allowed and held protected by the First Amendment.[21]

Applying the transformativeness tests to the Rush and Saderup prints is challenging, but the other tests do not fare any better. It is hard to predict the outcome of these cases under the predominant purpose test. Would both Saderup's and Rush's uses be deemed commercially exploitative because they both generated sales by using famous individuals' images and names, or instead as primarily expressive comments on Woods's victory at the Masters Tournament and the Three Stooges' underlying seriousness? The relatedness test would likely allow both portraits, as each is related to its underlying subjects—the Three Stooges and Tiger Woods. Some have criticized the relatedness test on this basis, as it sometimes seems that virtually any use could be a related one.[22]

If the relatedness test means something narrower, however, which some courts have concluded, then it too is challenging to evaluate. Consider the lawsuit brought by the civil rights hero Rosa Parks against the hip-hop group Outkast, in which Parks objected to the group's titling a song "Rosa Parks." The Sixth Circuit applied the relatedness test and rejected Outkast's First Amendment defense, at least as a matter of law. The court concluded that the band's use of her name appeared "wholly unrelated" because the lyrics

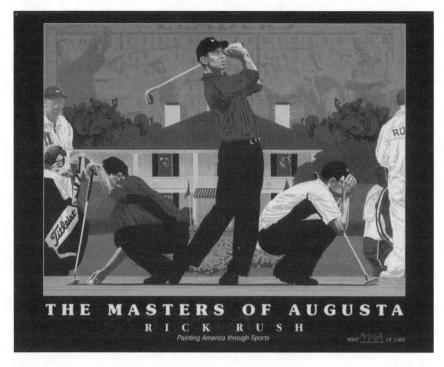

THE MASTERS OF AUGUSTA
R I C K   R U S H
Painting America through Sports
PRINT 1269 OF 5,000

Rick Rush, *The Masters of Augusta*, in author's collection.

of the song were not about the civil rights movement or about Parks's experiences. The assessment that her name was not related to the song is highly questionable. The district court judge had reasonably found a connection between the use of Parks's name and the song given that the song lyrics repeatedly called for "everybody to move to the back of the bus." The trial court explained the "obvious" relatedness of the use of her name:

> There can be no reasonable dispute that Rosa Parks is universally known for and commonly associated with her refusal in late 1955 to obey the segregation laws in Montgomery, Alabama and "move to the back of the bus." The song at issue makes unmistakable reference to that symbolic act a total of ten times. Admittedly, the song is not about plaintiff in a strictly biographical sense, but it need not be. Rather, defendants' use of plaintiff's name, along with the phrase "move to the back of the bus," is metaphorical and symbolic. As a matter of law, this obvious relationship between the content of the song and its title bearing plaintiff's name renders the right of publicity inapplicable.

Although the song was not a commentary on Parks, it was related in the sense that the band was evoking her and her experiences to conjure up an image and meaning in a new context. The band did not use her name to generate sales or in an exploitative manner. Nevertheless, the Sixth Circuit concluded that the use of Parks's name could not be held artistically relevant without additional fact-finding. Accordingly, the First Amendment defense failed at this stage of the proceeding, leading to the case settling. The terms of the settlement and likely payment to Parks are sealed, but allowed Outkast to continue to sell its album using Parks's name.[23]

Ultimately, these disparate tests used to evaluate First Amendment defenses to right of publicity claims do not provide sufficient speech protection or predictable results. Creators, defense attorneys, and free speech advocates saw a ray of hope in early 2017 when the Ninth Circuit applied a strict-scrutiny analysis in the context of evaluating a First Amendment defense to a right of publicity claim. The case, *Sarver v. Chartier*, involved a challenge to the alleged portrayal of Army Sergeant Jeffrey Sarver in the Academy Award–winning film *The Hurt Locker*. The screenwriter, Mark Boal, wrote a portrait of Sarver for *Playboy* magazine, which he later adapted for the screen. A condensed version of the *Playboy* profile was also printed in *Reader's Digest*. Sarver objected to all of these uses, but the focus here is primarily on the use in the movie. Sarver alleged that the main character in the movie, Will James, was based on his life as an explosive ordnance disposal technician in Iraq. The Ninth Circuit held that the use of Sarver's identity (if it was used) was allowed by the First Amendment.

The Ninth Circuit decided not to apply its usual transformative-use test in the context of *Sarver*. The appellate court distinguished the case from its decisions in the video game cases (in which it had applied that test and rejected the First Amendment defenses) because it viewed Sarver's right of publicity claim as a distinct type of claim—one that did not fit the IP paradigm set forth by the Supreme Court in *Zacchini*. Sarver was not a professional performer like Hugo Zacchini, or a student or professional athlete as in the video game cases. Nor was Sarver likely to have a successful endorsement career. Because the court concluded that Sarver did not have a commercially valuable personality and did not "'make the investment required to produce a performance of interest to the public' or invest time and money to build up economic value in a marketable performance or identity," he did not need the reward or incentives that a right of publicity could provide. The use of his identity by the filmmakers posed no "substantial threat to [his] economic value." Under such circumstances, the Ninth Circuit concluded that Sarver had a right of publicity, but the First Amendment would allow almost any use of his identity, at least in an expressive work, like a movie.[24]

The conclusion that the use of Sarver's identity—to the extent it was used at all in the movie—was allowed and protected by the First Amendment is unquestionably correct, but the route the Ninth Circuit took to get there is misguided and continues to jeopardize realistic depictions of public figures in movies and other expressive works. The tortured logic of *Sarver* likely arose because the panel was bound by its prior precedents that had rejected First Amendment defenses in the video game cases that involved the alleged use of realistic portraits of athletes playing football and basketball. The panel contrasted *Sarver* with the circumstances in two of these video game cases, *Keller v. Electronic Arts* and *Davis v. Electronic Arts,* claiming that those holdings apply only to uses that "appropriate[] the economic value of a performance or persona or seek[] to capitalize off a celebrity's image in commercial advertisements." It is not clear that the facts of *Keller* and *Davis* met this standard given that none of the plaintiffs were used in advertising or otherwise promoted or singled out. In addition, many student-athletes who play NCAA basketball or football (like the plaintiffs in *Keller* and the Third Circuit's similar case, *Hart v. Electronic Arts*) don't go on to successful professional careers and are not necessarily any more commercially valuable than Sarver, who was profiled in a national magazine and allegedly singled out as the main character in a film.[25]

Nor is it clear why those with commercially valuable identities should be given a vast property right, while others should not be. The movie studio is enriched (whether unjustly or not) regardless of whether a famous or obscure person's identity forms the basis of a film project. In both instances, the studio has created a movie that will (hopefully) profit by capturing the value of the person's identity. The benefit may sometimes differ in amount if a more famous individual's identity is used, but if a successful (and Oscar-winning) movie is made about an unknown explosives technician, then the studio is profiting from that person's identity.

Additionally, the Ninth Circuit's suggestion that Sarver did not invest in building his identity is unsupportable given that he devoted years to developing his skills in dealing with bombs and as a member of the military, skills that had both value to the country and clear economic value to the magazines and filmmakers who chose to use his identity. The court likely meant something different—that Sarver had not sought to commercialize his identity outside of his primary career. Yet, such individuals should have *more* rather than *less* control over how their identities are used and exploited by others. Private figures do not seek out the limelight, nor are the public and creators as likely to need to refer to them.

The analysis in *Sarver* gets things backward. The court gives the least protection to anonymous, fungible individuals, while boosting protection for the very individuals we most need to refer to and comment on in expressive works. *The Hurt Locker* need not have portrayed Sarver, a private figure; it could have portrayed an amalgamated fictional individual and made the same points—which is exactly what the filmmakers likely did with the fictionalized Will James character. In contrast, public figures often are not substitutable. The *Sarver* decision therefore continues to jeopardize realistic depictions of celebrities and other public figures in expressive works, and even magnifies the misguided treatment of their right of publicity claims as IP-based ones that will beat out First Amendment defenses. *Sarver* therefore continues to place at risk films about real people with commercially valuable identities. Such a reality jeopardizes the creation and independence of future films and television series like *Feud* (about Bette Davis and Joan Crawford), *Ray* (about Ray Charles), *The Theory of Everything* (about Stephen Hawking), and *Walk the Line* (about Johnny Cash).

At the same time, the Ninth Circuit's analysis of the First Amendment defense to Sarver's claim may bar legitimate claims by private figures (at least outside commercial advertising) when the use is of publicly available information, such as a person's name or likeness. This could greatly limit the role of the right of publicity (and privacy-based misappropriation claims) in addressing uses of private figures' identities, whether in revenge porn, on mug-shot sites, or on Twitter-approved trading cards. The Ninth Circuit's distinction between private figures and public ones is also difficult to sustain in a world in which social media increasingly turns so-called private figures into "popular nobodies" and "social media influencers." So rather than being a ray of hope, *Sarver* may only worsen matters. The court got the outcome correct in *Sarver*—the use was allowable—but its route to get there paves a treacherous road for future creators.[26]

If You Ask the Wrong Questions,
You Get the Wrong Answers

Courts, litigants, and scholars have gotten lost in the weeds of these various balancing tests and in figuring out which is the best one to apply when analyzing First Amendment defenses to right of publicity claims. In doing so, we have lost sight of the bigger picture questions that must be answered when evaluating such First Amendment defenses. The First Amendment will not block all right of publicity claims, but it must block some. Because the Supreme Court in *Zacchini* embarked on a balancing approach, courts are likely to continue to balance the identity-holder's interests against those of the speaker. As courts do such balancing, and creators and litigants try to navigate these treacherous and uncertain waters, there are some lessons that emerge from this book's reframing of the right of publicity that facilitate the evaluation of conflicts between right of publicity laws and free speech.

As an initial matter, the right of publicity should be pruned back in a number of ways that would reduce its conflicts with free speech. When a person's actual image, name, or voice is not used, there should have to be additional showings before liability should attach, such as demonstrating that viewers or listeners would think the person's name, likeness, or voice was in fact used. In the absence of such evidence, there should have to be a showing of a likelihood of confusion as to the identity-holder's sponsorship or endorsement. The right of publicity should also either not survive after death or be more modest in scope postmortem, with a far shorter duration than most states have, and should provide broad exemptions for uses in expressive works, news, and other commentary. These shifts alone would greatly reduce the frequency and extent of the conflicts of right of publicity laws with free speech. They would also provide greater clarity and predictability.

Short of such a paring back, moving away from the knee-jerk treatment of the right of publicity as a robust, powerful IP right will help rebalance First Amendment defenses in ways that are more protective of speech. The rights of publicity-holders should not be unduly favored simply because they are viewed as IP rights. Nor should the value of the speech be dismissed as pirating someone else's IP simply because a person's identity is used. Even if the right of publicity were appropriately analogized to IP, it should not benefit from the default preference for the rights of IP holders

THE BLACK HOLE OF THE FIRST AMENDMENT

over speakers given that right of publicity laws do not have the same built-in speech protections as other areas of IP and are not themselves speech-generating mechanisms.

Courts must evaluate and scrutinize the interests purportedly served by the right of publicity both generally and that are at stake in the particular case. When evaluating First Amendment defenses, then, courts must begin by better understanding and challenging the claimed justifications for the right of publicity—something that the Supreme Court did not fully engage with in *Zacchini* because of the case's anomalous facts and lack of sufficient briefing. If First Amendment defenses to right of publicity claims were reviewed under a strict scrutiny standard, which they should be (at least in the context of noncommercial speech), courts would need to identify a "compelling" interest that the right of publicity serves. But even if a lesser standard of review is applied, courts would still need to identify, at the very least, an "important" or "legitimate" justification for allowing a right of publicity claim at the expense of free speech.

As developed in Chapter 5, the best justifications, perhaps the only legitimate ones, for the right of publicity are not those rooted in analogies to IP but those focused on protecting a person's identity, particularly the person's name or likeness, when the uses are likely to cause dignitary, emotional, or economic harms. These injuries were the impetus behind the initial advocacy for and adoption of the right of privacy, and continue to best justify the right of publicity. Because courts have focused on the wrong interests when identifying the justifications behind the right of publicity, they have improperly weighed the competing interests when determining whether the First Amendment allows and protects uses of a person's identity in a particular instance.

Such a recalibration indicates that the First Amendment should usually prevail over right of publicity claims based solely or primarily on the bankrupt incentive-rationale or the more appealing (but equally unsatisfying) unjust enrichment justification. Many of the most troubling decisions denying First Amendment defenses to right of publicity claims have arisen when the sole basis for compensating plaintiffs is unjust enrichment, rather than for actual (or even likely) injuries. The simple fact that someone profits from the use of another's identity should not be sufficient to form a compelling (or even legitimate) interest that overcomes First Amendment protection. Although the unjust enrichment logic has some persuasive appeal, as discussed in Chapter 5, it fails to provide answers to the key questions of when the right of publicity should prevail over free speech, and how to distinguish uses that are just from those that are not. Andy Warhol was unquestionably enriched by using Marilyn Monroe and other celebrities' identities, as opposed to generic unknown faces. In fact, he profited much more financially (and reputationally) from their use than Gary Saderup did from his lithographs of the Three Stooges. But this doesn't mean Warhol needed to pay or get permission to paint these celebrities.

Favoring the First Amendment over right of publicity claims when those claims are based solely on unjust enrichment suggests that the video game cases were wrongly decided. The cases brought by athletes against Electronic Arts (EA) for the sports-based video games turned entirely on the unjust enrichment logic. The players were *not* harmed by the uses; instead, the complaint was that they deserved compensation either because they had a virtually absolute property right in their identities or because EA was deemed unjustly enriched by the use. Because the games did not use the players' names or actual photographs, the dignitary harms, if any, were minimal, and there was no suggestion that the uses would cause future economic injury to their earning potential in either their athletic careers or their endorsement careers. Given that no harm befell the players, this was an instance in which the free speech interests of EA should have weighed more heavily.

Courts that have appropriately focused on the likely harms to identity-holders have rejected such broad property-based entitlement claims when faced with competing First Amendment interests. The Eighth Circuit's analysis in C.B.C. provides a good example of this. Recall that in C.B.C. the court held that the First Amendment permitted fantasy sports games to use players' names and statistics because such uses would not materially undermine the baseball players' livelihoods, incentives to continue in their careers, or future endorsement deals. Even without revenue from fantasy baseball games, "major league baseball players are rewarded, and handsomely, too, for their participation in [real baseball] games and can earn additional large sums from endorsements and sponsorship arrangements."[27]

Focusing on likely harms rather than lost revenue also suggests that First Amendment defenses should be more potent in the context of uses of the identities of the dead. In such instances, the public's interest in engaging with the deceased celebrity will often far exceed the interests of heirs. There can be no personal injury, distress, or dignitary or economic harm to the dead. The heirs may lose out on some profits, but they do not deserve to reap all (perhaps any) of the economic rewards. To the extent heirs have a legitimate claim to rights of the deceased person's identity, the survivors' interests should primarily be to prevent their own distress at seeing their loved one commercialized or resurrected. Such claims would have the most force in advertisements, and perhaps merchandise. No doubt, survivors may also suffer distress from unflattering or critical portrayals of their deceased loved ones in movies, books, or video games, but the speech value and public interest in those uses will almost always outweigh the survivors' interests, which are more attenuated than those of living identity-holders.

In addition to better identifying and focusing on the interests furthered by the right of publicity and the likely harm to the identity-holder in a given case, courts must also evaluate the competing speech interests jeopardized by enforcing a right of publicity. Justice Powell in his dissent in *Zacchini* thought the majority had asked the wrong questions in the case, and therefore got the wrong answer. He contended that the Court should have asked *why* the footage of Zacchini was used, and *how* it was used, rather than *how much* of Zacchini's act was shown. Powell contended that the First Amendment defense should have prevailed unless the station was using the footage as a "subterfuge or cover for private or commercial exploitation," as opposed to doing what it did do, telling the story of his performance at the local fair.[28]

Courts should indeed consider the nature of the use, including how and why a particular use was made of a person's identity. Both copyright's fair use analysis and trademark law's nominative fair use analysis focus on these exact questions when determining whether uses of copyrighted works or trademarks are permissible. Copyright's fair use defense considers more than just transformativeness; it also evaluates the purpose of the use, even if it is not transformative, such as whether it is used for educational, commentary, parodic, or nonprofit purposes. Courts consider how much of the underlying work is used and whether it is the heart of the work that is taken or only a small amount. Courts also look at the likely impact on the market for the work. This focus on the nature of the use and likely market harm meshes with some considerations that could also apply to uses in the right of publicity context, and the potential injury to a person's livelihood.[29]

The Lanham Act (the federal trademark statute) provides similar defenses to uses of others' trademarks. Trademark laws expressly allow the use of others' marks and names to accurately describe the nature and characteristics of products and services, as well as to refer to others' trade-marks and names. The nominative fair use defense evaluates whether the use of a trademark or person's name (in false endorsement cases) was "reasonably necessary to identify the product or service," whether more of the mark was used than necessary, and whether anything was done to "suggest sponsorship or endorsement." Some courts also apply a variation of the relatedness or *Rogers* test in Lanham Act cases in which a person's name is used in an expressive work. Under this test, courts consider whether the use was artistically relevant and whether the user did anything to explicitly mislead consumers as to sponsorship or source. These considerations could also provide guidance in right of publicity cases.[30]

Although these speech-protective tests from copyright and trademark do not necessarily import wholesale to the right of publicity context (and are far from perfect themselves), the First Amendment defense in right of publicity cases must be at least as robust as they are. The right of publicity should be no less constitutionally constrained than trademark law or copyright law. In fact, First Amendment defenses to right of publicity claims should be far stronger given the right of publicity's less convincing and largely absent public-regarding goals, lack of internal speech protections, and far broader basis for liability. As the Second Circuit highlighted in *Rogers v. Grimaldi*, the right of publicity is "potentially more expansive" than trademark laws, given the lack of any requirement of a showing of likely confusion, and therefore must be at least equally checked by the First Amendment.[31]

Some degree of harmonization in defenses also is necessary, because right of publicity claims often arise in cases in which trademark and copyright claims can be made. In most instances when plaintiffs with commercially valuable personalities bring right of publicity claims, they will also have trademark or false endorsement claims, and claims often arise in the context of a copyrighted work. If First Amendment or other free speech defenses defeat copyright and trademark claims, we should not allow right of publicity claims to step in to thwart the speech protections provided for in these other bodies of law.

Yet, this is exactly what happened in the litigation surrounding the use of athletes' identities in video games. In *Brown v. Electronic Arts*, the same Ninth Circuit panel that rejected a First Amendment defense to right of publicity claims in the video game cases held that the very same uses were protected by the First Amendment and allowed in the context of a false endorsement claim brought under the Lanham Act. Given this discrepancy, after Brown lost his appeal on his false endorsement claim, he simply added a right of publicity claim to his complaint. Faced with this double standard, EA settled the case for $600,000. But if the First Amendment protected and allowed the use of Brown's likeness as to one claim, it should have protected it as to the other claim as well. Similarly, if a court holds that the use of a copyrighted work, such as someone else's photograph, is a fair use under copyright law, then the person who appears in such a photograph should not usually be able to block the fair use by asserting a right of publicity claim. The tests need not be identical, but they must be harmonized; otherwise, the right of publicity will continue to run roughshod over superior constitutional rights and federal laws.[32]

✧ ✧ ✧

The right of publicity should be pruned back on its own terms to reduce conflicts with the First Amendment. But even without such state-by-state improvements, courts can and should shift the framework of First Amendment analysis in right of publicity cases away from the rigid IP-like approach currently employed. Instead, courts should identify the compelling, or at least legitimate, justifications for the right, and whether those interests are implicated by the particular use. Litigants and courts should focus on whether the underlying identity-holder is likely to suffer injuries from the use—rather than on possible lost licensing fees or relying on the amorphous unjust enrichment rubric or unconvincing incentive rationale. Courts should then consider the nature, purpose, and extent of the use by the defendant. In the process, courts must not allow the right of publicity—which lacks built-in speech protections—to circumvent the speech protections provided by copyright and trademark laws. Even though difficult cases will remain, this reframed approach will facilitate greater speech protections and improve predictability when free speech and the right of publicity collide.

8

A Collision Course with Copyright

MOST RIGHT OF PUBLICITY claims arise in the context of uses of a person's identity in a copyrighted work. It should come as no surprise, then, that from the beginning, right of publicity laws (and privacy laws before them) have clashed with copyright law. The preceding chapters have already provided many examples of this conflict. *O'Brien v. Pabst Sales* involved a college football star who objected to the use of a copyrighted photograph of him on a calendar, even though the use was authorized by the publicity department of his university, which held the copyright to the photograph. In *Lugosi v. Universal Pictures*, Bela Lugosi's heirs objected to the movie studio's use of stills and images from its own movies on merchandise, including shirts, costumes, and cards, because they included Lugosi's likeness. *Wendt v. Host International* involved a dispute between a licensee who was authorized to use characters from a copyrighted television series in its airport bars and the actors who had played those characters on TV.[1]

Copyright law protects original works of expression that are in a fixed form, such as novels, movies, musical compositions, sound recordings, photographs, and paintings. Authors of such works or nonauthor copyright owners (to whom the rights have been assigned) are given the exclusive rights to reproduce, distribute, and display these works, as well as to prepare derivative works from them, and in some instances to publicly perform them. The conflicts between these exclusive rights of copyright holders and the right of publicity have grown as the right of publicity has risen to the status of IP. This treatment has made courts more willing to put the right of publicity on equal footing with federal copyright law and to mistakenly view the two laws as in harmony. The shift to the IP frame has also supported the expansion of the right of publicity in many ways, notably to allow liability for the mere evocation of a person's identity, which has further amplified the clash with copyright law.[2]

What should the law do when the exclusive rights granted to copyright holders clash with the interests of identity-holders who may object to the uses of their names, likenesses, voices, and other indicia of identity in copyrighted works? Copyright law tells us one thing—that copyright holders are free to make particular uses of their works, including to prepare derivative works (new works based on preexisting works, such as sequels, adaptations, and even merchandise). But right of publicity law tells us another—that additional permission from publicity-holders may be necessary. Resolving these conflicts has led to much litigation and confusion. Courts have struggled to determine whether and when movie studios can reuse footage of actors, sports leagues can sell images of their athletes, and advertisers can use licensed musical compositions of songs made famous by a particular singer. Reframing how we understand the right of publicity and shifting the mechanism for resolving its conflicts with copyright law provide the best opportunity for navigating our way out of the current maelstrom.

The Rabbit Hole of Section 301

When state and federal laws conflict, as the right of publicity and copyright sometimes do, the primary mechanism for resolving such conflicts is a legal doctrine known as "preemption." Preemption provides a defense against the enforcement of state laws when those laws interfere with federal ones. In such instances, federal laws take precedence over (or preempt) state laws. Such federal preemption is expressly provided for by the Supremacy Clause of the United States Constitution, which establishes that the Constitution and federal laws "shall be the supreme Law of the Land." Suppose the federal government establishes a standard that all new cars must come equipped with air bags (which it has). Then, under the preemption doctrine a state cannot pass a law prohibiting the use of air bags in cars in that state. The airbag statute itself might have an express provision that preempts (or limits) such state laws, but regardless of the existence of such an explicit statutory provision the Supremacy Clause of the Constitution would prohibit such a state law.[3]

The current Copyright Act has an explicit preemption provision, Section 301, but the provision has sowed confusion about whether (and when) federal copyright law preempts state right of publicity laws. Trying to make sense of the conflicting decisions applying the section is challenging, if not downright impossible. A leading treatise on copyright law has fairly described copyright preemption as having "more volatility than just about any other doctrine" in copyright law, and as being in "[t]remendous disarray." Section 301 was added as part of the major overhaul of U.S. copyright law in the 1976 Copyright Act. The preemption provision was included primarily to eliminate state copyright laws in an effort to create uniformity and consistency nationwide. Despite the fact that Section 301 likely was never intended to preempt most other state laws, courts usually rely exclusively on it to decide whether copyright law preempts state right of publicity claims.[4]

The reliance on this statutory provision has produced incoherent and irreconcilable decisions. To understand why, a brief sojourn into Section 301 is necessary. The statutory provision prohibits state laws that provide rights *equivalent to any of the exclusive rights*" provided to copyright holders, *and* that "come within the *subject matter* of copyright." Both requirements must be met for the state law to be barred or preempted by Section 301. Courts have struggled to interpret these elements. In the context of right of publicity cases, courts (even in the same jurisdiction) have interpreted what constitutes an "equivalent" right to copyright in two contradictory ways. The first interpretation is sometimes called the "extra element" test. Applying this approach, many courts have held that the right of publicity is not preempted because the cause of action has a number of extra elements beyond what copyright law requires to demonstrate infringement. These additional elements range from requiring the use of an individual's "identity" or "name or likeness" to requiring a "commercial use" or a use for "purposes of trade" to establish a violation of right of publicity laws.[5]

The second interpretation of the equivalent rights language considers a different question: whether the right of publicity claim arises out of the defendant's exercise of one of its exclusive rights as a copyright holder or licensee, such as displaying or reproducing a copyrighted work. As an example of this approach, suppose an actor agrees to appear in a television show. When the copyrighted show is broadcast she doesn't like how her performance is edited, and she sues, objecting to the use of her likeness in the show. Under this second interpretation of the equivalent rights language, her claim would be preempted or blocked by the Copyright Act because the copyright holder in the show was entitled under copyright law to distribute and display the episode, and the violation of the right of publicity occurred solely by exercising those rights.

Such a view would bar right of publicity claims anytime they arise out of a lawful use of a copyrighted work, which is to say almost always, even in the paradigmatic cases in which people object to the nonconsensual use of photographs of them in advertisements. The reproduction of the copyrightable photographs and their use in advertisements are both exercises of the copyright holder's exclusive rights—in particular, the rights to display and reproduce. So this second interpretation of the equivalent rights language cannot be correct, even if it occasionally leads to correct outcomes, as in the case of the actor objecting to her TV episode airing. The better explanation for why the actor should not have a right of publicity claim is that she consented to the use and therefore there is no violation of her right of publicity—such cases should not be analyzed under the copyright preemption rubric, even though they often are.[6]

There are similarly conflicting interpretations of the second requirement for preemption under Section 301—that the state law must protect material or works within copyright's "subject matter." Copyright law protects works of original authorship, fixed in a tangible medium of expression. There is agreement that a person's likeness, name, voice, and other aspects of their identity are not copyrightable, nor within the subject matter of copyright. Many courts and most commentators have therefore concluded that the right of publicity is almost never preempted by copyright law. Some courts, however, have adopted an alternative interpretation—that if the use is contained within a copyrighted (or copyrightable) work, then the claim falls within the scope of copyright. So the actor's performance in the TV show is captured within a copyrighted work, and therefore would be within the subject matter of copyright. Of course, so would almost all uses of a person's identity, such as a print advertisement that uses a photograph of the quarterback Tom Brady without his permission. Such an approach would make the right of publicity "virtually cease to exist" because claims usually arise in the context of copyrighted works.[7]

Section 301, then, either provides us with little to no guidance on the question of when copyright law should preempt a right of publicity claim or (likely the best interpretation of it) leads to the right of publicity never being preempted, even when it substantially interferes with the rights of copyright holders. Complaints over uses of one's identity are not within the subject matter of copyright, nor does the right of publicity provide equivalent rights to those that copyright offers. One of the reasons we likely have such an irreconcilable mess of decisions applying the statute's preemption provision is that Section 301 does not provide the option of a nuanced case-by-case approach. Instead, it was meant as an on-off switch that evaluates whether federal law preempts a state law writ large, rather than whether it obstructs federal copyright law in a particular instance.

Because courts recognize the need for a more specific evaluation in each case, they have tried to turn Section 301 into something it is not. This has led courts to make some questionable distinctions between types of uses of copyrighted works that have no relevance under Section 301 or copyright law, but that track courts' instincts about whether a particular use should be allowed. For example, courts have often favored copyright holders over publicity-holders when performances are captured in video or audio recordings, but not when a person's photograph is taken, even though copyright gives the same protections to moving pictures, photographs, and sound recordings. In contrast, courts have favored right of publicity claims over the rights of copyright holders when the uses are in advertising and merchandise, even though neither Section 301 nor copyright law provide a basis for making such blanket distinctions between those types of uses and ones in expressive works or news.[8]

Copyright's "Full Purposes and Objectives"

Thankfully, the Copyright Act's preemption provision is not the only way to preempt state laws. The act leaves intact independent consideration under the Supremacy Clause of the Constitution. This means that courts can independently evaluate whether a state law, like the right of publicity, or the application of the law in a specific case, obstructs the objectives of federal copyright law. Supremacy Clause preemption provides a better framework for resolving conflicts between publicity-holders and copyright holders, their licensees, and the public. Such a conflict preemption approach focuses on whether the right of publicity is being wielded in the particular instance in a way that "stands as an obstacle to the accomplishment and execution of the full purposes and objectives" of copyright law. To determine when (or if) a state law (such as the right of publicity) obstructs a federal law (such as copyright law), the Supreme Court has advised that one must "examine the objectives of both" the federal and state laws. The fact that enforcement of a right of publicity law limits what a copyright holder can do does not lead to the preemption of the state-law claim. Instead, enforcement of the state-law claim in the particular instance (and similar situations) must interfere more significantly with the copyright system. The analysis also takes into consideration the objectives of the state law, suggesting that when it works in harmony with federal law it will be given greater latitude. It also indicates that when the harms sought to be protected against are at their apex, more latitude may be given to enforce them, if the burden on the federal law is small.[9]

In Chapter 5, I considered the many posited justifications for the right of publicity. The right protects individuals against injuries stemming from unauthorized uses of their identities, including economic, personal, and dignitary injuries. The unjust enrichment rubric provides some overall support for the right, but, as discussed, provides limited to no guidance as to when uses are just or unjust. The interests served by the right of publicity are different from those sought to be protected by copyright law. Copyright law is not concerned with protecting one's identity or one's right to control publicity about oneself. Instead, it is focused on protecting and encouraging the production and distribution of original works that could be freely copied in the absence of laws prohibiting such reproduction.

Copyright laws are expressly provided for in the U.S. Constitution, which grants an "exclusive Right" to authors in their "Writings" for "limited Times" "[t]o promote [] Progress." This grant of power to Congress to create copyright laws highlights the primary justification for copyright in the United States—the goal of incentivizing the creation and distribution of original works of expression. Without copyright laws, works (like movies, books, and songs) could be freely copied without permission from or payment to authors (or copyright owners), making it more difficult to profit from, or at least receive adequate compensation for, such creative pursuits. Some (maybe many) people would continue to create in the absence of copyright's incentives, such as professors who are paid to write as part of their jobs or those with passion projects that keep them awake at night. But in the absence of copyright protection, others might pursue other careers, or have less time and energy to devote to their creative pursuits, as they may need to spend time earning an income elsewhere to support themselves. The incentive effect also extends to those who fund, publicize, and distribute creative works—like movie studios or record labels. If such producers and distributors could not recoup their costs, they would be less likely to fund films or television shows, or to print, distribute, and promote books and music.

The incentive rationale for copyright law is not solely for the benefit of authors (and copyright holders and their licensees), but is also and primarily directed at benefiting society overall. As the Supreme Court has explained: "The immediate effect of our copyright law is to secure a fair return for an 'author's' creative labor. But the ultimate aim is, by this incentive, to stimulate artistic creativity for the general public good. 'The sole interest of the United States and the primary object conferring the monopoly . . . lie in the general benefits derived by the public from the labors of authors.'" In part because of copyright's public-regarding interests, and in part to preserve an important zone for other creators and free speech, copyright laws have a number of built-in protections for the public domain and for uses of others' copyrighted works. This is an important aspect of copyright law—sometimes referred to as copyright's negative spaces—zones free from ownership. Ideas and facts, for example, are deemed "free as the air" for the public to use and build on.[10]

Copyright laws are also justified by several other goals, though ones less often highlighted in the American legal system. Copyright law rewards authors and copyright holders for their labor in creating, funding, and distributing expressive works, and prevents the unjust enrichment of others who would otherwise profit from such works. Authors have dignitary interests in their works. There are numerous ways in which our courts and copyright laws support these dignitary interests, from the rights of termination (allowing authors to reclaim their copyrights years after assigning them), to the availability of statutory damages, and to some extent the provision of the right to prepare derivative works. Our copyright laws also expressly convey "moral rights" to authors of works of visual arts (such as paintings and sculptures), providing a right of attribution and a right of integrity to authors of these works—meaning that the creator must be credited, and the work cannot be altered without the artist's permission.[11]

With this basic understanding of copyright and its objectives, it is possible not only to identify when the right of publicity and copyright clash, but also to better analyze what to do when such conflicts arise. When publicity-holders have consented to the use in the underlying work, then copyright holders most often should be able to use their copyrighted works in all the ways provided by the Copyright Act, including in some (though not all) derivative works. The public must also be able to use copyrighted works in ways expressly allowed by the Copyright Act. If such was not the case, the right of publicity could seriously interfere with copyright law in ways that would obstruct copyright law's incentive effect, the underlying rights of the authors and copyright holders, and the public benefit derived from the copyright regime.

In most other circumstances, the right of publicity should be enforced even in the context of uses in copyrighted works. Copyright laws do not justify abusing identity-holders. The simple fact that a person's identity is captured in a copyrighted work should not undermine legitimate right of publicity claims when the creator did not consensually capture or use that person's identity. Copyright holders and their licensees are not unduly burdened by needing to secure the consent of those whose likenesses and voices are captured. And to the extent they are, this is more likely an issue about free speech and the relevance of a First Amendment defense to the use than about a significant burden on the copyright system.

"No" Means No, but What Does "Yes" Mean?

The most frequently litigated conflicts between copyright law and the right of publicity arise when a publicity-holder sues over a use in a copyrighted work and the defendant is either the copyright holder in the original work or a licensee. In such instances, the dispute often revolves around the nature and scope of consent by identity-holders (or publicity-holders, if the right is transferable, which as discussed it should not be). Courts usually bar right of publicity claims when the original fixation of a person's identity (often in the form of an image or performance) is with permission and the offending use is of the original work. The centrality of such consent to the preemption analysis, however, is initially somewhat perplexing. A lack of consent is part of the prima facie case for a right of publicity claim (in other words, one of the required elements to show a violation). This means that preemption should not be necessary to decide cases in which consent was given—in such instances there simply is no right of publicity violation. Consent is also irrelevant to Section 301 preemption analysis—whether consent was given does not affect whether a use is within the subject matter of copyright or whether the law is equivalent to rights provided by copyright. The relevance of consent makes somewhat more sense under a

Supremacy Clause–based conflict preemption analysis. Allowing a right of publicity action when consent was given to the use significantly interferes with copyright's objectives by preventing the reproduction, display, distribution, and performance of a copyrighted work.

Copyright preemption should not apply when the original capturing and use of the person's identity was without consent. In such instances, right of publicity claims should usually be allowed. If such claims were blocked, the right of publicity would be preempted virtually every time it is raised because most uses of a person's name or likeness are in copyrightable works. It is not a significant burden on preplanned copyrighted works to seek permission of captured subjects; when such permission is not possible (such as in news reporting, street photography, or documentaries), First Amendment or similar defenses likely apply, rather than copyright preemption.

Preemption analysis is crucial in a third category of uses—where there was consent to the original use, but the use at issue exceeds the scope of consent (often in the context of a derivative work) or violates some condition upon which the consent for the original work was given. For example, the model June Toney gave permission to Johnson Products to use her photograph in national magazine advertising for hair care products for a one-year time period, but a successor company, Wella, used her photograph in advertising after the one-year period had expired. The use therefore exceeded the terms of her contract and Toney sued. In such an instance, copyright law expressly allowed the use of the copyrighted photograph by the copyright holder or licensee, but Toney's right of publicity was violated because the use exceeded what she had agreed to. The Seventh Circuit Court of Appeals in *Toney v. L'Oreal USA* concluded that under such circumstances Toney's right of publicity claim should be allowed despite limiting what the copyright holder and its licensees could do with the copyrighted photograph.[12]

Many of these cases simply turn on whether there is a right of publicity violation in the first place, and don't require any preemption analysis. But courts sometimes use preemption analysis to work through the question of whether a plaintiff should be limited to a contract claim if a defendant breaches the terms of a contract, or instead should also be able to bring a right of publicity claim. Two cases highlight this issue and suggest some possible bases for distinguishing the scenarios on preemption grounds. The first is *No Doubt v. Activision Publishing*—a case in which the famous ska-influenced rock band No Doubt sued the video game company Activision for violating the band members' rights of publicity in its video game *Band Hero*. No Doubt alleged that the company violated the terms of the contract under which the band members had agreed to appear in the game. The contract allowed Activision to create animated avatars of the band members, but limited uses only to those with No Doubt songs. Activision breached this contract provision (as well as many others) by allowing the avatars to perform sixty unapproved songs.[13]

Under such circumstances, a federal district court in California held that it was appropriate for the right of publicity claims to proceed against Activision, even though the company held the copyright in the recorded performances and video game. It is not an undue burden on authors and copyright holders to conform to terms that they agreed to and negotiated with a publicity-holder. If Activision and other content creators could use a person's likeness without regard to negotiated contract terms, then individuals once having agreed to one type of use would not be able to control other uses of their identity. This requirement of following through on agreements with actors, models, performers, and musicians is not a substantial obstacle to the achievement of the objectives of copyright law, and successors to the copyrighted works would have been able to tell simply by looking at the terms of the contract with No Doubt that the uses exceeded its terms. The same is true of the circumstances in *Toney*.

Contrast the scenarios in *No Doubt* and *Toney* with that of *Fleet v. CBS*. In *Fleet*, actors were not paid for their performances in a movie and sued when the film was released on video. Although the actors had originally agreed to appear in the film, their consent was given with the understanding that they would be paid. If their consent was contingent on timely payment, then one could conclude that their rights of publicity were technically violated. On the other hand, in contrast to the plaintiffs in *No Doubt* and *Toney*, it may be more appropriate to conclude that the actors should have only a breach of contract claim against the original producers. The actors' main objections and injuries did not stem from their right of publicity claims, but from not being paid. In contrast to the band members in *No Doubt*, the actors in *Fleet* did not suffer a dignitary injury by the use of their names and likenesses, and the nature of their economic injury was simply the failure to pay their salaries, rather than any broader economic injuries to their careers or future deals. The actors agreed to the use of their names and likenesses in the film in exactly the ways in which they were ultimately used. Their true complaint was not an "unauthorized" fixation and use of their performances, but simply that they were not paid. The remedy they were owed, therefore, was simply their salary as promised by the contract.[14]

Nevertheless, if a right of publicity claim can proceed in cases like *Fleet*, it is appropriate for copyright laws to take precedence over and preempt such state-based right of publicity claims, at least when the defendant is not an original contracting party. This is exactly what the California appellate court held. Although the copyright system is not seriously burdened by requiring a copyright holder or creator to pay actors as promised, allowing right of publicity claims in cases like *Fleet* produces unpredictability and uncertainty that would interfere with the copyright system in a larger way, particularly in the context of the distribution and licensing of copyrighted works. Downstream licensees and subsequent purchasers of the copyrights may reasonably assume that the actors agreed both to be captured on film and to the film's distribution.

Even if a licensee had reviewed the actors' contracts in *Fleet*, they would have reasonably presumed that payment had been tendered. In fact, in *Fleet* the main defendant was CBS, which paid $1.25 million for the rights to the film and did not appear to know that the actors had not been paid until after its purchase. Barring right of publicity claims in such instances would not leave performers without a remedy—they would still be able to recover against the producers for the breach of contract claims (presuming the producers were solvent and locatable—risks of all litigation). Notably, it appears that at least some (if not all) of the unpaid actors in *Fleet* were also producers of the film who had failed to pay themselves.[15]

Derivative Works and Art on a Coffee Mug

The role of consent becomes even more complicated when there has been consent to the underlying work and its distribution, but not consent to subsequent derivative uses of that work. Uses of a person's identity in a derivative work—such as in prequels, sequels, spin-offs, re-created or reanimated performances, and merchandise—often exceed what the parties anticipated when they agreed to the capturing of that person's likeness or voice. Under copyright law, however, the right to prepare derivative works is on equal footing with the other exclusive rights provided by the Copyright Act. Nevertheless, derivative uses are often treated differently by courts, and right of publicity claims are more likely to survive in such instances even when they conflict with copyright law.[16]

Conflict preemption analysis suggests some reasons why and provides a basis for determining when right of publicity claims arising out of derivative works should be allowed and when they should not. To the extent we wish to incentivize creative works (and reward authors and copyright holders), allowing copyright holders to harness income from derivative works is an important part of the copyright ecosystem. Derivative works are often a significant source of income for copyright holders. In the context of motion pictures, successful films, like *Star Wars*, and all of the derivative works from them, pay for movie studios' less profitable pictures. When an identity-holder agrees to appear in a copyrighted work, she usually understands that she is an "artist for hire" and will not have a copyright in the fixed form of her performance or image. She also likely understands that this consent extends to (unless otherwise objected to in the contract) the exclusive rights of copyright holders—such as the right to reproduce, distribute, and display the work, and to prepare at least some derivative works, such as posters and advertisements that promote the underlying work. Most movie merchandise is related to the underlying work, such as action figures or mugs and T-shirts with stills from the films on them.

Many of the conflicts between identity-holders and copyright holders can be and are addressed using contracts, as well as collective bargaining agreements. Merchandising and sequel rights are frequently addressed in performers' contracts. However, older contracts and those drafted by less sophisticated parties often do not address all of the issues that now arise. And, of course, sometimes contracts do not get signed, were not drafted, or fail to consider a novel use. When there is no contract or the contract does not address the conflict, there needs to be a default. Given the supremacy of federal copyright law, the default when contracts are silent or absent should be to allow at least some derivative works. The right to prepare such works was in existence at the time consent was given and either known to the actors or other identity-holders (or their agents or attorneys, if so represented) or should have been known. Identity-holders should not be able to use the right of publicity to get at the back end what they were unable to get at the front end during their negotiations. The right to prepare derivative works, at least those that would have been anticipated at the time consent was given for the original, or that are related to the exploitation of the original work, should usually overcome right of publicity claims.

On the other hand, derivative works that were unanticipated and that are not related to the exploitation of the original may well exceed the scope of the person's initial consent. In such an instance, right of publicity claims should often proceed. Right of publicity claims should also survive if a copyright holder (or licensee or assignee) unreasonably extracts and primarily trades off the value of a particular individual rather than the copyrighted work. Determining whether the derivative use is primarily exploiting the underlying copyrighted work or instead the particular person will indicate the degree of impact on the copyright system of limiting such uses.

When derivative works incorporate portions of original works to which identity-holders consented, copyright should often preempt right of publicity claims absent a contractual limitation on such uses. The 2016 decision by the Eighth Circuit Court of Appeals in *Dryer v. NFL* provides a good example of this. In *Dryer*, the court held that right of publicity claims brought by retired football players were preempted when the defendant used copyrighted footage of the players' games and interviews in a series of documentaries about "significant games, seasons, and players in NFL's history." The players had consented to both the original broadcasts and interviews. In such instances, the derivative uses were inextricably tied to the natural exploitation of the underlying work, and the players were not excessively or tangentially promoted other than as intertwined with the underlying content. The uses in *Dryer* also should have been allowed on the basis of a First Amendment defense.[17]

Copyright should also have preempted (blocked) the right of publicity claims in *Wendt*, even though the Ninth Circuit held otherwise. The copyright holder had the right to authorize derivative works, including the airport bars that used the characters from the television series. Neither the copyright holder nor the licensee in *Wendt* did anything to exploit or focus on the actors' identities instead of the copyrighted work itself. If the actors' likenesses had been used on the disputed robots that were used in the bars, which the district court concluded they were not, such a conclusion would be a closer call, largely because the copyright holders could exploit the copyrighted property without using the actors' specific likenesses. But, even so, there needs to be latitude given for the robots portraying the characters to look similar to the actors—copyright holders should not need to change the weight, body type, skin color, or hair of their characters to avoid infringing the right of publicity. And the copyright holder, licensees, and even members of the public should be able to use images from the series, including displaying lawfully procured posters and photographs that include actors' likenesses as memorialized in stills from the television show.

Tough calls will arise, particularly when the derivative works single out and promote individual identity-holders. A Ninth Circuit case from 2017 raises such a situation. In *Maloney v. T3Media*, the Ninth Circuit held that copyright preempted and barred student-athletes' right of publicity claims arising out of the sale of photographs of them on the defendant T3's paya.com website. The NCAA had authorized T3 to use and license the photographs to which the NCAA held the copyrights. When they were students, the plaintiff-athletes agreed (as part of their contract with the NCAA) to the taking of and use of such photographs. Presuming the validity of these contracts (which is far from certain), the NCAA, as the copyright holder in those photographs, should be able to sell, distribute, reproduce, and promote the sale of those photographs, absent a contractual provision to the contrary. To not let the NCAA do so would be a significant obstacle to copyright law, as virtually no uses of the original copyrighted works would be permissible.[18]

The more challenging question is what to do with derivative works produced from those underlying photographs that might appear on merchandise or that single out individual players (and likely sell because of the value of the identities of those specific players). Copyright law confers on the NCAA the right to use those photographs, including placing them on mugs or T-shirts or using them in advertising. On the other hand, if the players did not agree to these additional uses (via the contract or otherwise), they could have right of publicity claims arising out of such uses. The NCAA also is arguably unjustly enriched by such uses, for which the players are not paid. But the players' interests are no more affected by those uses than by widely circulated and sold photographs and posters.

Many courts and some scholars, including both the Ninth Circuit and the district court in *Maloney*, have suggested that there is a difference for purposes of preemption analysis between uses in photographs and those on a mug or T-shirt, or in advertising. But it is hard to see how. Copyright law makes no distinction between such uses, nor does its explicit preemption provision, Section 301. There may be broader policy reasons to limit right of publicity claims to uses in merchandising and advertising (primarily to create clearly protected free speech zones), but for copyright preemption analysis such distinctions are beside the point. Such a distinction has more relevance for First Amendment analysis, which treats commercial speech differently, but for purposes of copyright preemption analysis, courts have gone down the wrong path by focusing on whether uses are in advertising or on merchandise.[19]

Consider the NCAA's sale of a photograph of NFL superstar quarterback Eli Manning playing for the University of Mississippi. Purchasers will likely buy the photo because it depicts Manning, rather than because they seek memorabilia featuring any old quarterback who played for Ole Miss. The same goes for a mug with Manning's photograph on it. If Manning as a college athlete agreed to such photographs being taken and used by the NCAA, then the NCAA should be able to reproduce, distribute, and sell those photographs, accurately describe who appears in them, and even put the photographs on a mug, coaster, or T-shirt to incentivize the production and distribution of copyrighted works and reward the labor of the copyright-holders (and licensees). It may well be unfair that athletes do not receive a portion of the money earned from the sale of these photographs and related merchandise. And it may be that various solutions to this situation are appropriate, including some form of compensation to the athletes (and certainly more fair and limited contracts with student-athletes going forward). But allowing the right of publicity to run roughshod over copyright law is not the solution to such inequities in college athletics.

It is a somewhat different matter if the photograph is used to sell an orthogonal unrelated product, such as using the photograph of Eli Manning on a box of breakfast cereal or in a commercial for it. These uses are about selling cereal, not selling the underlying copyrighted work or various adaptations, translations, or expressive works based on it. It may be more appropriate in such instances to allow Manning a right of publicity claim; doing so will not place as significant a burden on copyright holders as would a broader limit on using the photograph in all advertisements or merchandise. Nevertheless, it is not clear that state law should be able to bar all derivative uses in advertising for unrelated products without showing some harm other than the bare use of the copyrighted photograph. The advertiser's reliance on the shield of copyright law to use the licensed photo would have less traction if the commercial highlighted Manning's name and likeness beyond simply using the photograph, or if the advertisement was likely to cause confusion as to Manning's endorsement of the cereal or participation in the ad. Notably, even if Manning's right of publicity claim arising out of the use of the photograph was blocked by copyright law, he would not be left without any recourse against the advertiser. He would still have a right of publicity claim if the advertisement used additional indicia of his identity (other than an accurate description of the photograph), and a Lanham Act false endorsement claim if the ad caused confusion as to whether he endorsed the cereal or approved the commercial. (A variety of other state laws and federal regulations would also limit uses of Manning's image in the advertisement without his permission.)

This analysis of how to address uses in derivative works holds true whether a public or private figure is involved. Consider a photograph of a child taken while at summer camp. Parents often sign (without noticing) forms that give camps permission to use their children's names and likenesses (usually in photographs) in camp communications, web postings, advertising, and brochures. When the camp takes photographs of the children, it (or potentially the photographer, if not judged a work-for-hire) will hold the copyright to those images. The camp might use a child's photograph on its website or in its brochures to generate business. The parents gave express consent for such uses—through the form (presuming it is valid)—but what if the camp has some financial woes and decides to sell the cute photographs of the children having fun at camp to advertisers for use in unrelated advertisements, say for bug spray? Such uses of the children's photographs from camp are not related to camp activities or promotion, nor were they anticipated when the parents sent their children off to camp or signed the forms. A right of publicity claim brought on behalf of the children should survive a preemption analysis in such an instance even though the use is of a copyrighted work consensually captured. The derivative use of the photograph would be unanticipated and unrelated, and exceed the scope of the agreed-to uses. This would be true even if the use was not in a commercial, but instead on trading cards that parodied particular camper types. This does not mean that no defense would apply to such uses—it may be that a First Amendment defense would apply to some uses of the photographs—but copyright should not bar right of publicity claims under such circumstances.

Synthespians and Delebs

Another compelling instance in which right of publicity claims should be allowed despite the use of a person's identity in otherwise lawful derivative works is when such uses could potentially destroy an identity-holder's career. A panel of judges raised this concern in oral arguments in the Ninth Circuit case *Keller v. Electronic Arts*. Recall that *Keller* involved a lawsuit by student-athletes who challenged the alleged use of their likenesses in a video game. The ultimate decision controversially rejected a First Amendment defense to the uses—a holding that I criticized in Chapter 7—but a question raised during the hearing is particularly salient to copyright preemption. The court expressed concern that the reanimation of actors could destroy the entire market for the actors' services. Judge Jay Bybee gave the example of reanimating Tom Cruise for use in sequels to *Top Gun* and questioned whether this should be allowed.[20]

The possibility of using such "synthespians" is not idle speculation. Filmmakers increasingly are able to use computer animation and previously captured footage to create "new" performances. Several dead celebrities, sometimes called "delebs," recently have been reanimated, from Tupac Shakur at the 2012 Coachella music festival to Michael Jackson moonwalking at the 2014 Billboard Music Awards. Computer-generated performances of the deceased actor Peter Cushing and of Carrie Fisher (then alive) appeared in the 2016 *Star Wars* installment, *Rogue One: A Star Wars Story*. These new performances were created by combining replacement actors with visual effects using previous footage of the original performers.[21]

Even before today's sophisticated computer technology, film companies could "reanimate" actors. In one notable case, the actor Crispin Glover, who played George McFly in the 1985 movie *Back to the Future*, sued Universal Pictures for violating his right of publicity when the film company used a prosthetic mask and makeup to make another actor look like him in the 1989 sequel, *Back to the Future Part II*. The film allegedly used footage of Glover from the first film, in addition to footage of the new actor. The studio had replaced Glover after he asked for more than the studio was willing to pay him to perform in the sequel. The case ultimately settled with a significant payout to Glover—close to his initial asking price.[22]

Filmmakers should be able to recast roles that they have developed and for which they hold the copyright. But reanimating performers goes to the heart of the performers' ability to make a living. Requiring copyright holders to compensate and negotiate with the living if their performances are reanimated does not obstruct the copyright system in a fundamental way. Copyright holders are free to recast, but they should not be able to use previously captured performances to reanimate a person against her will and then pass such a CGI performance off to customers as an authentic performance by the actor. Even if the audience knows that the performer did not agree to the reanimation, the living actor's livelihood is threatened and copyright law should allow right of publicity claims in such instances. There are ways that copyright holders can adequately exploit their original works, including uses in derivative works, without reanimating performers. There is some burden, but it is not great. Meanwhile, the identity-holder could suffer significant economic, dignitary, and emotional harms from such reanimation. Once again, a First Amendment defense might apply in some contexts, but copyright preemption usually should not.

Even so, studios should be able to reanimate actors without additional permission under a variety of circumstances, such as when an actor dies midstream. Deceased actors Philip Seymour Hoffman and Paul Walker were both reanimated to allow the completion of the films they were working on when they died. In *The Hunger Games: Mockingjay–Part 2*, the filmmakers used digital technology and existing footage to cover for Hoffman's physical absence. Similarly, Universal Pictures used CGI and Walker's younger brothers in *Furious 7* to finish the movie after Walker's death. Preventing a film company from completing a work that the actor was already paid for and agreed to participate in, such as was the case with Hoffman and Walker, would be a serious obstacle to the exploitation of the original copyrighted work. These reanimated uses could also be understood as consensual and therefore not violations of Hoffman's or Walker's postmortem publicity rights. They both agreed to be filmed and to appear in the very movies in which they did appear.[23]

Protecting Copyright's Negative Spaces

Although frequently overlooked, one of the major contexts in which copyright law should preempt and bar right of publicity claims is when the claims interfere with copyright's negative spaces—the places copyright law expressly leaves free from ownership or enforcement of copyright laws. These spaces are vital to the copyright system. In a series of decisions that developed the doctrine of conflict preemption in the context of IP laws, the Supreme Court emphasized that federal patent and copyright laws "determine not only what is protected, but also what is free for all to use."[24]

Copyright law leaves facts and ideas in the public domain, and has many other exemptions that facilitate public engagement with copyrighted works to promote the spread of knowledge and to facilitate the creation of new works. The right of publicity does not have the same public interest lodestar as copyright and has no built-in protections for the public domain. It therefore is crucial that copyright law steps in to protect these carefully constructed negative spaces. Our copyright law permits the "fair use" of copyrighted works without permission or payment when the uses are deemed appropriate in light of several considerations, such as the purpose and character of the use, the amount used, and any likely market harm caused by the use. As discussed in Chapter 7 in the context of First Amendment and free speech defenses to right of publicity claims, a finding that a particular use is fair under copyright law should not be circumvented by a finding that the use violates a person's right of publicity.

Copyright law expressly allows the resale and display of lawfully obtained works, private performances, and the public performance of sound recordings other than by digital transmission. It also provides a "home-style" exemption that allows bars and restaurants to play radio and television broadcasts under limited circumstances similar to those of in-home viewing. Actors, singers, and athletes should not be able to stop bars and restaurants from broadcasting their images and voices, or displaying lawfully purchased movie posters in contexts that copyright law expressly authorizes. The Copyright Act also provides the right to make sound-alike recordings or "covers" of musical compositions provided that a compulsory license (sometimes called a mechanical license) is obtained, fees are paid for the underlying musical composition, and the use is in a nondramatic work. The right of publicity cannot obstruct these expressly permitted uses by allowing liability for the bare use of a similar-sounding voice, in the absence of some additional showing, such as a likelihood of confusion as to sponsorship, or as to the use of the person's actual voice.[25]

❖ ❖ ❖

The right of publicity—a state law—cannot significantly obstruct the constitutionally-provided-for rights that copyright law grants to creators and the protection copyright affords to the public domain. When identity-holders agree to the original fixation and use of their images, voices, names, or other indicia of identity, copyright holders (and their licensees) usually should be able to exercise the exclusive rights conferred on them without fear of liability for violating the right of publicity. This remains true even in the context of some derivative works, including uses in merchandise and advertising, unless a contract limits the scope of the right to use a person's identity, or the use is unanticipated and unrelated to the original work, or primarily focuses on exploiting the underlying identity-holder, rather than the copyrighted work. When right of publicity claims obstruct copyright's negative spaces, copyright law should usually bar the state-law claims. Copyright laws, however, cannot be used as an excuse to trample on the right of individuals to control uses of their identities. Copyright should not bar right of publicity claims solely because a use appears in a copyrighted work, nor be wielded to extend the consent to appear in one context to consent to appear in any context.

Often, challenging whether there is a violation of the person's right of publicity in the first place or asserting a First Amendment defense is a more appropriate starting point. In many instances, uses of a copyrighted work should be allowed because of the speech value of the uses, rather than the superior rights of a copyright holder or licensee. Unfortunately, as Chapter 7 revealed, the First Amendment analysis in right of publicity claims is unpredictable and confusing, and often not doing the work it should be. In part because of this, courts and litigants often hope that copyright preemption (despite its own challenges) can stand in to decide these cases, even when it should not. This reality has sent copyright preemption analysis off track. We can set things right again in part by focusing on the lodestars of the objectives of both sets of laws to ensure that the right of publicity does not present a substantial obstacle to our copyright system. But the best way to limit copyright's clashes with the right of publicity is to rein in the ever-expanding scope of right of publicity laws, and put the right back on a path that will less frequently interfere with copyright law, as well as with individual liberty and free speech.

Epilogue
The Big Crunch

CALLS TO EXPAND and spread the right of publicity will continue in the years to come. States that have not considered whether there is a right of publicity separate from a right of privacy will likely move in the direction of adopting such a right. In the aftermath of the death of music legend Prince, the Minnesota legislature may add a postmortem right of publicity in that state. Celebrities and their heirs will continue their annual efforts to add such a postmortem provision to New York's narrow statutory right for the living. Despite the trend of an ever-growing right of publicity, this book has revealed ways to pare it back for the better.

It is time for a Big Crunch for the right of publicity. I borrow (with some liberties taken) the concept of the Big Crunch from physicists who have hypothesized that the Big Bang launched an expansion of the universe that one day will reverse itself, and a contracting phase will begin in which all matter rejoins through the forces of gravity, leading once again into a singularity of matter. The way forward for the right of publicity is by reclaiming its past. The best justifications for adopting a right of publicity are the same ones that justified the adoption of the right of privacy in the late 1800s—ones rooted in personal liberty and dignity, and the prevention of economic, reputational, and emotional harms to individuals. Such a conclusion suggests a variety of ways that the right of publicity should be contracted or limited going forward. It may be that, starting from a clean slate, there would be no need for a separate cause of action; instead, we would have a broader understanding of what we mean by privacy rights, and both public and private figures would be permitted to sue under that rubric and collect both economic and noneconomic damages. But the right of publicity is now well established in a majority of states, and there is likely little to be gained by trying to eliminate it at this point. Such acceptance does not mean, however, that the contours of the right should not be debated or challenged. It is time to take a hard look at why we have a right of publicity and at what work it should—and should not—be doing.

The proposed rebalancing of right of publicity laws, and the recognition that they are part and parcel of privacy law, shifts the right of publicity away from the current dominant paradigm of treating these rights as robust exclusionary and transferable IP rights, like copyrights or patents. Such a reconceptualization will limit clashes with other rights (such as copyright and free speech) and also better protect identity-holders from the dangers that such a transferable right of publicity poses. If we continue to go down the current misguided path of unmooring the right of publicity from its origins and its fundamental link to the right of privacy, then instead of protecting the interests of the underlying identity-holders, the right of publicity will become a tool to thwart those interests. Income from and control over the identities of athletes, performers, and even average citizens will shift away from these individuals and toward corporate owners who need not share the proceeds, nor consult in how these individuals are publicized.

Reuniting our conceptual understanding of right of publicity and right of privacy laws provides a road map for avoiding these harms and redesigning right of publicity laws. Without changing any laws on the books, courts with a better understanding of the legitimate purposes behind the right of publicity can limit its dark side. They can prevent the transfer of the right on the basis that it interferes with the rights of liberty and free speech of identity-holders. Courts can provide more robust First Amendment review, rather than wielding the less speech-protective IP model in the context of evaluating defenses to right of publicity claims. Courts can also better limit the right of publicity's interference with otherwise lawful uses of copyrighted works.

Changes to state laws could be made along the lines that this book has suggested, moving right of publicity law in a direction that would serve society for the twenty-first century rather than burden it. Given the many and disparate state laws on the subject, identity-holders and would-be users of others' identities would benefit from both greater certainty and consistency among state laws. Although I have been hesitant to recommend the adoption of a federal right of publicity, the increasing chaos created by the myriad, conflicting state laws suggests that it may be time for federal intervention. Whether it is a federal law or new state laws, legislators would do well to consider the lessons of this book, and even states that already have laws in place can amend them, ideally moving us toward a more uniform (and narrower) set of state laws.

A number of other insights flow from this book's demonstration that the rights of publicity and privacy are intertwined, and that they both are focused on the same interests—protecting individuals' identities rather than protecting a separable, purely economic interest. First, both public and private figures should be equally able to bring claims, without regard to whether they have actively (or otherwise) exploited their identities. Distinctions between public and private figures make little sense today as so-called private figures increasingly live public or quasi-public lives on Instagram, Twitter, Facebook, Pinterest, Periscope, and other online fora that likely will have already changed and evolved by the time this book goes to press. Because of this greater comfort with publicity, private figures today are not likely to collapse and suffer a nervous breakdown if their image appears in an advertisement for flour or in a sponsored ad on Facebook, as their counterparts like Abigail Roberson did at the turn of the nineteenth century. But this does not mean that we intend to cede control over our identities, nor that we cannot suffer injuries from such uses—even if the nature and scope of our injuries might differ from those of more than a century ago.

Second, public and private figures should be able to recover for both financial and personal injuries. It has done a disservice to public figures to deny the possibility that they too suffer dignitary and emotional harms from nonconsensual uses of their identities. Despite claims to the contrary, their sole objections are not pecuniary in nature, nor should they be forced to pretend that they are. Such requirements unfairly minimize their injuries, and dehumanize them. Nor should private figures be left out in the cold. Such individuals have sometimes been barred from bringing right of publicity claims because they lack commercial value, while also being denied the ability to bring privacy-based claims, because they have permitted their images or names to enter the public sphere. To adequately protect private figures, or at least those without (commercially) valuable identities, it is appropriate to provide statutory damages to deter unwanted uses when actual damages are likely small or nonexistent.

Third, given a better understanding of the legitimate justifications for the right of publicity, the right of publicity should be more limited in scope. Use of a person's actual name, likeness, or voice should be actionable, but when the use is more attenuated, such as simply evoking a person's identity or sounding or looking similar to the person, then an additional hurdle should have to be met before there can be liability. In the context of uses of sound-alikes or look-alikes, liability should attach only if listeners or viewers would think either that the person's actual voice or image was used or that the person sponsored or endorsed the use. Persona-based claims, at least those in which the claim is based on the mere evocation of an identity-holder, should usually not form the basis of a claim, absent a likelihood of confusion as to sponsorship or endorsement.

Fourth, the right should not be transferable. Regardless of whether it is understood as a property right in oneself or solely as a personal tort claim, the right to one's identity should not be capable of being transferred to others. To prevent the undermining of this prohibition, the licensing of one's name, likeness, voice, and other indicia of identity should be limited in scope and duration. This revised understanding will prevent both voluntary and involuntary transfers. Creditors and ex-spouses would still be able to receive income generated by the use and licensing of the debtors' names and likenesses, but would not obtain an ownership right. The IRS would still be able to tax income that flows from uses of a person's identity (whether of the living or dead), but should not be able to tax an estate on the imagined value of publicity rights—something that can force unwanted commercialization of the deceased.

Fifth, any postmortem right of publicity should be narrow in scope and duration, focused on protecting the noneconomic interests of heirs for no more than one generation, and perhaps for a shorter postmortem period of ten to twenty-five years. Postmortem rights should not be able to vest in corporate entities that lack any personal stake in the deceased. Given that the interests of heirs are more attenuated than would be true of the living identity-holder, the free speech rights of the public should have far more traction in the context of postmortem publicity claims. Postmortem rights, therefore, should not apply in the context of uses in news, commentary, or expressive works. It may be appropriate even outside these contexts to limit liability for merchandise (such as Martin Luther King Jr. busts) to instances in which consumers are likely to be confused as to whether the allegedly infringing use originated with or is sponsored by the estate.

Finally, a number of changes can be made to statutory right of publicity laws to limit their negative impact on speech and copyright holders without unduly burdening legitimate claims by identity-holders. Many states have a strict liability standard, but they could shift to require a defendant to know or have reason to know that the use was without permission. States should also add specific speech protections that allow fair uses of a person's identity, and provide some guidelines and specific (though not exclusive) exemptions. Although many have advocated for limiting right of publicity claims to uses in advertising or merchandise, such a limit would exclude legitimate claims arising out of other problematic uses of people's identities, such as uses in revenge porn, mug-shot sites, and catfishing (impersonating others to lure dates). It may be that exemptions for news and expressive works are appropriate, but limiting right of publicity laws solely to merchandise and advertising is too narrow.

In the years ahead, the right of publicity may increasingly become a tool to protect not only public figures but private ones as well. And that is as it should be. Properly understood (and cabined), the right of publicity can provide a path to addressing a number of twenty-first-century challenges. More than one hundred years ago people began to complain when their names and likenesses appeared on products, in advertisements, and in newspapers without their permission. These complaints reached a fever pitch toward the end of the nineteenth century in large part because of technological advancements that made it possible to capture and use the likenesses of both public and private individuals, and to spread these images and news stories widely across the country through the burgeoning mass media. A series of technological shifts broke down the boundaries of what was private and public in the late 1800s, just as we see in today's Internet Age, in which we face another series of technological, cultural, and commercial shifts. The right of publicity led to a narrowing of the right of privacy for the worse, but it now may also provide us with a path back—if only we can save it from itself. We must recognize and embrace its harmony (rather than its divergence) with our "old friend" the right of privacy, and set the two back on course together.

Notes

Abbreviations

The research for this book involved access to many libraries and archives. I am grateful to them all for their assistance. Where citations and documents are not available in the expected places, such as the original courthouses for cases, the notes provide additional information about where to locate the primary materials. The abbreviations below are used where appropriate to indicate some of these many locations.

CCNY   County Clerk of New York County, New York, NY

CCP   Charles Clark Papers, Yale University Library, New Haven, CT

CSA   California State Archives, Sacramento, CA

HAB   Harry A. Blackmun Papers, Library of Congress, Washington, DC

KCC   Kings County Clerk Supreme Court Building, Brooklyn, NY

LFP   Lewis F. Powell Jr. Papers, Supreme Court Case Files, Lewis F. Powell Jr. Archives, Washington & Lee University School of Law, Lexington, VA

LHP   Learned Hand Papers, Harvard Law School, Cambridge, MA

NAF   National Archives, Fort Worth, TX

NAN   National Archives, New York, NY

NAR   National Archives, Riverside, CA

NAW   National Archives, Center for Legislative Archives, Washington, DC

NYSA   New York State Archives, Albany, NY

NYSL   New York State Library, Albany, NY

UNC   North Carolina Supreme Court Records and Briefs Collection, Katherine R. Everett Law Library, University of North Carolina, Chapel Hill, NC

1. The Original "Right of Publicity"

1. Notions of privacy in a colloquial sense predated the 1800s. People had long expressed an interest in having space for seclusion from others, particularly for the performance of bodily functions and sexual activity. Paul Veyne, ed., *A History of Private Life*, trans. Arthur Goldhammer, vol. 1: *From Pagan Rome to Byzantium* (Cambridge, MA: Belknap Press of Harvard University Press, 1987).

2. Todd Gustavson, *Camera: A History of Photography from Daguerreotype to Digital* (New York: Sterling Publishing, 2009), 99–113, 129–143, 148–170; Beaumont Newhall, *The History of Photography*, 5th ed. (New York: Museum of Modern Art, 2012), 27–32, 124–129; Jean-Claude Lemagny and André Rouillé, eds., *A History of Photography: Social and Cultural Perspectives*, trans. Janet Lloyd (Cambridge: Cambridge University Press, 1987), 23–27, 36–37, 80–81; Helmut Gernsheim and Alison Gernsheim, *The History of Photography: From the Camera Obscura to the Beginning of the Modern Era* (New York: McGraw-Hill, 1969), 120–154, 234–242, 263–265, 298, 410–425; "The Right of Privacy," *New York Times*, August 23, 1902, p. 8; Kodak, Eastman Dry Plate & Film Co., *Photographic News*, November 9, 1888, xv.

3. "The Right of Privacy," p. 8.

4. Ibid.; Roberson v. Rochester Folding Box Co., 64 N. E. 442, 450 (N.Y. 1902) (Gray, J., dissenting).

5. Pollard v. Photographic Co. (1888) 40 Ch. D. 345 (Eng.); Samuel D. Warren and Louis D. Brandeis, "The Right to Privacy," *Harvard Law Review* 4 (1890): 193, 208–211.

6. Asa Briggs and Peter Burke, *A Social History of the Media: From Gutenberg to the Internet*, 3rd ed. (2009; repr., Cambridge: Polity Press, 2014), 105–108; David W. Bulla and David B. Sachsman, introduction to *Sensationalism: Murder, Mayhem, Mudslinging, Scandals, and Disasters in 19th-Century Reporting*, ed. David B. Sachsman and David W. Bulla (New Brunswick, NJ: Transaction Publishers, 2013), xix–xxv; Jack Breslin, "Naughty Seeds of Sensationalism: Gossip and Celebrity in 19th-Century Reporting," in *Sensationalism*, 115–126; David W. Bulla and Heather R. Haley, "Sensational Journalism in the Mid-19th Century," in *Sensationalism*, 75–95; W. Joseph Campbell, *Yellow Journalism: Puncturing the Myths, Defining the Legacies* (Westport, CT: Praeger, 2001), 1–13, 25–41, 51–63, 151–167, 175–186; Lemagny and Rouillé, *History of Photography*, 76–79; Gernsheim and Gernsheim, *History of Photography*, 452–455, 551–552; James Playsted Wood, *The Story of Advertising* (New York: Ronald Press, 1958), 87–88; "The Right of Privacy," p. 8; "The Cartoon Bill—Taking Their Own Medicine—Results of Yellow Journalism," *Sacramento Record-Union*, February 28, 1899, p. 6; "The Anti-

Cartoon Law," *Sacramento Record-Union*, February 24, 1899, p. 2; "The Caricature Bill," *Sacramento Record-Union*, January 28, 1899, p. 2; Comment, "An Actionable Right of Privacy? Roberson v. Rochester Folding Box Co.," *Yale Law Journal* 12 (1902): 35, 37–38.

Magazines began to print photographs in the late 1800s, but most newspapers instead copied the photographs using woodcuts or engravings until the 1920s. The "yellow journalism" of the late 1800s has more neutrally been dubbed "new journalism." This new journalism was indeed more sensationalistic than traditional papers had been, with increased coverage of scandals and high-society gossip, but it also had many other features, such as the use of larger type and font sizes, more engaging titles, an increase in the use of images, and the moving up of sports and society stories to the front pages. These legacies of new journalism remain today even in what were once the traditional papers that decried such changes. Campbell, *Yellow Journalism*.

7. Mark Tungate, *Adland: A Global History of Advertising* (2007; repr., London: Kogan Page, 2008), 7–18; Wood, *Story of Advertising*, 24–38, 152–157, 190, 207–208, 221–228, 343, 346, 377, 392–394; Stuart M. Blumin, "The Social Implications of U.S. Economic Development," in *The Cambridge Economic History of the United States*, ed. Stanley L. Engerman and Robert E. Gallman, vol. 2: The Long Nineteenth Century (Cambridge: Cambridge University Press, 2000), 813, 819–858; Briggs and Burke, *Social History of the Media*, 95–96; Robert Higgs, *The Transformation of the American Economy, 1865–1914: An Essay in Interpretation* (New York: John Wiley & Sons, 1971), vii, 39–49; Thomas Richards, *The Commodity Culture of Victorian England: Advertising and Spectacle, 1851–1914* (Stanford, CA: Stanford University Press, 1990), 1–2, 84–85, 200–259; Stephen Fox, *The Mirror Makers: A History of American Advertising and Its Creators* (New York: William Morrow, 1984), 13–45; Ivor Guest, *Fanny Elssler* (Middletown, CT: Wesleyan University Press, 1970), 128–145, 173–174, 200–201; Frederick Dwight, "The Significance of Advertising," *Yale Review* 18 (1909): 197, 199–200; Nath'l C. Fowler Jr., *Fowler's Publicity: An Encyclopedia of Advertising and Printing, and All That Pertains to the Public-Seeing Side of Business* (1900), 31–32, 276–277; *The Life of P. T. Barnum: Written by Himself* (New York: Redfield, 1855), 296–314; *The Papers of Benjamin Franklin*, ed. Leonard W. Labaree, vol. 1 (New Haven, CT: Yale University Press, 1959), 218–221, 271–280, 342–345.

8. Thomas M. Cooley, *A Treatise on the Law of Torts or the Wrongs Which Arise Independent of Contract*, 2nd ed. (Chicago: Callaghan, 1888), 29–33, 420–423; William L. Prosser, *Handbook of the Law of Torts* (St. Paul, MN: West, 1941), 1053–1054; G. Edward White, *Tort Law in America: An Intellectual History*, rev. ed. (New York: Oxford University Press, 2003), 4–5, 173–176.

9. Stuart Banner, *American Property: A History of How, Why, and What We Own* (Cambridge, MA: Harvard University Press, 2011), 28–30, 131–132; Noble E. Cunningham Jr., *Popular Images of the Presidency: From Washington to Lincoln* (Columbia, MO: University of Missouri Press, 1991), ix, 3, 19, 25, 114, 241–280; Michael Madow, "Private Ownership of Public Image: Popular Culture and Publicity Rights," *California Law Review* 81 (1993): 127, 147–167; Richards, *Commodity Culture*, 85–92 (describing Queen Victoria as the "great-grandmother not only of miniature Washington Monuments and piggy banks of the Statue of Liberty, but of mosaics of the Mormon Tabernacle and honorific portraits of the eternal Elvis").

10. Corliss v. E. W. Walker Co., 64 F. 280, 281 (C.C.D. Mass. 1894).

11. J. A. J., "The Legal Relations of Photographs," *American Law Register* 17 (1869): 1, 8; "Portrait Right," *Washington Law Reporter* 12 (1884): 353; "Current Topics," *Solicitors' Journal* 24 (1879): 1–2; Watkin Williams, "The Sale of Photographic Portraits," *Solicitors' Journal* 24 (1879): 4–5; "The Right to Privacy," *The Green Bag* 6 (1894): 498, 499.

12. Neil Richards, *Intellectual Privacy: Rethinking Civil Liberties in the Digital Age* (New York: Oxford University Press, 2015), 21; Richards, *Commodity Culture*, 105–110, 200–202, 226–235; Wood, *Story of Advertising*, 249–264, 377; 19 Cong. Rec. 1782 (1888); "A Bill to Protect Ladies," H.R. 8151, 50th Cong. (1888); "A Chivalrous Congressman," *San Francisco Chronicle*, March 6, 1888, p. 1; "A Question of Personal Right," *Sacramento Daily Record-Union*, March 31, 1888, p. 4.

For a recent exploration of women rising up during this era to object to the nonconsensual use of their images, see Jessica Lake, *The Face That Launched a Thousand Lawsuits: The American Women Who Forged a Right to Privacy* (New Haven, CT: Yale University Press, 2016). Although Lake claims that privacy laws were driven primarily by claims brought by women, the historical record provides ample evidence that men pushed for such a right for themselves. The nature of the claimed injuries was sometimes styled differently, and men more frequently included claims of damage to their professional and economic interests. But men also included claims of emotional distress and reputational harm from appearing in advertisements, and some women included claims for economic and professional injuries.

13. H.R. 8151; "A Chivalrous Congressman," p. 1; "A Question of Personal Right," p. 4; 19 Cong. Rec. 3916 (1888); Photographers of Buffalo, N.Y. to Honorable John M. Farquhar, received May 9, 1888, Boxes 147–148, E3/7/15/3, Collection of Petitions and Memorial Referred to the Committee on the Judiciary, NAW; Lake, *The Face*, 5, 45–50.

14. "A New Crusade," *Profitable Advertising* 8 (March 15, 1899): 561; Polly Larkin, *Marin Journal*, March 9, 1899, p. 1.

15. Mackenzie v. Soden Mineral Springs, 18 N.Y.S. 240 (N.Y. Sup. Ct. 1891); Dockrell v. Dougall (1899) 80 LT 556 (AC) (Eng.); Dockrell v. Dougall (1898) 78 LT 840 (QB) (Eng.); Clark v. Freeman (1848) 50 Eng. Rep. 759; 11 Beav. 112; Fox, *Mirror Makers*, 65–66.

16. "New York Legislature," *New York Times*, March 26, 1897, p. 4; "Tammany's Conventions: Candidates Named for Places on the County and Borough Ticket of the Hall," *New York Times*, October 8, 1897, pp. 1, 2; "Anti-Cartoon Bill Again," *New York Times*, December 17, 1897, p. 1; *Los Angeles Daily Times*, May 10, 1897, p. 6. Senator Ellsworth also introduced a bill to "prohibit and punish the publication and dissemination of licentious, indecent and degrading papers," which failed to proceed. *Journal of the Senate of the State of New York at Their One Hundred and Twenty-First Session* (New York, 1898), 83.

17. Act of Feb. 23, 1899, ch. 29, 1899 Cal. Stat. 28 (codified at Cal. Penal Code § 258) (Deering 1915); "The Anti-Cartoon Law," p. 2; "Senators Get Even with Newspapers," *San Francisco Call*, February 21, 1899, p. 3; *Los Angeles Herald*, January 20, 1899, p. 4; "Works' Cartoon Bill," *Los Angeles Herald*, February 21, 1899, p. 3; "Works' Anti-Cartoon Bill Was Passed," *San Francisco Call*, January 28, 1899, p. 4; "Johnson Worked His Cartoon Bill Through," *San Francisco Call*, January 29, 1899, p. 2; "Useless Anti-Cartoon Bill May Be Repealed," *San Francisco Call*, January 21, 1901, p. 4; "Cartoon Law," *Sacramento Union*, January 17, 1907, p. 1; Act of May 22, 1915, ch. 459, 1915 Cal. Stat. 761.

18. E. L. Godkin, "The Rights of the Citizen: To His Own Reputation," *Scribner's Magazine*, July 1890, 58, 65; Rollo Ogden, ed., *Life and Letters of Edwin Lawrence Godkin*, 2 vols. (New York: Macmillan, 1907).

19. Warren and Brandeis, "The Right to Privacy," 195–196, 213–214.

20. Ibid., 195–196n7; "Will Not Be Photographed in Tights: Miss Manola Will Wear Them, but There She Draws the Line," *Chicago Tribune*, June 13, 1890, p. 6; "Photographed in Tights: Marion Manola Caught on the Stage by a Camera," *New York Times*, June 15, 1890, p. 2; "Manola Gets an Injunction," *New York Times*, June 18, 1890, p. 3; "Miss Manola Seeks an Injunction," *New York Times*, June 21, 1890, p. 2; "Marion Manola," Our Gallery of Players, *Illustrated American*, September 26, 1891, 270; "The Rights and Tights of an Actress," *Baltimore Sun*, June 19, 1890, Supplement, p. 1.

21. Marks v. Jaffa, 26 N.Y.S. 908 (Sup. Ct. 1893). The case mirrors a case from the 1990s in which the boy band New Kids on the Block objected to polls run by two newspapers in which the public could vote (for a fee) for their favorite member of the band. The Ninth Circuit Court of Appeals rejected misappropriation, right of publicity, trademark, and false endorsement claims primarily because of free speech considerations. New Kids on the Block v. News Am. Publ'g, 971 F.2d 302 (9th Cir. 1992).

22. Schuyler v. Curtis, 42 N.E. 22 (N.Y. 1895); Schuyler v. Curtis, 15 N.Y.S. 787 (Sup. Ct. 1891); Schuyler v. Curtis, 42 N.E. at 27–29 (Gray, J., dissenting).

23. Roberson v. Rochester Folding-Box Co., 65 N.Y.S. 1109 (Sup. Ct. 1900).

24. Ibid., 1109–1113.

25. Roberson v. Rochester Folding-Box Co., 71 N.Y.S. 876 (App. Div. 1901); Roberson v. Rochester Folding Box Co., 64 N.E. 442 (N.Y. 1902).

26. Roberson v. Rochester Folding Box Co., 64 N.E. at 448–451 (Gray, J., dissenting); Pavesich v. New England Life Ins., 50 S.E. 68, 78–79 (Ga. 1905); Munden v. Harris, 134 S.W. 1076, 1078–1079 (Mo. Ct. App. 1911); Flake v. Greensboro News Co., 195 S.E. 55, 63–64 (N.C. 1938); Fegerstrom v. Hawaiian Ocean View Estates, 441 P. 2d 141, 143 (Haw. 1968); McGovern v. Van Riper, 43 A.2d 514, 518–519 (N.J. Ch. 1945); Canessa v. J. I. Kislak, Inc., 235 A.2d 62, 68–70 (N.J. Super. Ct. Law Div. 1967).

27. "The Right of Privacy," p. 8; Case Comment, "Right to Privacy: Injunction Denied a Young Woman to Restrain the Publication of her Portrait on Commercial Packages for the Purpose of Advertising," *American Law Review* 36 (1902): 614–620, 634–636 (note that due to an apparent printing error, the commentary and reporting on *Roberson* is discontinuous).

28. Act of April 6, 1903, ch. 132, 1903 N.Y. Laws 308. The law was amended and renumbered N.Y. Civ. Rights Law §§ 50–51 in 1909. Civil Rights Law, ch. 6, §§ 50–51, 1909 N.Y. Laws 317. The right of privacy was first codified in Virginia in 1904. Act of March 7, 1904, ch. 66, 1904 Va. Acts 111 (codified at Va. Code Ann. § 2897a); 10 Va. L. Reg. 824 (Jan. 1905). In 1919, Virginia added a postmortem provision to the section and renumbered the section as § 5782. Va. Code Ann. § 5782 (1919).

29. Pavesich v. New England Life, 78–81.

30. Ibid.

31. Foster-Milburn Co. v. Chinn, 120 S.W. 364 (Ky. 1909); Munden v. Harris, 1079; Itzkovitch v. Whitaker, 39 So. 499 (La. 1905); Edison v. Edison Polyform & Mfg., 67 A. 392 (N.J. Ch. 1907); Kunz v. Allen, 172 P. 532 (Kan. 1918). In *Itzkovitch*, the Supreme Court of Louisiana applied a right of privacy to enjoin the use of the plaintiff's portrait in a Rogue's gallery—similar to today's mug-shot websites—but expressly left open the question of whether a use like that of Roberson's photograph in advertising would violate such a right. Itzkovitch v. Whitaker, 500–501.

32. Melvin v. Reid, 297 P. 91 (Cal. Dist. Ct. App. 1931); Katzberg v. Regents, 58 P. 3d 339, 354n23 (Cal. 2002) (noting that "*Melvin* represents the foundation, in California, of the common law invasion of privacy tort"); Gill v. Curtis Publ'g, 239 P. 2d 630 (Cal. 1952); Prosser, *Handbook of the Law of Torts*, 1050, 1052.

33. Godkin, "The Rights of the Citizen," 65; Warren and Brandeis, "The Right to Privacy," 196; William M. McKinney and Burdett A. Rich, eds., *Ruling Case*

Law, vol. 21 (Northport, NY: Edward Thompson, 1918), 1196–1198; Brents v. Morgan, 299 S.W. 967, 970 (Ky. 1927); Marks v. Jaffa, 909–910; "Privacy," § 2, *American Jurisprudence,* vol. 41: Perjury to Procedendo (San Francisco: Bancroft-Whitney, 1942), 925; "Portrait Right," 353; "The Right of Privacy," p. 8.

34. Pavesich v. New England Life, 70.

35. Advertisement, Pears Soap, *New York Herald,* December 3, 1882, p. 13 (Henry Ward Beecher endorsement); Advertisement, Pears Soap, *New York Herald,* November 3, 1882, p. 7 (Lillie Langtry endorsement); Wood, *The Story of Advertising,* 24–25, 222–224, 249–250, 335–342, 377, 392–394; Benjamin McArthur, *Actors and American Culture, 1880–1920* (Iowa City, IA: University of Iowa Press, 2000), 42; Banner, *American Property,* 135–136; Richards, *Commodity Culture,* 84, 195–199; Tungate, *Adland,* 11–12; Roy Franklin Nichols, "Advertisement to the Public," in *The Papers of Benjamin Franklin,* ix (describing Franklin's successful efforts at self-advertisement in the 1700s).

36. Case Comment, "The Right to Immunity from Wrongful Publicity," *Columbia Law Review* 11 (1911): 566–568; Brents v. Morgan, 970 (emphasis added); George Ragland Jr., "The Right of Privacy," *Kentucky Law Journal* 17 (1929): 85, 115; Leon Green, "The Right of Privacy," *Illinois Law Review* 27 (1932): 237, 239.

37. *Restatement of the Law (First) Torts* (St. Paul, MN: American Law Institute, 1939), § 867; Prosser, *Handbook of the Law of Torts,* 1050, 1056 (emphasis added).

38. Fairfield v. Am. Photocopy Equip., 291 P. 2d 194, 197 (Cal. Dist. Ct. App. 1955) (emphasis added).

2. From the Ashes of Privacy

1. Edison v. Edison Polyform & Mfg., 67 A. 392 (N.J. Ch. 1907); Foster-Milburn Co. v. Chinn, 120 S.W. 364 (Ky. 1909); Eliot v. Jones, 120 N.Y.S. 989 (Sup. Ct. 1910); Redmond v. Columbia Pictures, 14 N.E.2d 636 (N.Y. 1938); Flake v. Greensboro News, 195 S.E. 55 (N.C. 1938); Marks v. Jaffa, 26 N.Y.S. 908 (Sup. Ct. 1893); Loftus v. Greenwich Lithographing, 182 N.Y.S. 428 (App. Div. 1920); "Astaire v. Esquire Magazine," *New York Law Journal,* February 11, 1936, 760.

2. "Manola Gets an Injunction," *New York Times,* June 18, 1890, p. 3; Samuel D. Warren and Louis D. Brandeis, "The Right to Privacy," *Harvard Law Review* 4 (1890): 193, 195–196n7; Dorothy Glancy, "Privacy and the Other Miss M," *Northern Illinois University Law Review* 19 (1990): 401, 401–419. The leading treatise on theater law at the time cited to the *Manola* case for its conclusion that "actors and actresses may control the public exhibition, use or sale of their own photographs." Samuel H. Wandell, *The Law of the Theatre: A Treatise*

upon the Legal Relations of Actors, Managers and Audiences (Albany, NY: James B. Lyon, 1891), 110–111.

3. "The Right of Privacy," *New York Times*, August 23, 1902, p. 8; "The Camera and the Prominent Person," *Current Literature*, July 1902, 390–391.

4. Riddle v. MacFadden, 101 N.Y.S. 606 (App. Div. 1906); Riddle v. MacFadden 115 N.Y.S. 1142 (App. Div. 1909) (affirming jury award); Binns v. Vitagraph Co. of Am., 103 N.E. 1108 (N.Y. 1913); Colyer v. Richard K. Fox Publ'g, 146 N.Y.S. 999 (App. Div. 1914); Loftus v. Greenwich Lithographing, 428; Franklin v. Columbia Pictures, 2 N.E.2d 691 (N.Y. 1936); Redmond v. Columbia Pictures, 636; Lane v. F. W. Woolworth Co., 11 N.Y.S.2d 199 (Sup. Ct. 1939), aff'd, 12 N.Y.S.2d 352 (App. Div. 1939); Negri v. Schering Corp., 333 F. Supp. 101 (S.D.N.Y. 1971); Andretti v. Rolex Watch U.S.A., 437 N.E.2d 264 (N.Y. 1982); Welch v. Mr. Christmas Inc., 440 N.E.2d 1317 (N.Y. 1982); Dzurenko v. Jordache, Inc., 451 N.E.2d 477 (N.Y. 1983); Ippolito v. Lennon, 542 N.Y.S.2d 3 (App. Div. 1989); Pavesich v. New England Life Ins., 50 S.E. 68, 80 (Ga. 1905); Flake v. Greensboro News, 55.

5. William L. Prosser, *Handbook of the Law of Torts* (St. Paul, MN: West, 1941), 1061n94; Marks v. Jaffa, 909–910; Samuel Spring, *Risks and Rights in Publishing, Television, Radio, Motion Pictures, Advertising, and the Theater* (New York: W. W. Norton, 1952), 3–10, 31–33, 244–245, 290; Bell v. Birmingham Broad., 96 So. 2d 263, 265–266 (Ala. 1957).

6. Harold R. Gordon, "Right of Property in Name, Likeness, Personality and History," *Northwestern University Law Review* 55 (1960): 553, 567–568, 581, 592 (claiming that recoveries by public figures were minimal or nonexistent); Stacey L. Dogan and Mark A. Lemley, "What the Right of Publicity Can Learn from Trademark Law," *Stanford Law Review* 58 (2006): 1161, 1171 (describing limits of privacy for "celebrities" as including inability to recover for economic value of uses); Lombardo v. Doyle, Dane & Bernbach, 396 N.Y.S.2d 661, 664 (App. Div. 1977); Cabaniss v. Hipsley, 151 S.E. 496, 504–506 (Ga. Ct. App. 1966); Prosser, *Law of Torts*, 1056–1060.

7. Riddle v. MacFadden, 101 N.Y.S. 606; Riddle v. MacFadden 115 N.Y.S. 1142; Extract from Minutes, Case on Appeal at 18, Riddle v. MacFaddden, 115 N.Y.S. 1142, available at https://www.rightofpublicityroadmap.com/case-archives; Binns v. Vitagraph, 1108; "Jack Binns to Get $12,500," *New York Times*, December 31, 1913, p. 5; Judgment, Record on Appeal at 75, Franklin v. Columbia Pictures, 2 N.E.2d 691 (NY 1936) (No. 554), NYSL; Franklin v. Columbia Pictures, 284 N.Y.S. 96 (App. Div. 1935); Redmond v. Columbia Pictures, 1 N.Y.S.2d 643 (App. Div. 1937); Redmond v. Columbia Pictures, 14 N.E.2d at 637 (awarding $1,500 in economic damages); O'Brien v. Pabst Sales, 124 F.2d 167, 170 (5th Cir. 1941); Ibid., 170–171 (Holmes, J., dissenting); Mackenzie v. Soden Mineral Springs, 18 N.Y.S. 240 (Sup. Ct. 1891); "Astaire v.

Esquire Magazine," 760. Present-day recovery values are calculated using the Consumer Price Index to assess the value as if awarded in June 2017.

8. Loftus v. Greenwich Lithographing, 182 N.Y.S. 428; Complaint, Case on Appeal at 5–9, Loftus v. Greenwich Lithographing, 182 N.Y.S. 428, NYSL; "Gladys Loftus Wins," *New York Clipper*, June 9, 1920, p. 32; Redmond v. Columbia Pictures, 14 N.E.2d 636; Redmond v. Columbia Pictures, 1 N.Y.S.2d 643; Complaint, Case on Appeal at 4–9, Redmond v. Columbia Pictures, 14 N.E.2d 636 (N.Y. App. Div.) (No. 859), available at https://www .rightofpublicityroadmap.com/case-archives (hereinafter references to the *Redmond* Case on Appeal will be indicated as "*Redmond* COA"); Testimony of Jack Redmond, *Redmond* COA at 34–64; Complaint, Record on Appeal at 6, Flake v. Greensboro News, 195 S.E. 55 (N.C. 1938) (No. 744), UNC; Affidavit of Harry E. Malcom in Opposition to Plaintiff's Motion for an Order En- joining Defendants at Exh. A, Astaire v. Esquire. (N.Y. Sup. Ct. 1936) (No. 1083) (July 10, 1935, letter from Kenneth E. Hallam of RKO Radio Pictures Inc. to Bernard Waldman of Modern Merchandising Bureau), CCNY.

9. Complaint, ¶¶ 8–11, Record and Case on Appeal at 8–9, Binns v. Vitagraph, 132 N.Y.S. 23 (App. Div. 1911), NYSL; Testimony of John R. Binns, Record and Case on Appeal at 68–94, Binns v. Vitagraph, 132 N.Y.S. 23.

10. Advertisement, Pears Soap, *New York Herald*, December 3, 1882, p. 13 (Henry Ward Beecher endorsement); Advertisement, Pears Soap, *New York Herald*, November 3, 1882, p. 7 (Lillie Langtry endorsement); Advertisement, Pears Soap, *New York Herald*, November 12, 1882, p. 13 (Adelina Patti endorsement); Riddle v. MacFadden, 101 N.Y.S. 606 ($3,000 damages award upheld by 115 N.Y.S. 1142); "Astaire v. Esquire Magazine," 760; Testimony of Redmond, *Redmond* COA at 36–64; Flake v. Greensboro News, 64; Complaint, Papers on Appeal at 6–7, Lane v. F. W. Woolworth Co., 12 N.Y.S.2d 352 (App. Div. 1939) (No. 2757), CCNY; Answer, Papers on Appeal at 8–10, Lane v. F. W. Wool- worth Co., 12 N.Y.S.2d 352; O'Brien v. Pabst, 170; Ibid., 170–171 (Holmes, J., dissenting); Philip G. Hubert Jr., *The Stage as a Career: A Sketch of the Actor's Life; Its Requirements, Hardships, and Rewards* (New York: G. P. Putnam's Sons, 1900), 126–134; Louis D. Frohlich and Charles Schwartz, *The Law of Motion Pictures* (New York: Baker, Voorhis, 1918), 97–98, 104, 139–140; James Playsted Wood, *The Story of Advertising* (New York: Ronald Press, 1958), 24–25, 222–224, 249–250, 335–342, 377–394; Daniel J. Boorstin, *The Image: A Guide to Pseudo-Events in America* (New York: Vintage Books, 2012), 45–65, 153–178, 217–228 (first printed in 1961); Stephen Fox, *The Mirror Makers: A History of American Advertising and Its Creators* (New York: William Morrow, 1984), 87–90, 116; Thomas Richards, *The Commodity Culture of Victorian England: Advertising and Spectacle, 1851–1914* (Stanford, CA: Stanford University Press,

1990), 84, 195–199; Benjamin McArthur, *Actors and American Culture,
1880–1920* (Iowa City, IA: University of Iowa Press, 2000), 42; Charles L. Ponce
de Leon, *Self-Exposure: Human-Interest Journalism and the Emergence of
Celebrity in America, 1890–1940* (Chapel Hill, NC: University of North
Carolina Press, 2002); Mark Tungate, *Adland: A Global History of Advertising*
(2007; repr., London: Kogan Page, 2008), 11–12; Amy Henderson, "Media and
the Rise of Celebrity Culture," *OAH Magazine of History* 6 (1992): 49.
Self-promotion, fame, and celebrity long predate the 1800s. Leo Braudy, *The
Frenzy of Renown: Fame and Its History* (New York: Vintage Books, 1997);
Roy Franklin Nichols, "Advertisement to the Public," in *The Papers of Benjamin
Franklin*, ed. Leonard W. Labaree, vol. 1 (New Haven, CT: Yale University
Press, 1959), ix.

11. Some examples of this include Melvin v. Reid, 297 P. 91 (Cal. Dist. Ct.
App. 1931) and Munden v. Harris, 134 S.W. 1076 (Mo. Ct. App. 1911).

12. Humiston v. Universal Film Mfg., 178 N.Y.S. 752 (App. Div. 1919); Martin v.
New Metropolitan Fiction, 248 N.Y.S. 359 (Sup. Ct. 1931); Kline v. Robert M.
McBride & Co., 11 N.Y.S.2d 674 (Sup. Ct. 1939); Lahiri v. Daily Mirror,
295 N.Y.S. 382, 389–390 (Sup. Ct. 1937); Gill v. Hearst Publ'g, 253 P. 2d 441
(Cal. 1953); Jacova v. S. Radio & Television, 83 So. 2d 34 (Fla. 1955); Neff v.
Time, Inc., 406 F. Supp. 858 (W.D. Pa. 1976). Even in cases in which private
figures recovered, courts noted that they would not have had claims if the uses
had been newsworthy. Melvin v. Reid, 93; Binns v. Vitagraph, 1110–1111. Many
of the early privacy cases also predate the Supreme Court's recognition in
Gitlow v. New York, 268 U.S. 652, 666 (1925), that the First Amendment applied
to the states, or were in the early days of its application to state law.

13. Corliss v. E. W. Walker Co., 64 F. 280 (C.C.D. Mass. 1894). Courts, litigants,
and scholars citing to *Corliss* for this erroneous proposition include: Branson v.
Fawcett Publ'ns, 124 F. Supp. 429, 433n11 (E.D. Ill. 1954); Koussevitzky v. Allen,
Towne & Heath, Inc., 68 N.Y.S.2d 779, 784 (1947); Elmhurst v. Pearson,
153 F.2d 467, 468n2 (D.C. Cir. 1946); Dogan and Lemley, "What the Right of
Publicity Can Learn," 1171n36; William L. Prosser, "Privacy," *California Law
Review* 48 (1960): 383, 411–412n232; Jack G. Johnson, Comment, "Torts—Right
of Privacy—Distinction between Right of Privacy and Proprietary Right in
Personality and History—*Sharkey v. National Broadcasting Co.*, 93 F.
Supp. 986 (S.D.N.Y. 1950)," *Texas Law Review* 29 (1951): 976; Appellee's Brief at
27–28, O'Brien v. Pabst, 124 F.2d 167 (No. 9892), NAF.

Ultimately, Massachusetts never adopted a common law right of privacy,
and only adopted such a right by statute many years later. Act of July 28, 1970,
ch. 592 (codified at Mass. Gen. Laws Ann. ch. 214, § 3A); Act of October 23, 1973,
ch. 941, 1973 Mass. Acts 968 (codified at Mass. Gen. Laws Ann. ch. 214 § 1B).

14. Cohen v. Marx, 211 P. 2d 320, 321 (Cal. Dist. Ct. App. 1949). A number of cases and articles cited to *Cohen* for the proposition that public figures waive their right of privacy. Gill v. Hearst Publ'g, 444–445; Branson v. Fawcett Publ'ns, 433n11; Peter L. Felcher and Edward L. Rubin, "Privacy, Publicity, and the Portrayal of Real People by the Media," *Yale Law Journal* 88 (1979): 1577, 1586n54; Prosser, "Privacy," 411–412n222; Melville B. Nimmer, "The Right of Publicity," *Law and Contemporary Problems* 19 (1954): 203, 206n25.

15. Gautier v. Pro-Football, 107 N.E.2d 485 (N.Y. 1952); Binns v. Vitagraph, 1108. Although many litigants had thought the distinction between uses in fiction and uses in nonfiction under New York law was no longer valid, several recent cases have suggested that it remains in force. Porco v. Lifetime Entm't Servs., 47 N.Y.S.3d 769 (App. Div. 2017); Messenger v. Gruner+Jahr Printing & Publ'g, 727 N.E.2d 549 (N.Y. 2000).

16. Gautier v. Pro-Football, 489–490 (Desmond, J., concurring). Courts and scholars citing to *Gautier* for the proposition that public figures waive their privacy rights include Falwell v. Flynt, 797 F.2d 1270, 1278 (4th Cir. 1986), aff'd on other grounds, Hustler Magazine v. Falwell, 485 U.S. 46 (1988); Man v. Warner Bros., 317 F. Supp. 50, 53 (S.D.N.Y. 1970); Felcher and Rubin, "Privacy, Publicity, and the Portrayal of Real People," 1588n60; Prosser, "Privacy," 411–412n223, 419–420n294; Gordon, "Right of Property in Name, Likeness, Personality and History," 588–590, 605n213; Nimmer, "The Right of Publicity," 204n10, 216n83, 218; Herman Finklestein, "Risks and Rights in Publishing, Television, Radio, Motion Pictures, Advertising, and the Theater," *Yale Law Journal* 62 (1953): 298, 300–301 (reviewing Spring, *Risks and Rights*); Joseph R. Grodin, Note, "The Right of Publicity: A Doctrinal Innovation," *Yale Law Journal* 62 (1953): 1123, 1127n21; John Randolph Ingram, Comment, "Privacy— Unauthorized Use of Photographs—Infringement of Personal and Property Rights," *North Carolina Law Review* 32 (1953): 125, 126–127n10. But other courts and litigants, particularly those in New York, have understood *Gautier*'s more nuanced message that public figures do *not* broadly waive their right of privacy. Messenger v. Gruner+Jahr Printing, 556; Ibid., 558 (Bellacosa, J., dissenting); Brinkley v. Casablancas, 438 N.Y.S.2d 1004, 1008 (App. Div. 1981); Ettore v. Philco Television Broad., 229 F.2d 481, 492–493 (3d Cir. 1956); Brief for Defendant-Appellee at 36, Haelan Labs. v. Topps Chewing Gum, 202 F.2d 866 (2d Cir. 1953) (No. 22564), NAN (describing a determination of whether a right of privacy exists based on the status of the plaintiff as an "invidious distinction. One star differeth from another star in glory—but not in its right to an inviolate personality").

17. Foster-Milburn v. Chinn, 366; Bell v. Birmingham, 265–266; Gautier v. Pro-Football, 488–489.

18. Martin v. F.I.Y. Theatre, 1 Ohio Supp. 19, 22 (Ct. Com. Pl. 1938).
19. Zacchini v. Scripps-Howard Broad., 351 N.E.2d 454 (Ohio 1976), rev'd on other grounds, 433 U.S. 562 (1977); Housh v. Peth, 133 N.E.2d 340 (Ohio Ct. App. 1956). Numerous scholars have cited to *Martin* for the proposition that public figures waive their privacy rights, including Dogan and Lemley, "What the Right of Publicity Can Learn," 1171n37; Mark P. McKenna, "The Right of Publicity and Autonomous Self-Definition," *University of Pittsburgh Law Review* 65 (2005): 225, 243n86 (2005); Michael Madow, "Private Ownership of Public Image: Popular Culture and Publicity Rights," *California Law Review* 81 (1993): 127, 169n210; Nimmer, "The Right of Publicity," 205; Grodin, "The Right of Publicity: A Doctrinal Innovation," 1123, 1127n21. A few courts have also pointed to *Martin* to suggest either more restricted privacy rights or outright waiver of such rights. Martin v. Senators, Inc., 418 S.W. 2d 660, 663–664 (Tenn. 1967); Bennett v. Valenti, No. 34894, 1976 WL 190968 (Ohio Ct. App. July 1, 1976).
20. O'Brien v. Pabst, 170.
21. Ibid.; Plaintiff's Original Petition at 4–5, O'Brien v. Pabst, 124 F.2d 167 (No. 9892), NAF.
22. Ibid., 170–171 (Holmes, J., dissenting).
23. Ibid., 170; Appellee's Brief at 4, 36, O'Brien v. Pabst, 124 F.2d 167.
24. O'Brien v. Pabst, 170–171 (Holmes, J., dissenting).
25. Kimbrough v. Coca-Cola / USA, 521 S.W.2d 719 (Tex. Civ. App. 1975). Law review articles, notes, and books citing to *O'Brien* for the claim that public figures waive their privacy rights include J. Thomas McCarthy, *The Rights of Publicity and Privacy*, vol. 1 (Thomson Reuters, 2016), § 1:25, 46–50 (suggesting that this conclusion from *O'Brien* set the "stage . . . for the right of publicity"); Samantha Barbas, *Laws of Image: Privacy and Publicity in America* (Stanford, CA: Stanford Law Books, 2015), 186; Mark Bartholomew, "A Right Is Born: Celebrity, Property, and Postmodern Lawmaking," *Connecticut Law Review* 44 (2011): 301, 310n22; Dogan and Lemley, "What the Right of Publicity Can Learn," 1171n36; Madow, "Private Ownership of Public Image," 169n210; Gordon, "Right of Property in Name," 564; Prosser, "Privacy," 411–412n221, 419–420n294; Nimmer, "The Right of Publicity," 205, 208n38, 220–221; Grodin, "The Right of Publicity: A Doctrinal Innovation," 1127n21; Case Comment, "Right of Privacy—Nature and Extent—Baseball Players' Right to Prevent Commercial Use of Photographs Held Transferred to Promisee by Contract for Exclusive Advertising Use," *Harvard Law Review* 66 (1953): 1536.

3. A Star Is Born?

1. As discussed in Chapter 1, *Pavesich v. New England Life Insurance* used the term "right of publicity" long before the *Haelan* court. Although the court in *Pavesich* likely meant a somewhat different concept than the court in *Haelan*, the concept of protecting public figures against unwanted "publicity" and against unauthorized uses of their identities dates back to the very beginning of privacy laws in this country. Pavesich v. New England Life Ins., 50 S.E. 68, 70 (Ga. 1905). It is no surprise that courts and scholars frequently repeat these mistaken or misleading assessments about *Haelan* given their overwhelming repetition over many decades, beginning with the very first scholarly and journalistic responses to *Haelan*. Here is a small sampling: Red Smith, "The Battle of Bubble Gum," Views of Sport, *New York Herald Tribune*, March 30, 1953, p. 14 (announcing that *Haelan* created a "new and fascinating principle of law"); Joseph R. Grodin, Note, "The Right of Publicity: A Doctrinal Innovation," *Yale Law Journal* 62 (1953): 1123, 1123–1127 (describing *Haelan* as a "doctrinal innovation"); Case Comment, "Right of Privacy—Nature and Extent—Baseball Players' Right to Prevent Commercial Use of Photographs Held Transferred to Promisee by Contract for Exclusive Advertising Use," *Harvard Law Review* 66 (1953): 1536–1537 (describing the case as having "for the first time termed" a "right of publicity" that "protects the advertising value of a person's name or photograph"); Melville B. Nimmer, "The Right of Publicity," *Law and Contemporary Problems* 19 (1954): 203, 204, 218–223 (describing *Haelan* as the first to "expressly recognize[] a 'right of publicity'"); Peter L. Felcher and Edward L. Rubin, "The Descendibility of the Right of Publicity: Is There Commercial Life after Death?," *Yale Law Journal* 89 (1980): 1125 (describing *Haelan* as "articulat[ing]" the right of publicity "to protect the ability of baseball players to profit from the use of their photographs on bubble gum cards"); Fleer Corp. v. Topps Chewing Gum, 658 F.2d 139, 148 (3d Cir. 1982) (describing *Haelan* as "establish[ing] a new 'right of publicity'"); Sheldon W. Halpern, "The Right of Publicity: Commercial Exploitation of the Associative Value of Personality," *Vanderbilt Law Review* 39 (1986): 1199, 1201 (describing *Haelan* as creating a "new right" and as about giving a right to a "celebrity" to collect "damages"); Jane M. Gaines, *Contested Culture: The Image, the Voice, and the Law* (Chapel Hill, NC: University of North Carolina Press, 1991), 187–189 (describing *Haelan* as creating a "brand-new right"); Arlen W. Langvardt, "The Troubling Implications of a Right of Publicity 'Wheel' Spun out of Control," *University of Kansas Law Review* 45 (1997): 329, 334 (giving *Haelan* credit for "provid[ing] the first formal recognition of a right of publicity cause of action" and as having "coined" the term); ETW Corp. v.

Jireh Publ'g, 332 F.3d 915, 929 (6th Cir. 2003) (describing *Haelan* as having "coined the phrase 'right of publicity'" and created a new "cause of action"); Stacey L. Dogan and Mark A. Lemley, "What the Right of Publicity Can Learn from Trademark Law," *Stanford Law Review* 58 (2006): 1161, 1172–1173 (describing *Haelan* as "vindicati[ng]" "[c]elebrities frustrated with the right of privacy" by creating a "new cause of action"); Mark Bartholomew, "A Right is Born: Celebrity, Property, and Postmodern Lawmaking," *Connecticut Law Review* 44 (2011): 301, 310–311 (describing *Haelan* as "call[ing] into being a new right" to address the "economic rewards of [the baseball players'] celebrity" as opposed to their "dignitary concerns"); Jessica Lake, *The Face That Launched a Thousand Lawsuits: The American Women Who Forged a Right to Privacy* (New Haven, CT: Yale University Press, 2016), 155, 179–181 (describing *Haelan* as "coin[ing]" the term and concept, and as "finally accord[ing] women and men quasi-property rights in their images"). See also Stuart Banner, *American Property: A History of How, Why, and What We Own* (Cambridge, MA: Harvard University Press, 2011), 154 (concluding that "the term 'right of publicity' does seem to have originated" in *Haelan*, but noting accurately that the concept of protecting celebrities' rights in their names and likenesses long predated the decision). J. Thomas McCarthy, the author of the leading treatise on the right of publicity, describes *Haelan* as having "coined" the term and "invent[ed] a new legal label," but also concedes the opposite in a footnote, observing that the "term" itself was not novel. Even the contention that the "concept" was new is not correct, other than the potential transferability of the right. *The Rights of Publicity and Privacy*, vol. 1 (Thomson Reuters, 2016), § 1:26, 52–55n1.

2. Judgment, Pakas Co. v. Leslie (N.Y. Sup. Ct. Mar. 19, 1915); Findings of Fact and Conclusions of Law, Pakas Co. v. Leslie (N.Y. Sup. Ct. Mar. 19, 1915); Complaint, Pakas Co. v. Leslie (N.Y. Sup. Ct. July 28, 1914). These documents were all submitted on March 13 and 14, 1952, to the district court in Bowman Gum v. Topps Chewing Gum, 103 F. Supp. 944 (E.D.N.Y. 1952) (No. 11852), NAN. All references to case files in *Bowman* and *Haelan Labs v. Topps Chewing Gum* are to the files located at the National Archives in New York, unless otherwise noted.

3. The case is often incorrectly referred to as *Pekas*, rather than *Pakas*, because of an error in the *New York Law Journal*, which in its brief report of the case cited to it as *Pekas Co. v. Leslie*. "Pekas [sic] Co. v. Leslie," *New York Law Journal* 52 (February 13, 1915): 1864; Judgment, Pakas Co. v. Leslie; Findings of Fact and Conclusions of Law, Pakas Co. v. Leslie.

4. Note, "Possible Interests in One's Name or Picture," *Harvard Law Review* 28 (1915): 689; Pollard v. Photographic Co. (1888) 40 Ch D 345 (Eng.); Prince Albert v. Strange (1849), 1 McN. & G. 25 (Eng.); Samuel D. Warren and

Louis D. Brandeis, "The Right to Privacy," *Harvard Law Review* 4 (1890): 193, 200–209; Brown Chem. v. Meyer, 139 U.S. 540 (1891); Mackenzie v. Soden Mineral Springs, 18 N.Y.S. 240 (Sup. Ct. 1891); Wood v. Lucy, Lady Duff-Gordon, 118 N.E. 214 (N.Y. 1917); Edison v. Edison Polyform & Mfg., 67 A. 392 (N.J. Ch. 1907); Munden v. Harris, 134 S.W. 1076, 1079 (Mo. Ct. App. 1911); Pavesich v. New England Life Ins., 79; Samuel Spring, *Risks and Rights in Publishing, Television, Radio, Motion Pictures, Advertising, and the Theater* (New York: W. W. Norton, 1952), 9–10, 31–33, 244–246, 290 (referring to the right of privacy as "akin to a property right"). Citations to the student note "Possible Interests in One's Name and Picture" include Haelan Labs. v. Topps Chewing Gum, 202 F.2d 866, 868 (2d Cir. 1953); Bowman Gum v. Topps Chewing Gum, 951; George M. Armstrong Jr., "The Reification of Celebrity Persona as Property," *Louisiana Law Review* 51 (1991): 443, 462–463nn105–106; "Right of Privacy—Nature and Extent," 1537; John Randolph Ingram, Comment, "Privacy—Unauthorized Use of Photographs—Infringement of Personal and Property Rights," *North Carolina Law Review* 32 (1953): 125, 126–127; Note, "Assignability of Rights in a Person's Name as Property," *Yale Law Journal* 45 (1936): 520, 521n7.

5. Trial Court Findings of Fact and Conclusions of Law, Transcript of Record at vol. 2, 837–839, Hanna Mfg. v. Hillerich & Bradsby Co., 78 F.2d 763 (5th Cir. 1935) (No. 7527), NAF.

6. Hanna Mfg. v. Hillerich & Bradsby, 766–768.

7. Case Comment, "Unfair Competition—Rights under Contract Granting Exclusive Advertising Use of Famous Name," *Harvard Law Review* 49 (1936): 496; Case Comment, "Trade-Marks and Trade Names—Right of Privacy—Action by Assignee of Baseball Player's Name against Use by Competing Bat Manufacturer," *Columbia Law Review* 36 (1936): 502–504.

8. "Assignability of Rights," 520–523; Haelan Labs. v. Topps Chewing Gum, 869; Memorandum by Judge Charles Edward Clark, Jan. 19, 1953, Folder 111, Box 37, Series II, CCP; Judge Clark to Judge Jerome N. Frank, memorandum, February 6, 1953, CCP; Judge Frank to Judge Clark, memorandum, February 7, 1953, CCP; Brief for Defendant at 29–33, Bowman Gum v. Topps Chewing Gum, 103 F. Supp. 944; Defendant's Memorandum in Opposition to Motions for Preliminary Injunction and Summary Judgment at 19–21, Bowman Gum v. Topps Chewing Gum, 103 F. Supp. 944.

9. Testimony of Jack Griffith Rensel, Transcript of Record at 212–219, Haelan Labs. v. Topps Chewing Gum, 202 F.2d 866 (No. 22564) (all further references to *Haelan* Transcript of Record are to "*Haelan* TR"); Testimony of Joseph J. Donahue, *Haelan* TR at 84, 88–117, 182; Dean Hanley, *Bubble Gum Card War: The Great Bowman & Topps Sets from 1948 to 1955* (San Bernardino, CA: Mighty Casey Books, 2016), 5–11, 49–55; Dave Jamieson, *Mint Condition: How*

Baseball Cards Became an American Obsession (New York: Atlantic
Monthly Press, 2010), 16–29, 49–67, 89–113; J. Gordon Hylton, "Baseball
Cards and the Birth of the Right of Publicity: The Curious Case of *Haelan
Laboratories v. Topps Chewing Gum*," *Marquette Sports Law Review* 12
(2001): 273, 275–283.

10. Bowman Gum v. Topps Chewing Gum, 944; Amended Complaint, Bowman
Gum v. Topps Chewing Gum, *Haelan* TR at 5–23; Complaint, Bowman Gum
v. Topps Chewing Gum, 103 F. Supp. 944.

11. Bowman Gum v. Topps Chewing Gum, 947–948.

12. Haelan Labs. v. Topps Chewing Gum, 202 F.2d at 868; Memorandum by Judge
Clark, January 19, 1953, pp. 1–2.

13. Plaintiff's Brief as Appellant at 3–14, Haelan Labs. v. Topps Chewing Gum,
202 F.2d 866; Brief for Defendant-Appellee at 41–47, Haelan Labs. v. Topps
Chewing Gum, 202 F.2d 866; Plaintiff's Reply Brief at 23–40, Bowman Gum v.
Topps Chewing Gum, 103 F. Supp. 944; Plaintiff's Proposed Findings of Fact
and Conclusions of Law at 10–45, Bowman Gum v. Topps Chewing Gum,
103 F. Supp. 944; Topps Amended Answer, *Haelan* TR at 31, 37–41, Testimony
of Sol Rogovin, *Haelan* TR at 403–417; Testimony of Sid Gordon, *Haelan* TR
at 418–435; Testimony of Wesley Westrum, *Haelan* TR at 135, 139–161; Trial
Transcript, *Haelan* TR at 69–76, 81–82, 127–161; Testimony of Rensel, *Haelan*
TR at 264–275; Plaintiff's Exhibits 30–40, *Haelan* TR at 516–533; Defendant's
Exhibits M, X, & Y, *Haelan* TR at 679–681, 687–692, 694–702; Defendant's
Memorandum in Opposition to Plaintiff's Motion for a Temporary Injunction at 27, Haelan Labs. v. Topps Chewing Gum (E.D.N.Y.) (No. 11852)
(on remand).

14. Testimony of Westrum, *Haelan* TR at 135–161; Plaintiff's Exhibit 39: Bowman
Contract with Westrum, September 7, 1950, *Haelan* TR at 529; Plaintiff's
Exhibit 40: Bowman Contract with Westrum, May 28, 1951, *Haelan* TR at
531–533.

15. Trial Transcript, *Haelan* TR at 48–50, 77–80, 194–195.

16. Ibid.

17. Brief for Defendant at 29–39, 66, Bowman Gum v. Topps Chewing Gum,
103 F. Supp. 944; Reply Brief for Defendant at 11–24, Bowman Gum v. Topps
Chewing Gum, 103 F. Supp. 944.

18. Brief for Defendant at 64, Bowman Gum v. Topps Chewing Gum, 103 F.
Supp. 944; Reply Brief for Defendant at 6, 11, Bowman Gum v. Topps
Chewing Gum, 103 F. Supp. 944.

19. Bowman Gum v. Topps Chewing Gum, 948–954.

20. Plaintiff's Brief as Appellant at 2, 15–32, Haelan Labs. v. Topps Chewing Gum,
202 F.2d 866; Plaintiff's Reply Brief at 3–18, Haelan Labs. v. Topps Chewing
Gum, 202 F.2d 866.

21. Supplemental Affidavit of Jonas J. Shapiro at 3, December 31, 1952, Haelan Labs. v. Topps Chewing Gum, 202 F.2d 866 (claiming that an "assignable property right" was at issue and could be enforced via contract); Plaintiff's Brief as Appellant at 2, 15–32, Haelan Labs. v. Topps Chewing Gum, 202 F.2d 866; Plaintiff's Reply Brief at 3–18, Haelan Labs. v. Topps Chewing Gum, 202 F.2d 866.

22. Haelan Labs. v. Topps Chewing Gum, 202 F.2d 866, 867–869.

23. Ibid., 868–869; Memorandum by Judge Frank, January 17, 1953, CCP.

24. Haelan Labs. v. Topps Chewing Gum, 202 F.2d 866, 868; Memorandum by Judge Clark, January 19, 1953, pp. 1–2; Memorandum by Frank.

25. Haelan Labs. v. Topps Chewing Gum, 202 F.2d 866, 868; Rensel Testimony, *Haelan* TR at 216–218, 251; Gordon Testimony, *Haelan* TR 421–422; Memorandum by Judge Clark, January 19, 1953, pp. 1–2; Memorandum by Frank. As discussed in Chapter 2, paid endorsements had been increasingly common from the turn of the nineteenth century on.

26. Clark to Frank, Feb. 6., 1953; Herman Finkelstein, *"Risks and Rights in Publishing, Television, Radio, Motion Pictures, Advertising, and the Theater,"* Yale Law Journal 62 (1953): 298, 300 (reviewing Spring, *Risks and Rights*); Charles E. Clark, *"Cases and Materials on Modern Procedure and Judicial Administration,"* Yale Law Journal 62 (1953): 292 (reviewing Arthur T. Vanderbilt, *Cases and Materials on Modern Procedure and Judicial Administration* (New York: Washington Square, 1952)); Frank to Clark, February 7, 1953.

27. Jansen v. Hilo Packing, 118 N.Y.S.2d 162 (Sup. Ct. 1952); Brief for Defendant-Appellee at 47–48, app. iii–iv, Haelan Labs. v. Topps Chewing Gum, 202 F.2d 866 (citing *Jansen* and including a copy of the case in the appendix to its brief).

28. Erie R.R. Co. v. Tompkins, 304 U.S. 64 (1938); Jansen v. Hilo Packing, 162; Stephano v. News Grp. Publ'ns, 474 N.E.2d 580, 583–585 (N.Y. 1984).

29. Haelan Labs. v. Topps Chewing Gum, 202 F.2d 866, 869 (Swan, C. J., concurring in part); Memorandum by Judge Thomas Walter Swan, Jan. 16. 1953, CCP; Transcript of Record at 6–7, June 8, 1955, Haelan Labs. v. Topps Chewing Gum (E.D.N.Y.) (No. 11852).

30. Petition for Writ of Certiorari at 18–19, 21–24, Topps Chewing Gum v. Haelan Labs., 346 U.S. 816 (1953) (No. 82286).

31. Respondent's Brief in Opposition to Petition for Writ of Certiorari at 4, 8–15, Topps Chewing Gum v. Haelan Labs., 346 U.S. 816 (No. 82286); Topps Chewing Gum v. Haelan Labs., 816 (denying petition); Affidavit in Opposition to Defendant's Motion for a Stay, Haelan Labs. v. Topps Chewing Gum, 202 F.2d 866 (No. 22564).

32. Haelan Labs. v. Topps Chewing Gum, 202 F.2d 866, 869; Transcript of Record, June 8, 1955, Haelan Labs. v. Topps Chewing Gum (No. 11852); Memorandum of Judge Galston, Haelan Labs. v. Topps Chewing Gum (No. 11852), February 9,

1955; Supplemental Complaint, Haelan Labs. v. Topps Chewing Gum
(No. 11852), May 17, 1954; Answer to Supplemental Complaint, Haelan Labs. v.
Topps Chewing Gum (No. 11852), June 22, 1954; Notice of Cross Motion and
Answering Affidavits, Haelan Labs. v. Topps Chewing Gum (No. 11852),
January 12, 1955.
33. Complaint, Haelan Labs. v. Topps Chewing Gum (N.Y. Sup. Ct. April 26,
1955) (No. 04430), KCC; Jamieson, *Mint Condition*, 100–101; Hylton, "Baseball
Cards," 291.
34. Stephano v. News Grp., 538–585.

4. A Star Explodes

1. Red Smith, "The Battle of Bubble Gum," Views of Sport, *New York Herald
Tribune*, March 30, 1953, p. 14; Martin Kane, "The Baseball Bubble Trouble,"
Sports Illustrated, August 16, 1954, 38.
2. Joseph R. Grodin, Note, "The Right of Publicity: A Doctrinal Innovation," *Yale
Law Journal* 62 (1953): 1123, 1125; Case Comment, "Right of Privacy—Nature
and Extent—Baseball Players' Right to Prevent Commercial Use of Photo-
graphs Held Transferred to Promisee by Contract for Exclusive Advertising
Use," *Harvard Law Review* 66 (1953): 1536; John Randolph Ingram, Comment,
"Privacy—Unauthorized Use of Photographs—Infringement of Personal and
Property Rights," *North Carolina Law Review* 32 (1953): 125; Donald A.
Macksey, Comment, "Torts—A Person Has the Right to the Publicity Value of
His Photograph, Independent of His Right of Privacy, Which May Be Trans-
ferred in Gross Vesting an Assignee with Sufficient Interest to Maintain a Suit
against Unauthorized Use by Third Parties," *Georgetown Law Journal* 41
(1953): 583–586. Many scholars and courts cited to these student notes. Wil-
liam L. Prosser, "Privacy," *California Law Review* 48 (1960): 383, 407n194;
Edward J. Bloustein, "Privacy as an Aspect of Human Dignity: An Answer to
Dean Prosser," *New York University Law Review* 39 (1964): 962, 988n146;
Uhlaender v. Henricksen, 316 F. Supp. 1277, 1281 (D. Minn. 1970); Motschenbacher v. R. J. Reynolds Tobacco, 498 F.2d 821, 825 (9th Cir. 1974); Zacchini v.
Scripps-Howard Broad., No. 33713, 1975 WL 182619, at n3 (Ohio Ct. App. July 10,
1975); PETA v. Bobby Berosini, Ltd., 895 P.2d 1269, 1284 (Nev. 1995); J. Thomas
McCarthy, *The Rights of Publicity and Privacy*, vol. 1, § 1.26 (Thomson Reuters,
2016), 56.
3. Melville B. Nimmer, "The Right of Publicity," *Law and Contemporary
Problems* 19 (1954): 203. Many courts have cited to Nimmer's article. Examples
include Motschenbacher v. R. J. Reynolds, 825; Hirsch v. S. C. Johnson & Son,
280 N.W.2d 129, 134 (Wis. 1979); Lugosi v. Universal Pictures, 603 P. 2d 425, 438

(Cal. 1979); Memphis Dev. Found. v. Factors Etc., 616 F.2d 956, 958n1 (6th Cir. 1980); Baltimore Orioles v. MLB Players Ass'n, 805 F.2d 663, 679 (7th Cir. 1986); Cardtoons, L. C. v. MLB Players Ass'n, 95 F.3d 959, 967 (10th Cir. 1996) (describing Nimmer's article as "seminal" and as "cultivat[ing]" the "new intellectual property right"); McCarthy, *Rights of Publicity and Privacy*, vol. 1, § 1.27, 57 (describing Nimmer and his article as the "first builder" and the "intellectual foundation" of the right of publicity).

4. Paramount Pictures v. Leader Press, 106 F.2d 229, 229–230 (10th Cir. 1939); Jane M. Gaines, *Contested Culture: The Image, the Voice, and the Law* (Chapel Hill, NC: University of North Carolina Press, 1991), 143–207; De Havilland v. Warner Bros. Pictures, 153 P. 2d 983 (Cal. Dist. Ct. App. 1944); David Denby, "Fallen Idols: Have Stars Lost Their Magic?," *The New Yorker*, October 22, 2007, 104, 108. After de Havilland was freed from her contract with Warner Brothers, she took more of the roles she had been craving, including two that led to Academy Awards for her. Judith M. Kass, *Olivia de Havilland* (New York: Pyramid, 1976), 40–86; Daniel Bubbeo, *The Women of Warner Brothers: The Lives and Careers of 15 Leading Ladies, with Filmographies for Each* (Jefferson, NC: McFarland, 2002), 54–73.

5. Nimmer, "The Right of Publicity," 203–204, 210.

6. Ibid., 209–210.

7. Ibid., 204–218. The district court in *Paramount Pictures v. Leader Press* dismissed Paramount's claim based on its assertion that the actors did not have privacy rights because as stars they sought "constant publicity," but the case was reversed by the Tenth Circuit on other grounds without affirming or supporting that conclusion. Nimmer cited the reversed district court decision as evidence that public figures waive privacy rights, even though the court did not consider whether the actors could directly sue the defendant Leader Press for the posters, and the case was decided in a state, Oklahoma, where at that time no court had held that a right of privacy existed. Paramount Pictures v. Leader Press, 24 F. Supp. 1004 (W.D. Okla. 1938), rev'd, 106 F.2d 229 (10th Cir. 1939).

8. Nimmer, "The Right of Publicity," 203; see note 3.

9. Chaplin v. NBC, 15 F.R.D. 134, 138–140 (S.D.N.Y. 1953); Hogan v. A. S. Barnes & Co., 114 U.S.P.Q. 314 (Pa. Ct. Com. Pl. 1957); Strickler v. NBC, 167 F. Supp. 68, 69 (S.D. Cal. 1958); Sharman v. C. Schmidt & Sons, 216 F. Supp. 401 (E.D. Pa. 1963).

10. Paulsen v. Personality Posters, 299 N.Y.S.2d 501, 508–509 (Sup. Ct. 1968); Selsman v. Universal Photo Books, 238 N.Y.S.2d 686 (App. Div. 1963); Russell v. Marboro Books, 183 N.Y.S.2d 8, 27–28 (Sup. Ct. 1959); Spahn v. Julian Messner, Inc., 250 N.Y.S.2d 529, 536 (Sup. Ct. 1964), vacated and remanded on other grounds, Julian Messner, Inc. v. Spahn, 387 U.S. 239 (1967), aff'd, Spahn v. Julian Messner, Inc., 233 N.E.2d 840 (N.Y. 1967); Stephano v. News Grp.

Publ'ns, 474 N.E.2d 580 (N.Y. 1984); Strickler v. NBC, 70; Sharman v. C. Schmidt, 407; Hogan v. A. S. Barnes, 314.

11. Cepeda v. Swift & Co., 415 F.2d 1205, 1206 (8th Cir. 1969) (rejecting baseball player's claim because he consented to the use); Uhlaender v. Henrickson, 1280.

12. Ettore v. Philco Television Broad., 229 F.2d 481, 486 (3d Cir. 1956); Prosser, "Privacy," 383, 389, 401–407.

13. Ibid., 401–410; *Restatement (Second) of Torts* (St. Paul, MN: American Law Institute, 1977), §§ 652C, 652I (allowing exclusive licensing, but not assignability in one section, but suggesting that the right may be assignable in another).

14. *Restatement (Second) of Torts*, §§ 652C, 652H, 652I. Prosser resigned in the later stages of the *Restatement's* drafting, and his duties were taken over by John W. Wade. *Restatement (Second) of Torts*, Introduction, vii–viii. The draft form of the *Restatement (Second)* was known to courts and scholars and cited even before its 1977 publication date. Zacchini v. Scripps-Howard Broad., 433 U.S. 562, 567–568, 571–573 (1977); Ibid., 581 (Powell, J., dissenting); Zacchini v. Scripps-Howard Broad., 351 N.E. 2d 454, 456–458, 461 (Ohio 1976); Ibid., 465 (Celebrezze, J., dissenting in part); Cabaniss v. Hipsley, 151 S.E.2d 496, 499–504 (Ga. Ct. App. 1966); Canessa v. J. I. Kislak, Inc., 235 A.2d 62, 66 (N.J. Super. Ct. Law. Div. 1967). Several scholars have noted the likely and actual influence of Prosser's approach. Bloustein, "Privacy as an Aspect of Human Dignity," 962–964; Harry Kalven Jr., "Privacy in Tort Law—Were Warren and Brandeis Wrong?" *Law and Contemporary Problems* 31 (1966): 326, 332 ("It's not easy to know just what to make of this new schema, except that given the legal mind's weakness for neat labels and categories and given the deserved Prosser prestige, it is a safe prediction that the fourfold view will come to dominate whatever thinking is done about the right of privacy in the future.").

15. Harold R. Gordon, "Right of Property in Name, Likeness, Personality and History," *Northwestern University Law Review* 55 (1960): 553; "Capone Kin to Sue on Film," *Los Angeles Times*, October 25, 1959, p. 4; "Capone's Sister Sues TV Show for $1,000,000," *Sheboygan Press*, December 30, 1959, Section II, p. 1; Maritote v. Desilu Prods., 345 F.2d 418 (7th Cir. 1965); Maritote v. Desilu Prods., 230 F. Supp. 721 (N.D. Ill. 1964).

16. "Leopold Assailed as 'Ingrate' for Suit," *Los Angeles Times*, October 4, 1959, p. 35; Leopold v. Levin, 259 N.E.2d 250 (Ill. 1970); Elmer Gertz, *A Handful of Clients* (Chicago: Follett, 1965), 166–192.

17. Gordon, "Right of Property in Name," 554–557, 562–564, 610–613; Zacchini v. Scripps-Howard, 433 U.S. at 572n9; Zacchini v. Scripps-Howard, 351 N.E.2d at 465 (Celebrezze, J., dissenting in part); Price v. Hal Roach Studios, 400 F. Supp. 836, 843–844n5 (S.D.N.Y. 1975); Grant v. Esquire, Inc., 367 F. Supp. 876, 879–880 (S.D.N.Y. 1973); Uhlaender v. Henricksen, 1280; Canessa

v. J. I. Kislak, 66–74; Cabaniss v. Hipsley, 504; Lugosi v. Universal Pictures, 603 P.2d at 444 (Bird, C.J., dissenting) (describing the conflation of the right of privacy and publicity as "procrustean jurisprudence").

18. Zacchini v. Scripps-Howard, 433 U.S. 562; Petition for a Writ of Certiorari at app. A49–A50, Zacchini v. Scripps-Howard, 433 U.S. 562 (No. 76-577) (hereinafter cited as "*Zacchini* Petition") (Complaint); Glenn Collins, "Mario Zacchini, Sensational Human Cannonball, Dies at 87," *New York Times*, February 3, 1999, p. B9; Jacquin Sanders, "'It's Lonely at the Top': Human Cannonball Reflects on an Explosive Career," *St. Petersburg Times*, June 14, 1987, p. 1B; John T. McQuiston, "Hugo Zacchini, 77, Dies; First Human Cannonball," *New York Times*, October 21, 1975, p. 40.

19. *Zacchini* Petition at app. A49–A50 (Complaint); Ibid., app. A57 (Exhibit B-1 to Motion for Summary Judgment by Defendant, Scripps-Howard Broad., Transcript of Script Relating to Film Clip of The Fabulous Zacchini Read by David F. Patterson on Defendant's Eyewitness News Program on September 1, 1973).

20. Ibid. at app. A49–A50 (Complaint).

21. Zacchini v. Scripps-Howard, 1975 WL 182619.

22. Zacchini v. Scripps-Howard, 351 N.E.2d at 455–459, 461 (citing both Prosser's article and the draft *Restatement (Second) of Torts*, which adopted that rubric).

23. Zacchini v. Scripps-Howard, 351 N.E.2d at syllabus 3. Under Ohio law, the court's syllabus sets forth its legal holdings. Memorandum by Gene Comey, p. 4, April 25, 1977, Box 43, LFP.

24. *Zacchini* Petition at 2.

25. Zacchini v. Scripps-Howard Broad., 429 U.S. 1037 (1977) (granting petition for writ of certiorari); Zacchini v. Scripps-Howard Broad., 433 U.S. at 569–573.

26. *Zacchini* Petition at 9–11; Brief for Petitioner at 15–23, Zacchini v. Scripps-Howard, 433 U.S. 562; Zacchini v. Scripps-Howard, 433 U.S. at 571–573.

27. Zacchini v. Scripps-Howard, 433 U.S. at 572–573. Richard A. Meserve, then clerk to Justice Harry A. Blackmun, circulated a memorandum that used the Prosser rubric to describe the four privacy torts, and identified this as a case involving the privacy-based appropriation tort. Memorandum by Richard A. Meserve, pp. 2–3, Folder 3, Box 254, HAB. I will discuss more about *Zacchini* in Chapter 7 and provide more insights into the internal working and thinking of the Supreme Court about the case. Lee Levine and Stephen Wermiel have also provided a useful history of the Court's review of the case. Lee Levine and Stephen Wermiel, "The Court and the Cannonball: An Inside Look," *American University Law Review* 65 (2016): 607.

28. Oral Arguments at 8, 19, 33–34, Zacchini v. Scripps-Howard, 433 U.S. 562.

29. Zacchini v. Scripps-Howard, 433 U.S. at 572–577.

30. Ibid., 573–578.

31. Ibid., 573n10, 576 (quoting Kalven, "Privacy in Tort Law," 331); Kalven, "Privacy in Tort Law," 331–341.

32. The settlement was for something "considerably less" than the $25,000 sought, but more than $10,000. "Human Cannonball, WEWS Settle Suit in Out-of-Court Pact," *Plain Dealer*, August 24, 1979, p. 2-B; Mary Strassmeyer, "Inflation Hits the Courts," *Plain Dealer*, August 23, 1979, p. 3-A.

33. Lugosi v. Universal Pictures, 172 U.S.P.Q. 541 (Cal. Super. Ct. 1972). Bela Lugosi played Dracula in Universal Studios' *Dracula* (1931) and *Abbott and Costello Meet Frankenstein* (1948). A wax bust of him appeared in the 1936 movie *Dracula's Daughter*, which was also released by Universal. Bela Lugosi Jr. attended and spoke at an event in which I was a participant. During the conversation, he acknowledged his motivation for the lawsuit. He was not concerned about Lugosi's reputation or propriety, but instead held the view that if someone was making money from his father's likeness and personality, it should be him. Kobe Matthys (artist and curator of event), Thing 001211 (Count Dracula), *Assembly (Before and After the Split Second Recorded)*, Redcat, Walt Disney Concert Hall, Los Angeles, CA, April 1, 2015.

34. Because of various probate issues, the initial complaint that was filed in 1963 was withdrawn and then refiled in 1966. Lugosi v. Universal Pictures, 172 U.S.P.Q. 541.

35. Maritote v. Desilu Prods., 345 F.2d 418; Miller v. Commissioner, 299 F.2d 706, 709 (2d Cir. 1962); Lugosi v. Universal Pictures, 172 U.S.P.Q. 541.

36. Price v. Hal Roach, 845; Stephano v. News Grp. Publ'ns, 474 N.E.2d 580 (N.Y. 1984) (holding that no independent right of publicity exists in New York).

37. Lugosi v. Universal Pictures, 139 Cal. Rptr. 35, 39–40 (Ct. App. 1977).

38. Lugosi v. Universal, 603 P. 2d 425; Ibid., 434–449 (Bird, C. J., dissenting). In a companion case to *Lugosi*, the California Supreme Court also rejected a claim by Rudolph Valentino's nephew that this famous actor (who had died in 1926) had rights of publicity that survived his death. Guglielmi v. Spelling-Goldberg Prods., 603 P.2d 454, 455 (Cal. 1979).

39. Lugosi v. Universal, 603 P. 2d at 437–447 (Bird, C.J., dissenting).

40. Act of Sept. 30, 1984, ch. 1704, 1984 Cal. Stat. 6169 (codified at Cal. Civ. Code § 990) (this provision has since been amended and renumbered as Cal. Civ. Code § 3344.1); Senator William Campbell to Governor George Deukmejian, August 31, 1984, Governor's Chaptered Bill File, CSA; Report of Assembly Committee on Judiciary on SB 613, June 18, 1984, Assembly Committee on Ways and Means, Minority, CSA; Letter Log on SB 613, Assembly Republican Caucus Materials, CSA.

 California had previously passed a statutory provision, California Civil Code § 3344, that we now think of as the statutory right of publicity in the state. But at the time it was passed and codified, it was understood as protecting the right of *privacy*. It was adopted primarily to provide statutory damages to protect those whose names and likenesses were used without permission, but who did not have commercially valuable identities that would provide for a sufficient monetary recovery to discourage such uses. Act of Nov. 22, 1971, ch. 1595, 1971 Cal. Stat. 3426 (codified at Cal. Civ. Code § 3344) (describing as "relating to the invasion of privacy"); Assemblyman John Vasconcellos to Governor Ronald Reagan, November 10, 1971, Governor's Chaptered Bill File, CSA.

41. Factors Etc. v. Creative Card, 444 F. Supp. 279 (S.D.N.Y. 1977).

42. Ibid., 280–283; Robert Hilburn, "Eternal Revenue: Elvis' Millions Were Disappearing When Priscilla Presley Took Charge and Rebuilt the King's Fortune," *Los Angeles Times Magazine*, June 11, 1989, 10, 18; "Parker Is Accused of Cheating Presley in Royalty Dealings," *Globe and Mail*, August 3, 1981, p. 15.

43. Factors Etc. v. Creative Card, 282; Factors Etc. v. Pro Arts, 444 F. Supp. 288 (S.D. N.Y. 1977); Factors Etc. v. Pro Arts, 579 F.2d 215, 221–222 (2d Cir.1978).

44. Memphis Dev. Found. v. Factors Etc., 441 F. Supp. 1323, 1329–1330 (W.D. Tenn. 1977); Memphis Dev. Found. v. Factors Etc., 616 F.2d 956, 958–960 (6th Cir. 1980).

45. Factors Etc. v. Pro Arts, 652 F.2d 278, 279–284 (2d Cir. 1981); Factors Etc. v. Pro Arts, 701 F.2d 11, 11–13 (2d Cir. 1983); Personal Rights Protection Act of 1984, ch. 945, § 1, 1984 Tenn. Pub. Acts 950 (codified at Tenn. Code Ann. § 47-25-1101); Hilburn, "Eternal Revenue," 42. After this legislation passed, a Tennessee appellate court also held that the right of publicity at common law was descendible. State ex rel. Elvis Presley Int'l Mem'l Found. v. Crowell, 733 S.W.2d 89 (Tenn. Ct. App. 1987). It is an open question whether there is both a statutory postmortem right and a common law right in Tennessee today. At least one federal court has suggested that the statute supplants the common law, but the statute itself suggests its provisions are cumulative. Marshall v. ESPN, 111 F. Supp. 3d 815, 824–826 (M.D. Tenn. 2015), aff'd 668 Fed. Appx. 155 (6th Cir. 2016).

46. Even though privacy law was narrowing in the context of tort law, it was expanding in constitutional law during this era. See Roe v. Wade, 410 U.S. 113 (1973); Griswold v. Connecticut, 381 U.S. 479 (1965).

5. A Star Expands

1. J. Thomas McCarthy, "The Human Persona as Commercial Property: The Right of Publicity," *Columbia-VLA Journal of Law & the Arts* 19 (1995): 129, 131 ("[T]he only kind of speech impacted by the right of publicity is commercial

speech—advertising. Not news, not stories, not entertainment and not entertainment satire and parody—only advertising and similar commercial uses."); Harold R. Gordon, "Right of Property in Name, Likeness, Personality and History," *Northwestern Law Review* 55 (1960): 553, 575, 582–588, 590–593, 608–613 (advocating here and in his work for plaintiffs that the right should apply to movies, television shows, books, and plays); Porco v. Lifetime Entm't Servs., 47 N.Y.S.3d 769 (App. Div. 2017); Redmond v. Columbia Pictures, 14 N.E.2d 636 (N.Y. 1938); Melvin v. Reid, 297 P. 91 (Cal. Dist. Ct. App. 1931); Binns v. Vitagraph Co. of Am., 103 N.E. 1108 (N.Y. 1913); Doe v. TCI Cablevision, 110 S.W.3d 363 (Mo. 2003); Hart v. Electronic Arts, 717 F.3d 141 (3d Cir. 2013); Martin Luther King, Jr., Ctr. for Soc. Change v. Am. Heritage Prods., 296 S.E.2d 697 (Ga. 1982); Zacchini v. Scripps-Howard Broad., 433 U.S. 562 (1977); Browne v. McCain, 611 F. Supp. 2d 1062 (C.D. Cal. 2009). For a developed discussion of the mistaken view that the right of publicity is limited to commercial speech, particularly advertising, see Jennifer E. Rothman, "Commercial Speech, Commercial Use, and the Intellectual Property Quagmire," *Virginia Law Review* 101 (2015): 1929, 1950–1959.

2. The New York privacy statute, understood as that state's right of publicity, initially limited claims to those for uses of a person's "name, portrait or picture," but in 1995 added voice to the list. Many other states have also added use of a person's voice to their rights of publicity, or include it in privacy-based misappropriation claims. Act of Aug. 9, 1995, ch. 674, 1995 N.Y. Laws 3642 (codified at N.Y. Civ. Rights Law § 51); Cal. Civ. Code §§ 3344, 3344.1 (West 2017); S.D. Codified Laws § 21-64-1-64-2 (2017); Okla. Stat. tit. 12, § 1448 (2017).

3. Memorandum by Robert P. Patterson, June 29, 1940, Box 202–3, HOLLIS No. 601605, LHP. The Second Circuit rejected efforts to "restrain the [radio] broadcasting of phonograph records of musical performances by Whiteman's orchestra." RCA Mfg. v. Whiteman, 114 F.2d 86, 87 (2d Cir. 1940). Al Smith was a governor of New York who ran an unsuccessful presidential campaign against Herbert Hoover and was known for wearing a brown derby hat, which became the symbol of his campaign. David Burner, "The Brown Derby Campaign," *New York History* 46 (1965): 356.

4. Motschenbacher v. R. J. Reynolds Tobacco, 498 F.2d 821 (9th Cir. 1974); Carson v. Here's Johnny Portable Toilets, 698 F.2d 831 (6th Cir. 1983); Lombardo v. Doyle, Dane & Bernbach, 396 N.Y.S.2d 661 (App. Div. 1977).

5. White v. Samsung Elecs. Am., 971 F.2d 1395, 1396 (9th Cir. 1992).

6. Ibid., 1397–1399; Cal. Civ. Code § 3344; Ellen Joan Pollock, "Vanna White Wins Suit," Legal Beat, *Wall Street Journal*, January 24, 1994, p. B2. The contemporary value is determined as of June 2017 using the Consumer Price Index.

7. White v. Samsung Elecs. Am., 989 F.2d 1512, 1514 (9th Cir. 1993) (Kozinski, J., dissenting from denial of rehearing en banc) (emphasis in original).

8. Wendt v. Host Int'l, 125 F.3d 806, 809–812 (9th Cir. 1997); Paramount Pictures Brief as Appellee at 2, Wendt v. Host Int'l, 125 F.3d 806 (No. 96-55243); Appellant's Brief at 4–13, 31–33, Wendt v. Host Int'l, 50 F.3d 18 (9th Cir. 1995) (No. 93-56510) (appeal in case, prior to Wendt v. Host Int'l, 125 F.3d 806); Complaint, Wendt v. Host Int'l (C.D. Cal. Jan. 12, 1993) (No. 93-0142); Judgment, Wendt v. Host Int'l (C.D. Cal. Jan. 19, 1996) (No. 93-0142); Defendant in Intervention Paramount Pictures Separate Statement of Uncontroverted Facts and Conclusions of Law at 2–3, Wendt v. Host Int'l (C.D. Cal. Jan. 19, 1996) (No. 93-0142) (adopted by court as its own); Findings of Uncontroverted Facts and Conclusions of Law, at 3–5, Wendt v. Host Int'l (C.D. Cal., April 18, 2001) (No. 93-0142); Cecilia Deck, "A Round for the Robots," *Detroit Free Press*, February 12, 1991, p. 1E; "Norm and Cliff Cheered by Lawsuit," *Chicago Tribune*, June 22, 2001, p. C2.

9. Wendt v. Host Int'l, 197 F.3d 1284, 1285–1286 (9th Cir. 1999) (Kozinski, J., dissenting from denial of rehearing en banc).

10. Waits v. Frito-Lay, Inc., 978 F.2d 1093 (9th Cir. 1992); Midler v. Ford Motor, 849 F.2d 460 (9th Cir. 1988).

11. The website is located at http://www.rightofpublicityroadmap.com.

12. Utah Code Ann. § 45-3-3 (West 2017); N.Y. Civ. Rights Law §§ 50, 51; Tyne v. Time Warner Entm't, 901 So. 2d 802 (Fla. 2005); Va. Code Ann. § 8.01-40 (2015); Mass. Gen. Laws Ann. ch. 214, § 3A (West 2017); Wash. Rev. Code Ann. § 63.60.010 (West 2016); Ala. Code § 6-5-770 (2015); 765 Ill. Comp. Stat. 1075/5, 1075/10 (West 2017); Cal. Civ. Code § 3344; Eastwood v. Superior Court, 198 Cal. Rptr. 342, 346–347 (Ct. App. 1983).

13. Ohio Rev. Code Ann. §§ 2741.01, 2741.06 (West 2017); Neb. Rev. Stat. § 20-207 (1979); Ind. Code Ann. § 32-36-1-0.2-1-20 (West 2017); Hauf v. Life Extension Found., 547 F. Supp. 2d 771 (W.D. Mich. 2008); Tropeano v. Atlantic Monthly, 400 N.E.2d 847 (Mass. 1980); Kelley v. CVS Pharmacy, No. 98-0897-BLS2, 2007 WL 2781163 (Mass. Super. Ct. Aug. 24, 2007); 42 Pa. Const. Stat. § 8316 (2003).

14. Cohen v. Facebook, No. C10-5282 RS, 2011 WL 5117164 (N.D. Cal. Oct. 27, 2011); Fraley v. Facebook, 830 F. Supp. 2d 785, 799–800, 807–809 (N.D. Cal. 2011); Cal. Civ. Code § 3344; Act of Nov. 22, 1971, ch. 1595, 1971 Cal. Stat. 3426; Assemblyman John Vasconcellos to Governor Ronald Reagan, November 10, 1971, Governor's Chaptered Bill File, CSA. These Facebook cases eventually settled, and Facebook changed its terms of service to grant it express permission to use names and likenesses in this way.

15. Neb. Rev. Stat. § 20-208 (West 2017); Cal. Civ. Code § 3344.1; Ariz. Rev. Stat. Ann. § 12-761 (West 2017); Ark. Code Ann. § 4-75-1107-75-1111 (2016); Fla. Stat. § 540.08

(2017); Ind. Code § 32-36-1-0.2; 42 Pa. Const. Stat. § 8316; Wash. Rev. Code Ann. §§ 63.60.020, 63.60.040 (West 2017); Haw. Rev. Stat. Ann. §§ 482P-2–482P-4 (West 2017); Tenn. Code Ann. § 47-25-1104 (2017).

16. Zacchini v. Scripps-Howard, 573, 576.

17. Lugosi v. Universal Pictures, 603 P. 2d 425, 441–442 (Cal. 1979) (Bird, C.J., dissenting); Roberta Rosenthal Kwall, "Is Independence Day Dawning for the Right of Publicity?," *University of California, Davis Law Review* 17 (1983): 191, 197–198; Peter L. Felcher and Edward L. Rubin, "The Descendibility of the Right of Publicity: Is There Commercial Life after Death?," *Yale Law Journal* 89 (1980): 1125; Peter L. Felcher and Edward L. Rubin, "Privacy, Publicity, and the Portrayal of Real People by the Media," *Yale Law Journal* 88 (1979): 1577, 1601.

18. William M. Landes and Richard A. Posner, *The Economic Structure of Intellectual Property Law* (Cambridge, MA: Belknap Press of Harvard University Press, 2003), 223 (describing any incentive effect as likely "minimal" or "incremental"); Richard A. Posner, "Misappropriation: A Dirge," *Houston Law Review* 40 (2003): 621, 634 (noting that a "person is unlikely to invest less than he would otherwise do in becoming a movie star or other type of celebrity merely because he'll be unable to appropriate the entire income from the franchising of his name and likeness; there is free riding but not the type that threatens to kill the goose that lays the golden eggs").

19. Hilton v. Hallmark Cards, 599 F.3d 894, 899 (9th Cir. 2010). The Ninth Circuit in *Hilton* was likely evoking Daniel Boorstin's definition of a celebrity as "a person who is known for his well-knowness." Daniel J. Boorstin, *The Image: A Guide to Pseudo-Events in America* (1961; repr., New York: Vintage Books, 2012), 57.

20. Michael Madow, "Private Ownership of Public Image: Popular Culture and Publicity Rights," *California Law Review* 81 (1993): 125, 215–219.

21. James M. Treece, "Commercial Exploitation of Names, Likenesses, and Personal Histories," *Texas Law Review* 51 (1973): 637, 647; Madow, "Private Ownership," 228–238.

22. Mark F. Grady, "A Positive Economic Theory of the Right of Publicity," *UCLA Entertainment Law Review* 1 (1994): 97.

23. Landes and Posner, *The Economic Structure*, 222–227; Posner, "Misappropriation," 634.

24. Landes and Posner, *The Economic Structure*, 223–227; Richard A. Posner, "How Long Should a Copyright Last?," *Journal of the Copyright Society of the U.S.A.* 50 (2002–2003): 1, 9–10. For a thoughtful analysis of the parallels and differences between trademark and right of publicity laws, see Stacey L. Dogan and Mark A. Lemley, "What the Right of Publicity Can Learn from Trademark Law," *Stanford Law Review* 58 (2006): 1161.

25. Landes and Posner, *The Economic Structure*, 222–227; Richard A. Posner, "The Right of Privacy," *Georgia Law Review* 12 (1978): 393, 411. In his 1978 essay,

Posner limits his consideration to the advertising context, concluding that other uses are very different. He does consider transaction costs, but only in the context of crowd scenes, not with regard to negotiating rights with an identity-holder or identifying who would most value a person's name or likeness in a commercial context.

26. Zacchini v. Scripps-Howard, 573, 576 (quoting Harry Kalven Jr., "Privacy in Tort Law—Were Warren and Brandeis Wrong?," *Law and Contemporary Problems* 31 (1966): 326, 331); Treece, "Commercial Exploitation," 646; Kwall, "Is Independence Day Dawning?," 198–200; Grady, "A Positive Economic Theory," 99–102, 109–110; Sheldon W. Halpern, "The Right of Publicity: Commercial Exploitation of the Associative Value of Personality," *Vanderbilt Law Review* 39 (1986): 1199, 1236. In his short essay, Kalven criticized the right of privacy as a "mistake," but suggested that Prosser's appropriation tort, sometimes termed a "right of publicity," could be justified by such an unjust enrichment logic. Kalven, "Privacy in Tort Law," 327, 331.

27. Kwall, "Is Independence Day Dawning?," 198; Seana Valentine Shiffrin, "Intellectual Property," in *A Companion to Contemporary Political Philosophy*, ed. Robert E. Goodin, Philip Pettit, and Thomas Pogge, vol. 1, 2nd ed. (Malden, MA: Blackwell Publishing, 2007), 653, 656–660.

28. Melville B. Nimmer, "The Right of Publicity," *Law and Contemporary Problems* 19 (1954): 203, 216; Treece, "Commercial Exploitation," 647; Lugosi v. Universal Pictures, 437–438, 446 (Bird, C.J., dissenting).

29. Madow, "Private Ownership," 185–191; Marshall Missner, "Why Einstein Became Famous in America," *Social Studies of Science* 15 (1985): 267, 281–288.

30. Halpern, "The Right of Publicity," 1242; Jessica Litman, "Breakfast with Batman: The Public Interest in the Advertising Age," *Yale Law Journal* 108 (1999): 1717, 1728–1735; Associated Press, "Judge Declares Prince's 6 Siblings the Heirs to His Estimated $200M Estate," *Chicago Tribune*, May 19, 2017, http://perma.cc/BEH6-M38D.

31. Leon Neyfakh, "Life, the Aftermarket: New Laws to Protect Celebrities Push the Bounds of What Part of a Human Life Can Be Considered Property," *Boston Globe*, August 19, 2012, p. K1, K11; Louis Sahagun, "Bettie Page," Obituaries, *Los Angeles Times*, December 12, 2008, p. B6; Tamar Brott, "Grateful Dead," *Los Angeles Magazine*, December 2004, 93.

32. Rosemary J. Coombe, *The Cultural Life of Intellectual Properties: Authorship, Appropriation, and the Law* (Durham, NC: Duke University Press, 1998); Rosemary J. Coombe, "Author/izing the Celebrity: Publicity Rights, Post-modern Politics, and Unauthorized Genders," *Cardozo Arts and Entertainment Law Journal* 10 (1992): 365; Madow, "Private Ownership," 127–147; Mark A. Lemley, "Property, Intellectual Property, and Free Riding," *Texas Law Review* 83 (2005): 1031.

33. Edward J. Bloustein, "Privacy as an Aspect of Human Dignity: An Answer to Dean Prosser," *New York University Law Review* 39 (1964): 962, 990; Alice Haemmerli, "Whose Who? The Case for a Kantian Right of Publicity," *Duke Law Journal* 49 (1999): 383, 408–409, 416; Jonathan Kahn, "Bringing Dignity Back to Light: Publicity Rights and the Eclipse of the Tort of Appropriation of Identity," *Cardozo Arts & Entertainment Law Journal* 17 (1999): 213; Pavesich v. New England Life Ins., 50 S.E. 68, 80 (Ga. 1905). Other scholars have also noted the restrictions on fundamental rights of liberty when an individual cannot control uses of her name, likeness, and other indicia of identity—a subject addressed in Chapter 6. Jennifer E. Rothman, "The Inalienable Right of Publicity," *Georgetown Law Journal* 185 (2012): 185, 209–217, 228–232; Mark P. McKenna, "The Right of Publicity and Autonomous Self-Definition," *University of Pittsburgh Law Review* 67 (2005): 225; Felcher and Rubin, "Privacy, Publicity, and the Portrayal of Real People," 1599–1600.

6. The (In)alienable Right of Publicity

1. This chapter is adapted in part from Jennifer E. Rothman, "The Inalienable Right of Publicity," *Georgetown Law Journal* 101 (2012): 185.
2. Terrance McConnell, "The Nature and Basis of Inalienable Rights," *Law and Philosophy* 3 (1984): 25, 27; Lee Anne Fennell, "Adjusting Alienability," *Harvard Law Review* 122 (2009): 1403; Susan Rose-Ackerman, "Inalienability and the Theory of Property Rights," *Columbia Law Review* 85 (1985): 931; Margaret Jane Radin, "Market-Inalienability," *Harvard Law Review* 100 (1987): 1849, 1849–1855; J. Thomas McCarthy, *The Rights of Publicity and Privacy*, vol. 2 (Thomson Reuters, 2016), § 10:13; Martin Luther King, Jr., Ctr. for Soc. Change v. Am. Heritage Prods., 296 S.E.2d 697, 704 (Ga. 1982); *Restatement (Third) of Unfair Competition* (St. Paul, MN: American Law Institute, 1995), § 46 cmt. g; Haw. Rev. Stat. Ann. § 482P-3 (West 2017); Ind. Code Ann. § 32-36-1-16 (West 2017); Nev. Rev. Stat. Ann. § 597.800 (West 2017).
3. Rothman, "The Inalienable Right of Publicity," 187.
4. Peter L. Felcher and Edward L. Rubin, "The Descendibility of the Right of Publicity: Is There Commercial Life after Death?," *Yale Law Journal* 89 (1980): 1125; Jessica Lake, *The Face that Launched a Thousand Lawsuits: The American Women Who Forged a Right to Privacy* (New Haven, CT: Yale University Press, 2016), 155, 179–181 (describing *Haelan* as "finally accord[ing] women and men quasi-property rights in their images"); Stacey L. Dogan and Mark A. Lemley, "What the Right of Publicity Can Learn from Trademark Law," *Stanford Law Review* 58 (2006): 1161, 1172 (describing *Haelan* as "vindication" for "[c]elebrities"); Sheldon W. Halpern, "The Right of Publicity: Commercial

Exploitation of the Associative Value of Personality," *Vanderbilt Law Review* 39 (1986): 1199, 1201 (describing *Haelan* as furthering "celebrity" rights); Mark Bartholomew, "A Right Is Born: Celebrity, Property, and Postmodern Law-making," *Connecticut Law Review* 44 (2011): 301, 310 (describing *Haelan* as about protecting the "economic rewards" for the players).

5. "Right of Publicity," SAG-AFTRA, accessed July 27, 2017, http://perma.cc /SE3Q-BYQY; Jennifer E. Rothman, "New York Legislature Amends Right of Publicity Bill for the Worse," *Rothman's Roadmap to the Right of Publicity*, June 14, 2017, http://perma.cc/9YXN-ZZS6; Assemb. B. A08155A (N.Y. 2017); O'Bannon v. NCAA, Nos. C 09-1967 CW, C 09-3329 CW, C 09-4882 CW, 2010 WL 445190, at *1 (N.D. Cal. Feb. 8, 2010); Complaint at 4–5, O'Bannon v. NCAA (Nos. C 09-1967 CW, C 09-3329 CW, C 09-4482 CW) (hereafter cited as "*O'Bannon* Complaint"); "Facebook Terms of Service," ¶¶ 2, 9, last modified January 30, 2015, accessed July 27, 2017, http://perma.cc/W35F -GCYL; "Twitter Terms of Service," last modified September 30, 2016, accessed July 27, 2017, http://perma.cc/J9GG-FMUY; "Instagram Terms of Use," last modified January 19, 2013, accessed July 27, 2017, http://perma.cc /Y9F2-B4KZ.

6. In re Lorraine Brooke Assocs., No. 07-12641-BKC-AJC, 2007 WL 7061312, at *1–3 (Bankr. S.D. Fla. July 2, 2007); Goldman v. Simpson, No. SC036340, 2006 WL 6845603, slip op. at 12 (Cal. Super. Ct. Oct. 31, 2006).

7. Sarah Schmalbruch, "9 Rich and Famous People Who Filed for Bankruptcy," *Business Insider*, July 13, 2015, http://perma.cc/ZB5C-ZAWL.

8. Neb. Rev. Stat. Ann. § 20-207 (West 2017); Avalos v. IAC /Interactivecorp., No. 13-CV-8351 (JMF), 2014 WL 5493242, at *4 (S.D.N.Y. Oct. 30, 2014) (applying Nebraska law and citing Rothman, "Inalienable Right," 192); 765 Ill. Comp. Stat. Ann. 1075 /15 (West 2017); The Frank Broyles Publicity Rights Protection Act of 2016, Ark. Code § 4-75-1101-75-1113 (West 2017); Alabama Right of Publicity Act, Ala. Code § 6-5-770-5-774 (West 2017); Assemb. B. A08155A; H.R. 415, 2017 Reg. Sess. (La. 2017).

9. Stephanie Merry, "The Story behind Why Prince Changed His Name to a Symbol," *Washington Post*, April 22, 2016, https://perma.cc/U4ZC-QV8J; Geoffrey Himes, " 'Emancipation': Prince-ly Freedom," *Washington Post*, January 10, 1997, Weekend, p. N12.

10. Cory v. Nintendo of Am., 592 N.Y.S.2d 6, 7–8 (App. Div. 1993); Sample Recording Contract Language from Record Executive, David Lessoff (on file with author) (granting perpetual right to use artist's name, likeness, and other indicia of identity "for all purposes of trade . . . and the general goodwill of Company"); Flim and the B.B.'s Contract with Warner Bros. Music, August 31, 1989 (on file with author) (prohibiting band members from authorizing use of name, likeness, voice, or other indicia of identity, or performing in the context

of the music industry for a term of up to twelve years); Andy Dehnart, "Survivor Contestant Contract: The Waivers, Agreements That Cast Members, Families Sign," *Reality Blurred,* May 31, 2010, http://perma.cc/2V9J-FJF5; Eric Olson, "Slaves of Celebrity," *Salon,* September 18, 2002, http://perma.cc/4J4J-NKZ5; Grant of Rights, Release, Confidentiality and Arbitration Agreement, *The Voice* Applicant Casting Application Packet, 2015, http://perma.cc/7LQN-S9AC; *Fear Factor* Season 6 Contestant Application § 65 (on file with author); Perfect 10 v. CCBill LLC, 488 F.3d 1102, 1108 (9th Cir. 2007); Complaint at 4, Perfect 10 v. Netsaits B. V., No. 10-cv-1773 BEN (NLS), 2011 WL 531302 (S.D. Cal. Feb. 8, 2011); Complaint at 8, 18, 22–23, 26, 33, 44–46, Perfect 10 v. CCBill, LLC, 488 F.3d 1102 (Nos. 07-57143, 04-57207); O'Bannon v. NCAA, 2010 WL 445190, at *1; *O'Bannon* Complaint at 4–5; "Facebook Terms of Service"; "Twitter Terms of Service," ¶¶ 2, 9; "Instagram Terms of Use."

11. Faloona ex rel. Fredrickson v. Hustler Magazine, 799 F.2d 1000 (5th Cir. 1986); Shields v. Gross, 448 N.E.2d 108, 109, 111 (N.Y. 1983).

12. "Coogan Law," SAG-AFTRA, accessed July 27, 2017, http://perma.cc/P9HW -BVX9; Cal. Fam. Code Ann. §§ 6750, 6753 (West 2017); Complaint, Gonzales v. Gonzales, No. CV-15-5498-DMG (AJWx) (C.D. Cal. July 20, 2015); Order of Dismissal, Gonzales v. Gonzales, No. CV-15-5498 (C.D. Cal. Jan. 5, 2016).

13. McCarthy, *The Rights of Publicity and Privacy,* § 10:14; Catherine L. Fisk, *Working Knowledge: Employee Innovation and the Rise of Corporate Intellectual Property, 1800–1930* (Chapel Hill, NC: University of North Carolina Press, 2009); Rothman, "Inalienable Right," 198–199n54–57.

14. 11 U.S.C. §§ 541(a)(1), (b)(5), (7) (2012); 11 U.S.C. §§ 522(b)(3)(c)–(4)(d)(2) (2012); Cusano v. Klein, 264 F.3d 936, 946–947 (9th Cir. 2001); Chesapeake Fiber Packaging v. Sebro Packaging, 143 B.R. 360, 372 (Bankr. D. Md. 1992) (citing United States v. Inslaw Inc., 932 F.2d 1467, 1471 (D.C. Cir. 1991)); Melissa B. Jacoby and Diane Leenheer Zimmerman, "Foreclosing on Fame: Exploring the Uncharted Boundaries of the Right of Publicity," *New York University Law Review* 77 (2002): 1322. The right of publicity has come up in several bankruptcy cases, but to date none has awarded a transfer to a creditor. Marradi v. Capital Entm't Indus., No. CV 01-02622 DDP (CWx), 2002 U.S. Dist. LEXIS 28488, *22–24 (C.D. Cal. Nov. 22, 2002); In re Jones, 445 B.R. 677, 688, 726n132, 730–731 (Bankr. N.D. Tex. 2011). Although the court in *Marradi* noted that the debtor's settlement with creditors assigned his right of publicity in the limited context of particular copyrighted works, the court suggested that if the works at issue were altered, the debtor might continue to have a right of publicity claim against the creditors.

15. In re Marriage of Worth, 241 Cal. Rptr. 135, 137–139 (Ct. App. 1987); Rodrigue v. Rodrigue, 218 F.3d 432, 435–443 (5th Cir. 2000). Only courts in New York and New Jersey have thus far suggested that something akin to a right of

publicity, "celebrity goodwill," might be marital property subject to division upon the dissolution of a marriage. Golub v. Golub, 527 N.Y.S.2d 946, 949–950 (Sup. Ct. 1998); Elkus v. Elkus, 572 N.Y.S.2d 901, 904–905 (App. Div. 1991); Piscopo v. Piscopo, 557 A.2d 1040, 1042–1043 (N.J. Super. Ct. App. Div. 1989). The concept of goodwill and its inclusion in divorce assets has been controversial, and not all states have agreed to recognize it. Ahern v. Ahern, 938 A.2d 35, 39–40 (Me. 2008); Taylor v. Taylor, 386 N.W.2d 851, 857–859 (Neb. 1986). One court in California suggested in dicta that the right of publicity (at least under the postmortem statute) is separate property rather than divisible community property. Crosby v. HLC Properties, 167 Cal. Rptr. 3d 354 (Ct. App. 2014).

16. Examination Technique Handbook for Estate Tax Examiners, I.R.M.M.T. 4350–31, Ch. 600 reprinted in Michael F. Beausang Jr., *Valuation: General and Real Estate* (BNA 1986), 132–3rd Tax Mgmt Est., Gifts & Tr. Portfolios, B-1001 (BNA 1986); Jeffrey K. Eisen and Allan E. Biblin, Estate Planning for Clients in the Entertainment Business, *Estate Planning*, Feb. 2006, at 26, 32–33; Ray D. Madoff, "Taxing Personhood: Estate Taxes and the Compelled Commodification of Identity," *Virginia Tax Review* 17 (1998): 759, 761–762; Ray D. Madoff, *Immortality and the Law: The Rising Power of the American Dead* (New Haven, CT: Yale University Press, 2010), 139; Senator William Campbell to Governor Deukmejian, Aug. 31, 1984, Senate Bill 613, Governor's Chaptered Bill File, CSA; Act of Sept. 30, 1984, ch. 1704, 1984 Cal. Stat. 6169; Mitchell M. Gans et al., "Postmortem Rights of Publicity: The Federal Estate Tax Consequences of New State-Law Property Rights," *Yale Law Journal Pocket Part* 117 (2008): 203; Joshua C. Tate, "Immortal Fame: Publicity Rights, Taxation, and the Power of Testation," *Georgia Law Review* 44 (2009): 1.

17. Miller v. Commissioner, 299 F.2d 706 (2d Cir. 1962); Miller v. Commissioner, 35 T.C. 631 (1961); Answer at Exh. A, Estate of Michael J. Jackson v. Commissioner, No. 17152-13 (T.C. Aug. 20, 2013) (Schedule F); Eriq Gardner, "Michael Jackson's Executor, Manager Ordered to Testify in Billion-Dollar Tax Battle," *Hollywood Reporter,* December 8, 2016, http://perma.cc/M7LB-DTFU.

18. Amended Exhibit A to Petition for Instructions at 8, In the Matter of the Robin Williams Trust, No. 14-298367 (Cal. Super. Ct. Mar. 30, 2015) (Second Amendment to and Complete Restatement of Trust Agreement of the Robin Williams Trust); Eriq Gardner, "Robin Williams Restricted Exploitation of His Image for 25 Years after Death," *Hollywood Reporter*, March 30, 2015, http://perma.cc/4XNP-M544.

19. David Westfall and David Landau, "Publicity Rights as Property Rights," *Cardozo Arts & Entertainment Law Journal* 23 (2005): 71, 72–74; Rothman, "Inalienable Right," 204–208.

20. George M. Armstrong Jr., "The Reification of Celebrity: Persona as Property," *Louisiana Law Review* 51 (1991): 443, 465.

21. Radin, "Market-Inalienability," 1852, 1891–1898.
22. Ibid., 1880–1881; Margaret Jane Radin, *Reinterpreting Property* (Chicago, IL: University of Chicago Press, 1993), 191–196.
23. Herman Miller, Inc. v. Palazzetti Imps. & Exps., 270 F.3d 298, 325–326 (6th Cir. 2001); Estate of Presley v. Russen, 513 F. Supp. 1339, 1354–1355 (D. N.J. 1981); Richard B. Hoffman, "The Right of Publicity—Heirs' Right, Advertisers' Windfall, or Courts' Nightmare?," *DePaul Law Review* 31 (1981): 1, 25, 27–29; Robert C. Post, "Rereading Warren and Brandeis: Privacy, Property, and Appropriation," *Case Western Reserve Law Review* 41 (1991): 647, 668; McCarthy, *The Rights of Publicity and Privacy*, § 10:8.
24. Halpern, "The Right of Publicity," 1239–1255.
25. Guido Calabresi and A. Douglas Melamed, "Property Rules, Liability Rules, and Inalienability: One View of the Cathedral," *Harvard Law Review* 85 (1972): 1089, 1112–1113.
26. Radin, "Market-Inalienability," 1899–1903; John Stuart Mill, *On Liberty*, 2nd ed. (Boston, MA: Ticknor & Fields, 1863), 198–201; Calabresi and Melamed, "Property Rules," 1112; Rose-Ackerman, "Inalienability," 961–968.
27. Mark P. McKenna, "The Right of Publicity and Autonomous Self-Definition," *University of Pittsburgh Law Review* 67 (2005): 225, 229, 291; Goldman v. Simpson, slip op. at 12; Pavesich v. New England Life Ins., 50 S.E. 68, 80 (Ga. 1905).
28. Jacoby and Zimmerman, "Foreclosing on Fame," 1357–1367.
29. O'Bannon v. NCAA, 802 F.3d 1049 (9th Cir. 2015). Some of the cases against the NCAA have settled, but others are ongoing. "NCAA Agrees to Pay $208 Million Settlement in Antitrust Case," *Chicago Tribune*, February 4, 2017, http://perma.cc/S4CB-U2ZG.
30. Mill, *On Liberty*, 199; Richard A. Epstein, "Why Restrain Alienation?," *Columbia Law Review* 85 (1985): 970, 970–972.
31. Epstein, "Why Restrain Alienation?," 972–988; Rose-Ackerman, "Inalienability," 932–940; Calabresi and Melamed, "Property Rules," 1101.
32. Christopher R. Knittel and Victor Stango, "Shareholder Value Destruction following the Tiger Woods Scandal," *Management Science* 60 (2014): 21–37; Jonathan Mahler, "The Tiger Bubble," *New York Times Magazine*, March 28, 2010, 30.
33. Ohio Rev. Code Ann. §§ 2741.01, 2741.06 (West 2017); 42 Pa. Stat. and Cons. Stat. Ann. § 8316(b) (West 2017). The Ohio provision suggests that an identity-holder could object to an assignee's claim, and the Pennsylvania statute suggests that the natural person on whom the rights are based can sue, as well as other authorized people. Neither aspect of these laws has been considered by courts.
34. Sterling v. Sterling, No. 310833/99, 2001 WL 968262, at *10 (N.Y. Sup. Ct. July 31, 2001) (describing outcomes in other cases).
35. Goldman v. Simpson, slip op. at 12; Rothman, "Inalienable Right," 190–204.

7. The Black Hole of the First Amendment

1. A small sampling of some of the scholarship on the conflicts between the right of publicity and the First Amendment include Rebecca Tushnet, "A Mask That Eats Into the Face: Images and the Right of Publicity," *Columbia Journal of Law & the Arts* 38 (2015): 157; David S. Welkowitz and Tyler T. Ochoa, "The Terminator as Eraser: How Arnold Schwarzenegger Used the Right of Publicity to Terminate Non-defamatory Political Speech," *Santa Clara Law Review* 45 (2005): 651; F. Jay Dougherty, "All the World's Not a Stooge: The 'Transformativeness' Test for Analyzing a First Amendment Defense to a Right of Publicity Claim against Distribution of a Work of Art," *Columbia Journal of Law & the Arts* 27 (2003): 1; Mark S. Lee, "Agents of Chaos: Judicial Confusion in Defining the Right of Publicity-Free Speech Interface," *Loyola of Los Angeles Entertainment Law Review* 23 (2003): 471; Eugene Volokh, "Freedom of Speech and the Right of Publicity," *Houston Law Review* 40 (2003): 903; Diane Leenheer Zimmerman, "Fitting Publicity Rights into Intellectual Property and Free Speech Theory: Sam, You Made the Pants Too Long!," *DePaul Journal of Art and Entertainment Law* 10 (2000): 283; Alice Haemmerli, "Whose Who? The Case for a Kantian Right of Publicity," *Duke Law Journal* 49 (1999): 383, 441–485; Pamela Samuelson, "Reviving *Zacchini*: Analyzing First Amendment Defenses in Right of Publicity and Copyright Cases," *Tulane Law Review* 57 (1983): 836. Some other useful works on the dangers of the right of publicity's speech suppression that do not primarily focus on the First Amendment include Rochelle Cooper Dreyfuss, "We Are Symbols and Inhabit Symbols, So Should We Be Paying Rent? Deconstructing the Lanham Act and Rights of Publicity," *Columbia-VLA Journal of Law & the Arts* 20 (1996): 123; Michael Madow, "Private Ownership of Public Image: Popular Culture and Publicity Rights," *California Law Review* 81 (1993): 127; Rosemary J. Coombe, "Author/izing the Celebrity: Publicity Rights, Postmodern Politics, and Unauthorized Genders," *Cardozo Arts & Entertainment Law Journal* 10 (1992): 365.
2. Zacchini v. Scripps-Howard Broad., 433 U.S. 562 (1977); Zacchini v. Scripps-Howard Broad., 351 N.E.2d 454 (Ohio 1976).
3. Memorandum by Wayne Drinkwater, December 7, 1976, Box 43, LFP; Memorandum by Gene Comey, April 25, 1977, LFP; Lewis F. Powell Jr., Certiorari Petition Conference Notes, October 23, 1976, LFP; Lee Levine and Stephen Wermiel, "The Court and the Cannonball: An Inside Look," *American University Law Review* 65 (2016): 607, 621.
4. Zacchini v. Scripps-Howard, 433 U.S. at 576; "Human Cannonball, WEWS Settle Suit in Out-of-Court Pact," *Plain Dealer*, August 24, 1979, p. 2-B; Mary Strassmeyer, "Inflation Hits the Courts," *Plain Dealer*, August 23, 1979, p. 3-A.

Most courts continue to consider newsworthiness defenses in right of publicity cases questions of state law, and either do not consider this aspect of *Zacchini* or view it as limited to Ohio law. Keller v. Electronic Arts, 724 F.3d 1268, 1282 (9th Cir. 2013). Justice John Paul Stevens dissented on these grounds in *Zacchini* because he thought the question was one of state law even in Ohio. Zacchini v. Scripps-Howard, 433 U.S. at 582–583 (Stevens, J., dissenting).

5. Zacchini v. Scripps-Howard, 433 U.S. at 576; Transcript of Oral Arguments at 5, 10, 15, 24–26, 30–33, Zacchini v. Scripps-Howard, 433 U.S. 562 (No. 76-577) (hereinafter "*Zacchini* Transcript"); Program from Gustav Mahler, Symphony No. 2 in C Minor, Minnesota Orchestra Performance, John F. Kennedy Center for the Performing Arts, April 23, 1977, Supreme Court Case File, Folder 3, Box 254, HAB; Lewis F. Powell Jr. Oral Argument Notes, April 25, 1977, LFP.

6. Brief for Respondent, Zacchini v. Scripps-Howard, 433 U.S. 562 (No. 76-577); *Zacchini* Transcript at 23–25, 31–32.

7. Memorandum by Comey, p. 3; Levine and Wermiel, "The Court and the Cannonball," 622; Brief for National Association of Broadcasters as Amicus Curiae Supporting Respondent, Zacchini v. Scripps-Howard, 433 U.S. 562 (No. 76-577), microformed on U.S. Supreme Court Records and Briefs (Cong. Info. Serv.) (hereafter cited as "NAB Brief"); "Orders in Pending Cases: No. 76-577," *Supreme Court Journal* 1976 (1977): 594 (denying leave to file amicus brief).

8. Zacchini v. Scripps-Howard, 433 U.S. at 579–582 (Powell, J., dissenting); NAB Brief at 7; "Family of Dr. King Charged Group Building His Monument," *New York Times*, April 18, 2009, p. A15; Jennifer E. Rothman, "Occupy the Public Domain," *San Francisco Chronicle*, February 6, 2012.

9. U.S. Const., amend. I; United States v. Alvarez, 567 U.S. 709, 717–719 (2012); Central Hudson Gas & Elec. v. Pub. Serv. Comm'n, 447 U.S. 557 (1980). The First Amendment applies to state law through the Fourteenth Amendment. In recent years, the Supreme Court has suggested that even commercial speech deserves "heightened scrutiny." Sorrell v. IMS Health, 564 U.S. 552, 566 (2011).

10. Reed v. Town of Gilbert, 135 S. Ct. 2218, 2226 (2015); Sarver v. Chartier, 813 F.3d 891, 903 (9th Cir. 2016); Gerald Gunther, "Foreword: In Search of Evolving Doctrine on a Changing Court," *Harvard Law Review* 86 (1972): 1, 8; Adarand Constructors v. Pena, 515 U.S. 200, 202 (1995) (questioning the assessment that strict scrutiny is always "fatal").

11. Melville B. Nimmer, "Does Copyright Abridge the First Amendment Guarantees of Free Speech and Press?," *UCLA Law Review* 17 (1970): 1180, 1192, 1203–1204; Eldred v. Ashcroft, 537 U.S. 186, 218–219 (2003); S.F. Arts & Athletics v. U.S. Olympic Comm., 483 U.S. 522, 535–541 (1987) (hereinafter "SFAA"); Lloyd Corp., Ltd. v. Tanner, 407 U.S. 551 (1972); Eugene Volokh, *The First Amendment and Related Statutes: Problems, Cases and Policy Arguments*,

4th ed. (New York: Foundation Press, 2011), 221–229; Volokh, "Freedom of Speech and the Right of Publicity," 903; Mark A. Lemley and Eugene Volokh, "Freedom of Speech and Injunctions in Intellectual Property Cases," *Duke Law Journal* 48 (1998): 147, 226–229; John O. McGinnis, "The Once and Future Property-Based Vision of the First Amendment," *University of Chicago Law Review* 63 (1996): 49, 79–85; Eugene Volokh, "Freedom of Speech and Intellectual Property: Some Thoughts after *Eldred, 44 Liquormart*, and *Bartnicki*," *Houston Law Review* 40 (2003): 697.

12. Eldred v. Ashcroft, 218–219; Nimmer, "Does Copyright Abridge the First Amendment," 1192, 1203–1204. Some scholars, including me, have criticized the engine of free-expression argument for suppressing speech. Jennifer E. Rothman, "Liberating Copyright: Thinking Beyond Free Speech," *Cornell Law Review* 95 (2010): 463, 476–493; Rebecca Tushnet, "Copyright as a Model for Free Speech Law: What Copyright Has in Common with Anti-pornography Laws, Campaign Finance Reform, and Telecommunication Regulation," *Boston College Law Review* 42 (2000): 1.

13. SFAA, 541. Some have claimed that this lower level of scrutiny is permissible because trademark law applies only (or usually) to commercial speech. I have questioned this conclusion elsewhere, but even if it were true, commercial speech increasingly receives the same "heightened" level of scrutiny as noncommercial speech. Jennifer E. Rothman, "Commercial Speech, Commercial Use, and the Intellectual Property Quagmire," *Virginia Law Review* 101 (2015): 1929.

14. C.B.C. Distribution & Mktg. v. MLB Advanced Media, 505 F.3d 818, 823–824 (8th Cir. 2007).

15. Comedy III Prods. v. Gary Saderup, Inc. 21 P.3d 797, 799, 811 (Cal. 2001); Campbell v. Acuff-Rose Music, 510 U.S. 569 (1994); 17 U.S.C. § 107 (1992).

16. Hilton v. Hallmark Cards, 599 F.3d 894, 910–11 (9th Cir. 2009); Davis v. Electronic Arts, 775 F.3d 1172 (9th Cir. 2015); Keller v. Electronic Arts, 1268; Hart v. Electronic Arts, 717 F.3d 141 (3d Cir. 2013).

17. *Restatement (Third) of Unfair Competition* (St. Paul, MN: American Law Institute, 1995), § 47; Parks v. LaFace Records, 329 F.3d 437, 460–461 (6th Cir. 2003); Montgomery v. Montgomery, 60 S.W.3d 524, 528–530 (Ky. 2001); Matthews v. Wozencraft, 15 F.3d 432, 440 (5th Cir. 1994); Romantics v. Activision Publ'g, 574 F. Supp. 2d 758, 765–766 (E.D. Mich. 2008); Rogers v. Grimaldi, 875 F.2d 994, 1003–1005 (2d Cir. 1989). Although the test is thought to originate with *Rogers*, the approach predated that case. Guglielmi v. Spelling-Goldberg Prods., 603 P.2d 454, 457n6 (Cal. 1979) (Bird, C.J., concurring); Frosch v. Grosset & Dunlap, Inc., 427 N.Y.S.2d 828, 829 (App. Div. 1980).

18. Doe v. TCI Cablevision, 110 S.W.3d 363, 374 (Mo. 2003) (citing and quoting Lee, "Agents of Chaos," 500).

19. C.B.C. Distribution v. MLB Advanced, 820–824; Keller v. Electronic Arts, 1270–1272, 1275–1279; Hart v. Electronic Arts, 145–147, 158–170; Davis v. Electronic Arts, 1175–1178; Doe v. TCI Cablevision, 374; Winter v. DC Comics, 69 P. 3d 473, 476–477, 478–480 (Cal. 2003); Comedy III v. Gary Saderup, Inc., 800–801, 809–811; ETW Corp. v. Jireh Publ'g, 332 F.3d 915, 918–919, 936–938 (6th Cir. 2003).

20. Comedy III v. Gary Saderup, Inc., 808, 811.

21. Ibid., 809, 810–811n12; ETW Corp. v. Jireh Publ'g, 936–938; Tushnet, "A Mask That Eats Into the Face," 169–177; Volokh, "Freedom of Speech and the Right of Publicity," 913–925; Dougherty, "All the World's Not a Stooge," 1–7, 28–40, 45–52; Lee, "Agents of Chaos," 491–493.

22. Hart v. Electronic Arts, 157–158; Montgomery v. Montgomery, 530–536 (Keller, J., dissenting); Doe v. TCI Cablevision, 374; Lee, "Agents of Chaos," 496–497.

23. Parks v. LaFace Records, 329 F.3d. at 437; Parks v. LaFace Records, 76 F. Supp. 2d 775, 780 (E.D. Mich. 1999); Joint Stipulation of Dismissal With Prejudice, April 14, 2005, Parks v. LaFace Records, 76 F. Supp.2d 775 (No. 99-76405).

24. Sarver v. Chartier, 903–905 (internal citation omitted).

25. Ibid.

26. Amanda Hess, "Popular Nobodies: A Celebrity Underclass Is Now Feeding the Gossip Machine," *New York Times*, September 1, 2016, p. C1; Karen Kay, "Millennial 'Influencers' Who Are the New Stars of Web Advertising," *Observer* (UK), May 28, 2017, http://perma.cc/6H9M=7PZM.

27. C.B.C. Distribution v. MLB Advanced, 823–824; Cardtoons, L.C. v. MLB Players Ass'n, 95 F.3d 959, 972–973 (10th Cir. 1996); Stacey L. Dogan, "*Haelan Laboratories v. Topps Chewing Gum:* Publicity as a Legal Right," in *Intellectual Property at the Edge: The Contested Contours of IP*, eds. Rochelle Cooper Dreyfuss and Jane C. Ginsburg (Cambridge: Cambridge University Press, 2014), 17–18 (suggesting things went awry when courts "abandoned a harms-based approach to celebrity publicity rights in favor of an approach centered on unjust enrichment").

28. Zacchini v. Scripps-Howard, 433 U.S. at 581 (Powell, J., dissenting).

29. A number of scholars have suggested that copyright's fair use defense could be a useful approach to import into right of publicity laws and evaluations of First Amendment defenses to those claims. Samuelson, "Reviving *Zacchini*," 915–939; Roberta Rosenthal Kwall, "Is Independence Day Dawning for the Right of Publicity?," *University of California Davis Law Review* 17 (1983): 191, 229–255; Haemmerli, "Whose Who?," 464–473; Stephen R. Barnett, "First Amendment Limits on the Right of Publicity," *Tort & Insurance Law Journal* 30 (1995): 635, 650–657; Randall T. E. Coyne, "Toward a Modified Fair Use

Defense in Right of Publicity Cases," *William and Mary Law Review* 29 (1988): 781, 812–820.

30. 15 U.S.C. § 1115(b)(4) (2002); New Kids on the Block v. News Am. Publ'g, 971 F.2d 302, 308 (9th Cir. 1992); Rogers v. Grimaldi, 1000–1002; Stacey L. Dogan and Mark A. Lemley, "What the Right of Publicity Can Learn from Trademark Law," *Stanford Law Review* 58 (2006): 1161, 1213–1220 (suggesting that trademark laws provide guidance for limiting the right of publicity).

31. Rogers v. Grimaldi, 1004.

32. Brown v. Electronic Arts, 724 F.3d 1235 (9th Cir. 2013); Complaint, Brown v. Electronic Arts, No. BC 520019 (Cal. Super. Ct., Aug. 30, 2013); Darren Rovell, "Jim Brown receives $600,000 to dismiss lawsuit against Electronic Arts," *ESPN*, June 28, 2016, http://perma.cc/5DUZ-SA2B.

8. A Collision Course with Copyright

1. O'Brien v. Pabst Sales, 124 F.2d 167 (5th Cir. 1941); Lugosi v. Universal Pictures, 603 P. 2d 425 (Cal. 1979); Wendt v. Host Int'l, 125 F.3d 806 (9th Cir. 1997).
   I have previously addressed some of these issues. Jennifer E. Rothman, "Copyright Preemption and the Right of Publicity," *University of California, Davis Law Review* 36 (2002): 199; Jennifer E. Rothman, "The Other Side of *Garcia*: The Right of Publicity and Copyright Preemption," *Columbia Journal of Law & the Arts* 39 (2016): 441. At the time of the 2002 article, courts most often rejected preemption defenses to right of publicity claims, but the pendulum has since swung in the other direction and courts are now more willing to hold right of publicity claims preempted by copyright law. Maloney v. T3Media, 853 F.3d 1004 (9th Cir. 2017); Dryer v. NFL, 814 F.3d 938 (8th Cir. 2016); Laws v. Sony Music Entm't, 448 F.3d 1134 (9th Cir. 2006).

2. 17 U.S.C. §§ 101, 103, 106 (2015); Wendt v. Host, 806; White v. Samsung Elecs. Am., 971 F.2d 1395 (9th Cir. 1992); Midler v. Ford Motor, 849 F.2d 460 (9th Cir. 1988); Waits v. Frito-Lay, Inc., 978 F.2d 1093 (9th Cir. 1992). The right of public performance under copyright law is limited and does not apply to sound recordings unless they are performed via digital audio transmission.

3. U.S. Constitution, article VI; Capital Cities Cable v. Crisp, 467 U.S. 691, 698–699 (1984).

4. 17 U.S.C. § 301 (2015); Melville B. Nimmer and David Nimmer, *Nimmer on Copyright*, rev. ed. (New York: Matthew Bender, 2017), § 1.01; J. Thomas McCarthy, *The Rights of Publicity and Privacy*, vol. 2 (Thomson Reuters, 2016), §§ 11:47, 11:50, 11:52, 11:54; Paul Goldstein, *Goldstein on Copyright* (New York: Wolters Kluwer, 2017), § 17.2.1; Thomas F. Cotter and Irina Y. Dmitrieva, "Integrating the Right of Publicity with First Amendment and Copyright

Preemption Analysis," *Columbia Journal of Law & the Arts* 33 (2010): 165, 183–187; Rothman, "Copyright Preemption," 208, 225–236; H.R. Rep. No. 94-1476, at 24, 129–133 (1976); Dryer v. NFL, 942–944; Laws v. Sony Music, 1137–1145; Toney v. L'Oreal USA, 406 F.3d 905, 909 (7th Cir. 2005); Landham v. Lewis Galoob Toys, 227 F.3d 619, 623–624 (6th Cir. 2000).

The effect of Section 301 on right of publicity laws is further muddied by a last-minute deletion from the bill. As the 1976 Copyright Act neared passage, the draft § 301 specifically enumerated state laws that were *not* to be preempted and included in this list "rights against misappropriation not equivalent to any of such exclusive rights [of copyright], breaches of contract, breaches of trust, trespass, conversion, invasion of privacy, defamation, and deceptive trade practices such as passing off and false representation." The accompanying Senate Report specifically identified the "evolving common law rights of 'privacy,' [and] 'publicity'" as laws that would not be preempted as long as the underlying claims were not merely the "equivalent of copyright protection." Shortly before the vote in the House on the Senate version of the 1976 Copyright Act, Representative John F. Seiberling introduced an amendment that struck the provision. He noted that he was doing so because the Department of Justice was concerned that vague and broad state misappropriation claims, which were also in the list of state laws, could protect ideas and limit "nondeceptive copying of uncopyrighted and unpatented subject matter." The deletion has left courts with dueling interpretations of what the omitted language means for the preemption of right of publicity laws. 122 Cong. Rec. 2823 (1976); H.R. Rep. No. 94-1476, at 24 (1976); S. Rep. No. 94-473, at 20, 115–116 (1975); 122 Cong. Rec. 31997, 32015 (1976); 122 Cong. Rec. 3836–3837 (1976) (letter from Thomas E. Kauper, Dep't of Justice); Copyright Law Revision: Hearing on S. 597 Before the Subcomm. on Patents, Trademarks, & Copyrights of the S. Comm. on the Judiciary, 90th Cong. 1175–1178 (1967) (letter from Barbara A. Ringer, Registrar of Copyright, U.S. Copyright Office); Copyright Law Revision: Hearing on H.R. 2223 Before the Subcomm. on Courts, Civil Liberties & the Admin. of Justice of the H. Comm. on the Judiciary, 94th Cong. 126–127, 137–138, 157 (1975) (testimony of Irwin Goldbloom, Dep't of Justice); Ibid. at 159–161, 164–165 (1975) (statement of Rene D. Tegtmeyer, Assistant Comm'r for Patents, Dep't of Commerce); 122 Cong. Rec. 31982 (1976) (statement of Representative Hutchinson); H.R. Rep. No. 94-1733, at 78–79 (1976); 122 Cong. Rec. 33678, 33680–33681 (1976) (joint explanatory statement of the committee of conference).

5. 17 U.S.C. § 301 (emphasis added); Facenda v. NFL Films, 542 F.3d 1007, 1027 (3d Cir. 2008); Toney v. L'Oreal, 909–910. The "extra element" test suffers from a number of other faults, including its failure to preempt the only laws we know the provision was added specifically to block—state copyright laws. These laws

had an extra element—that the works not be published. H.R. Rep. No. 94-1476, at 24, 129–133; Nimmer and Nimmer, *Nimmer on Copyright*, § 1.01[A].

6. Baltimore Orioles v. MLB Players Ass'n, 805 F.2d 663, 676 (7th Cir. 1986); Fleet v. CBS, 58 Cal. Rptr. 2d 645, 650–653 (Ct. App. 1996).

7. 17 U.S.C. § 301; Dryer v. NFL, 942; Laws v. Sony Music Entm't, 1139; Landham v. Lewis Galoob Toys, 623.

8. McCarthy, *The Rights of Publicity and Privacy*, § 11:55 (distinguishing performance cases); Maloney v. T3Media, 853 F.3d at 1012–1016 (distinguishing performance cases); Nimmer and Nimmer, *Nimmer on Copyright*, § 1.01[B][3][b][iv] (distinguishing advertising cases); Toney v. L'Oreal, 911 (distinguishing uses in advertising); Facenda v. NFL, 1028–1033 (distinguishing uses in commercial and noncommercial speech, but potentially solely because of contractual limits on uses).

9. Geier v. Am. Honda Motor, 529 U.S. 861, 872 (2000); Capital Cities Cable v. Crisp, 698–699; Kewanee Oil v. Bicron Corp., 416 U.S. 470, 479–480 (1974) (quoting Hines v. Davidowitz, 312 U.S. 52, 67 (1941)). Only a few courts have considered conflict preemption analysis in addition to Section 301 when analyzing preemption in the context of right of publicity claims. Facenda v. NFL, 1028–1032; Brown v. Ames, 201 F.3d 654, 659–661 (5th Cir. 2000).

10. U.S. Const. art. I, § 8, cl. 8; Twentieth Century Music v. Aiken, 422 U.S. 151, 156 (1975) (quoting Fox Film v. Doyal, 286 U.S. 123, 127 (1932)); International News Serv. v. Associated Press, 248 U.S. 215, 250 (1918) (Brandeis, J., dissenting).

11. 17 U.S.C. §§ 106, 106A, 203, 304, 504 (2015); Seana Shiffrin, "Intellectual Property," in *A Companion to Contemporary Political Philosophy*, ed. Robert Goodin, Philip Pettit, and Thomas Pogge, vol. 1, 2nd ed. (Malden, MA: Blackwell, 2007), 653; Jeanne C. Fromer, "Expressive Incentives in Intellectual Property," *Virginia Law Review* 98 (2012): 1745; Neil Netanel, "Alienability Restrictions and the Enhancement of Author Autonomy in United States and Continental Copyright Law," *Cardozo Arts & Entertainment Law Journal* 12 (1994): 1.

12. Toney v. L'Oreal, 907–910.

13. No Doubt v. Activision Publ'g, 702 F. Supp. 2d 1139 (C.D. Cal. 2010).

14. Fleet v. CBS, 645.

15. Ibid., 1914; Respondents' Opening Brief at 4, 18n7, 18n28, Fleet v. CBS, 58 Cal. Rptr. 2d 645 (No. B100377).

16. Wendt v. Host, 809 (allowing right of publicity claims arising out of licensed use of fictional characters from television series); Landham v. Lewis Galoob, 623 (holding that right of publicity claims by actors are not preempted in the context of licensed action figures of movie characters); Shamsky v. Garan, 632 N.Y.S.2d 930 (Sup. Ct. 1995) (allowing right of publicity claims when

defendant used a photograph of the 1969 World Champion New York Mets on a shirt, even though it had paid licensing fees to use the copyrighted image).

17. Dryer v. NFL, 941–944.

18. Maloney v. T3Media, 853 F. 3d at 1007–1016.

19. Ibid., 1011–1016; Maloney v. T3Media, 94 F. Supp. 3d 1128, 1138–1139 (C.D. Cal. 2015); Dryer v. NFL, 942–944; Facenda v. NFL, 1028–1033; Toney v. L'Oreal, 911 (suggesting that use in advertising context distinguished court's holding in *Baltimore Orioles*, even though plaintiff agreed to use of her likeness in advertising); Dent v. Renaissance Mktg., No. 14 C 02999, 2015 WL 3484464 (N.D. Ill. June 1, 2015); Nimmer and Nimmer, *Nimmer on Copyright*, § 1.01[B][3][b][iv] (suggesting that differentiating between "entertainment works" and advertising is the "magic vessel" out of the current preemption "tempest"); Cotter and Dmitrieva, "Integrating the Right of Publicity," 169, 208–218.

20. Oral Argument at 9:26, Keller v. Electronic Arts, 724 F.3d 1268 (9th Cir. 2013) (No. 10-15387), http://perma.cc/8U9E-VAR3.

21. Gregory Zinman, "Going 'Full Tupac,'" *The Atlantic*, August 26, 2016, http://perma.cc/RZV2-HG9W; Eriq Gardner, "Hollywood Hologram Wars: Vicious Legal Feud behind Virtual Mariah, Marilyn and Mick," *Hollywood Reporter*, May 28, 2015, http://perma.cc/ER4E-LU9B; Ashley Cullins, "Carrie Fisher, 'Star Wars' and the Legal Issues of Dead but In-Demand Actors," *Hollywood Reporter*, May 1, 2017, http://perma.cc/M26R-GNTY; Ahn v. Midway Mfg., 965 F. Supp. 1134 (N.D. Ill. 1997) (allowing reuse of performances in subsequent video games under copyright preemption analysis).

22. Eriq Gardner, "'Back to the Future II' from a Legal Perspective: Unintentionally Visionary," October 21, 2015, http://perma.cc/DH94-MM29. One federal district court held that the right of publicity claims of martial artists and dancers who had given their permission to a video game company to use their performances were preempted by copyright law even when the performers were reanimated in multiple versions of the games. Ahn v. Midway, 1134.

23. Benjamin Lee, "Discretion, Not CGI: How Philip Seymour Hoffman was kept in the Hunger Games," *Guardian* (U.S.), November 17, 2015, http://perma.cc /3G4P-P8HC; Carolyn Giardina, "How 'Furious 7' Brought the Late Paul Walker Back to Life," *Hollywood Reporter*, December 11, 2015, http://perma.cc /6TPG-YEKQ.

24. Sears, Roebuck & Co. v. Stiffel Co., 376 U.S. 225 (1964); Compco Corp. v. Day-Brite Lighting 376 U.S. 234 (1964); Bonito Boats v. Thunder Craft Boats, 489 U.S. 141, 151 (1989).

25. 17 U.S.C. §§ 102, 106–112, 114–122 (2015).

Acknowledgments

I could not have completed the massive undertaking of this book, which spanned many years, without the support of many people in my life.

All projects have a start, so I want to particularly thank Paul Goldstein for sending this project on its way, both by telling me this was a book I had to write and for introducing me to my excellent editor at Harvard University Press, Thomas LeBien. Thomas has been a passionate advocate for this project from the moment we first spoke.

I am very appreciative of the thoughtful feedback from my anonymous outside reviewers, who led me to think even bigger, as well as the many readers who were known to me. In particular, I want to thank Jessica Litman for her insightful, encouraging, and tremendously helpful suggestions. Rebecca Tushnet, who read an early draft of the book, was particularly helpful in my thinking about the last two chapters. I am also grateful to Eugene Volokh for his comments on those same chapters, and more generally for being instrumental in encouraging me in my career as a scholar, and for his friendship over the years.

I could not have made this book what it is without the support of my colleagues at Loyola Law School. I am particularly grateful to Elizabeth Pollman, who encouraged me every step of the way, insisted that I let her read a draft earlier than I was inclined to share, and provided excellent feedback on both that draft and a later one. My other colleagues at Loyola, Lee Petherbridge, Justin Levitt, Adam Zimmerman, and Jay Dougherty, participated in a very helpful roundtable. I also thank Bob Brain for providing comments on a draft chapter.

Early versions of some chapters benefited from the University of Michigan's Intellectual Property Workshop, led by Rebecca Eisenberg and Paul Courant, and the Intellectual Property Section's panel "Federalism in IP" at the 2017 annual meeting of the Association of American Law Schools.

I want to thank the dean of Loyola Law School, Michael Waterstone, for supporting this project. I am grateful to Dan Martin, the director of our library, who put the library's full resources behind this research-intensive project that spanned many states and many, many decades. One of the true heroes of this project is the talented reference librarian Caitlin Hunter. I am most indebted to her for her excellent detective skills, commitment, and enthusiasm for this project. I am also appreciative of the many other reference librarians who chipped in on this project, particularly Laura Cadra and Amber Madole.

I had many wonderful research assistants over the last few years who contributed in ways large and small to this project, but I particularly want to single out the significant contributions of Nicole Goss during the final stages of this project. Her dedication and excellent work were instrumental in getting this project over the finish line.

I also want to acknowledge the influence of two people who are no longer with us. The first is Gary Schwartz, a great torts scholar, who introduced me to the Flying Zacchini and encouraged me to become a scholar myself. I wish he were here to read this. The second is Millie Barish, my first high school English teacher, who knew I could write before I did. Without her this book would not have been possible.

And then, of course, there are those for whom words will never be enough. Top of this list is my spouse, Sarah, who read many more drafts than she wanted, all with good cheer and great advice. Her support, enthusiasm, and love made this multiyear project possible. I also want to thank my parents for their support and understanding of how much work this project entailed during a very difficult time in their lives.

Last, but far from least, I want to thank both of my children for their constant encouragement and faith that one day Mommy would finish this book. I am particularly appreciative of Elijah's wanting to keep me company, read over my shoulder, and ask me tough questions about what I was writing; and of Hazel's offering to bring me snacks, all the while creating a very long list of post-book activities to do. She also often channeled my own feelings by exclaiming, out of exasperation, "Isn't your book done yet?!" Well now it is.

Index

Page numbers in *italics* indicate illustrations.

Winter, Edgar and Johnny, and *Winter v. D.C. Comics*, 148
women and rights of publicity and privacy: Manola case (objection to being photographed in tights), 20–21; 19th century objections by and on behalf of, 17–18, 190n12; *Schuyler v. Curtis*, 22, 24. *See also* Roberson, Abigail, and *Roberson v. Rochester Folding Box*
Wood, James Playsted, 35
Woods, Tiger, 134, 148–149, 150
Writers Guild of America, 84

Yale Law Journal, 61, 68
yellow journalism, 15, 20, 31, 189n6

You Bet Your Life, 37
YouTube, 4, 121, 142

Zacchini, Hugo, 76–77. See also *Zacchini v. Scripps-Howard Broadcasting*
Zacchini v. Scripps-Howard Broadcasting: First Amendment implications of, 76, 77, 79, 86, 139–143, 145, 154, 155, 157; IP model of right of publicity and, 76, 78–81, 83–85, 87, 99–100, 140, 143, 145, 151; justifications for right of publicity and, 98, 105, 109–110; newsworthiness defense in, 220n4; support for independent right of publicity, 75–81, 83
Zimmerman, Diane, 122, 130–131